PRAISE FOR ANDREW SALTER'S WORK:

I have read [Salter's work] with admiration and approval. (1943)
— H.G. Wells

Most interesting and fundamentally sound. (1943)
— Aldous Huxley

... a founder of behavior therapy ... [Salter] helped develop the theoretical underpinnings and clinical applications of behavior therapy decades before the field became popular. (1996)
— *New York Times*

A pioneering behavior therapist. (2002)
— Albert Ellis, PhD; President, Albert Ellis Institute; Developer of Rational Emotive Behavior Therapy

PRAISE FOR *CONDITIONED REFLEX THERAPY*:

In the field of psychology, this work may well become a landmark of the order of Darwin's Origin of Species. (1949)
— Paul de Kruif, PhD; Leading medical writer from the 1930's through the 1950's, author of *Microbe Hunters* and many other books.

Andrew Salter blazed a trail into new territory, paving the way for what has become known as cognitive behavior therapy. (2002)
— Arnold Lazerus, PhD, ABPP; Distinguished Professor of Psychology (Emeritus), Rutgers University; Past-President, Association for the Advancement of Behavior Therapy

CRT remains decades ahead of the field. A half a century later, it is still an extraordinarily effective classic. The vision of Andrew Salter lives on. (2002)

> – Pat de Leon, PhD; Former President, American Psychological Association; former Chief of Staff, Senator Daniel Inouye

In lively, literate, and sometimes puckishly provocative prose, Salter courageously and successfully challenged the establishment and articulated a vision and a set of techniques that have become so widely accepted and applied that he is often not formally cited. Salter ... used learning principles as a guide to devising new therapeutic methods. [T]he techniques Salter derived from the theory were effective for a wide variety of disorders. Like other trail-blazing and creative thinkers, Salter's ongoing influence extends beyond behavior therapy and psychology generally. (2002)

> – Gerald Davison, PhD; Professor and Chair, Department of Psychology, University of Southern California; Past-President, Association for the Advancement of Behavior Therapy

The book is remarkably engaging, clinically astute, and of great practical value; it anticipated much of contemporary behavior therapy. Salter's leap from learning theory and research to treatments for clinical practice was groundbreaking. He focused primarily on action in everyday life and expression of how one feels to achieve therapeutic change. Concretely, this meant encouraging expression of emotions and positive actions. Clients were instructed on how to perform in everyday life situations and were given extra-therapeutic tasks (i.e., homework assignments.) (2018)

> – Alan Kazdin, PhD, ABPP; Sterling Professor of Psychology & Professor of Child Psychiatry (Emeritus), Yale University; former President, American Psychological Association; Past-President, Association for the Advancement of Behavior Therapy

It is a pleasure to see the new release of Andrew Salter's Conditioned Reflex Therapy. *Although initially published in 1949, the book has been largely unavailable for more than a decade, when the publisher's archives were destroyed by Hurricane Katrina. Salter's conviction that "psychotherapy can be quite rapid and extremely efficacious" helped forge an important new path in psychological healing, and the procedures he delineates in the book can now continue to help people for many years to come.* (2018)

> – Francine Shapiro, PhD; Senior Research Fellow (Emeritus), Mental Research Institute; Originator of Eye Movement Desensitization and Reprocessing (EMDR) Therapy

What jumps out at you from Conditioned Reflex Therapy *is its energy and boldness. This is not a book full of weasel words and conditional sentences. This is a statement book – direct, wise without being complex, and ready to take on the world. No wonder it lit the match that became behavior therapy. Although based on Pavlovian principles it is oddly contemporary, including precursors of interoceptive exposure; abandoning useless control agendas; encouraging more direct emotional expression and many other such topics. Salter's genius is his intuitive grasp of what moves human beings and his willingness to charge straight in that direction. I think this book is of more than historical interest – I suggest it especially for beginning behavioral and cognitive therapists. If they absorb the spirit of it, they will be emboldened to be more fully themselves in therapy, and that can only be for the good.* (2019)

    – Steven C. Hayes, PhD; Foundation Professor of Psychology, University of
    Nevada, Reno; Developer of Acceptance and Commitment Therapy and
    Relational Frame Theory

Much of the science and wisdom on which modern day, powerful, evidence-based psychotherapeutic interventions are based comes from this book. With its fascinating case studies described in lucid and vigorous prose, and edited lightly for relevance in today's world, this timeless classic should be read by every therapist and most of their patients. (2019)

    – David H. Barlow Ph.D, ABPP; Professor of Psychology and Psychiatry
    Emeritus; Founder, Center for Anxiety and Related Disorders at
    Boston University; Past-President, AABT

CONDITIONED

REFLEX

THERAPY

Andrew
Salter

CONDITIONED

REFLEX

THERAPY

The Practical Keys to Unlocking
Your Confidence, Authenticity
and Happiness – and Leaving
Anxiety, Loneliness and
Depression Behind

WATKINS
Sharing Wisdom Since 1893

This edition first published in the UK and USA in 2019 by
Watkins, an imprint of Watkins Media Limited
Unit 11, Shepperton House
89-93 Shepperton Road
London
N1 3DF

enquiries@watkinspublishing.com

Design and typography copyright © Watkins Media Limited 2019

1 3 5 7 9 10 8 6 4 2

Typeset by Lapiz

Printed and bound in the United Kingdom by TJ International, Padstow, Cornwall

A CIP record for this book is available from the British Library

ISBN: 978-1-786782-90-8

www.watkinspublishing.com

CONTENTS

WHY AND HOW TO READ
CRT

Mark R. Davis
Director and Principal,
UK College of Hypnosis and Hypnotherapy

I discovered Andrew Salter's *Conditioned Reflex Therapy* (*CRT*) in 2007 during a course at the UK College of Hypnosis and Hypnotherapy – www.ukhypnosis.com. I am now its Director and have successfully used the ideas and techniques *CRT* contains with well over a thousand therapy clients and taught them to hundreds of hypnotherapy students on our courses, both in the UK and in China, where, remarkably, they are considered a return to Lao Tsu's naturalism and emphasis on being at one with oneself and nature.

I'm in excellent company in the belief that *CRT* is invaluable to therapists. In blurbs for this edition, two of the most important contemporary psychologists developing therapeutic techniques and training therapists agree: "This timeless classic should be read by every therapist and most of their patients" (David H. Barlow). "I suggest it especially for beginning behavioral and cognitive therapists. If they absorb the spirit of it, they will be emboldened to be more fully themselves in therapy, and that can only be for the good" (Steven C. Hayes).

Nearly every client and student who encounters *CRT* and Salter's excitatory-inhibitory model of neurosis—that is, of unhappiness—finds his ideas and techniques simple to understand, practical in application, and dramatic in effects. Salter's ideas and techniques are inseparable: he stressed the importance of "homework," of practicing the methods learned in therapy in the client's real life, in interactions with strangers, with friends and partners and colleagues. Positive feedback from those interactions then strengthens the learning.

Deep themes underscore Salter's writing: authenticity and sincerity, a return to our original nature, "know thy self," responsiveness, spontaneity, freedom, unselfconsciousness, awareness of others and of the world around us. These ideas appeal to something deep within us yearning to connect with others and to be free again, escaping the inhibition (in Salter's terms) or repression (in other terms) responsible for most of our psychological entanglements and much human unhappiness.

From its initial publication in 1949, *CRT* drew comments and praise. It stressed mindfulness and assertion—though neither term appears—and introduced specific methods clients can use. It not only presents Salter's ideas, but also embodies them: it's forceful and opinionated, filled with "feeling talk."

I invite the reader of this new edition to apply Salter's approach when reading it: grab a pen and underline; highlight and scribble in the margins; laugh (or scowl) at his one-liners; contemplate his occasional seeming inconsistencies; recognize yourself and others in his poignant client cases. It is not dry scholarly writing, so don't try to keep an academic distance. It is as vigorous and alive as a dynamic and characterful therapist, as Salter himself was. Read it, feel it, interact with it! Have an opinion! Disagree! Tell others what you feel about it! Feelings, as Salter says, are to be felt out loud.

The ideas contained in this book have truth and meaning only to the extent that they work for us, as readers, and as individuals living our lives. The best way to benefit from them is to try them out. Don't read *CRT* as just the vigorous exposition of interesting ideas that it is; it gives not just permission, but an invitation and specific techniques to change your behavior and see how it feels. It explicitly encourages experimentation: become aware of your feelings and be more genuine and expressive in response to them, then notice how the world responds to those experiments and experience how that makes you feel. Such experimentation—such work in the world—will reveal the value and deep truths of *CRT*.

In applying Salter's approach with hundreds of clients, it's become clear to me that psychotherapy is not primarily talking about feelings in the office, which can paradoxically maintain distance from how we actually feel; good psychotherapy is helping clients learn how to talk and act with genuine feeling in their lives, how to bring their primary emotions into whatever they say and do. Salter would certainly have agreed.

As you read this new edition you will discover that Salter's ideas are just as relevant, alive, and important now as they were in 1950s America. This is because they are about the integration of emotion, thought, and behavior into the whole organism, an eternal theme in human striving for self-actualization and happiness. Much socialization in all cultures is about controlling emotion and splitting it off from behavior.

Salter's ideas about healing this schism between feeling and behavior through the practice of deliberate disinhibition allows us to discover—by actually experiencing—how our emotions can work for us; they are both timeless and shockingly contemporary, despite the seventy years that have passed since its original publication. Put emotion into everything you say and do and see what happens. As Salter said, if you don't like it, you can always go back to your old ways, and you know how that makes you feel.

Salter leads us towards awareness, acceptance, and integration of our emotions. This is essential if we are to truly grow emotionally and become whole and authentic. Our needs for integration of emotion into the core of our being, for self-expression and the sense of personal and political self-efficacy are, I believe, the primary drivers behind personal and social change. Now, just as when *CRT* was published, restriction of emotion leads to neurosis and unhappiness. Salter's ideas are both personally and politically important. Let them be alive for you. I encourage you to put them into practice. And spread the news!

INTRODUCTION

Gerald Davison, Ph.D.
Professor of Psychology and Gerontology
University of California, Dornsife

There is a regrettable tendency nowadays to disregard the seminal contributions of some of our most creative thinkers, the true pioneers of our field. This reissue of Andrew Salter's classic book will, I hope, go some way to educating younger cohorts to the important role that Salter played in launching behavior therapy in the 1950's. Reading *Conditioned Reflex Therapy*, even for the second time for some people, will reveal how forward-looking his ideas were and how much both specialists and laypeople owe to this remarkable scholar and psychotherapist.

Andrew Salter, whom I was privileged to have as a colleague and friend for many years, was an unconventional person. Calling himself a "clinical psychologist" in the early 1940's, before that was an official designation, he was eventually officially grandfathered into the profession he had helped to found over the objections of the New York State Psychological Association, then dominated by Freudians. And many are glad that this happened because he established a thriving Manhattan-based practice, with but a bachelor's degree, and as a fulltime clinician (often to the rich and famous), he is widely recognized as one of the founders of behavior therapy along with distinguished people like H.J. Eysenck, Arnold Lazarus, and Joseph Wolpe.

While earning his B.S. Degree from New York University in 1937, Salter immersed himself in the intellectual riches of the New York Public Library. Impressed by Clark Hull's little known work in hypnosis and conditioning, he published a paper on autohypnosis in 1941 and a book on the topic in 1944, reporting successful applications to some of the problems (e.g., insomnia, smoking, overeating) he was treating in his newly established practice.

Using his clinical experiences in a thoughtful and creative fashion ("creative" is a word I always think of when I think of him), Salter went on to publish two other books that form the basis of behavior therapy today, *Conditioned Reflex Therapy* (1949) and *The Case Against Psychoanalysis* (1952). These works occupy an honored place for those with an appreciation of original, paradigm-breaking ideas in clinical psychology, psychiatry, and especially behavior therapy. At the time these works were published, it was not fashionable—indeed, it was downright risky—to critique psychoanalysis or to propose that clinical interventions could be based on experimental data. Dollard and Miller's classic *Personality and Psychotherapy* (1950) was published a year later than Salter's second book and was important in its own right, but it was much different in purpose and ultimate effect than *Conditioned Reflex Therapy*; whereas Dollard and Miller attempted to explain existing psychoanalytic procedures in terms of well-established principles of learning, Salter (and, later, Wolpe) used learning principles as a guide to devising new therapeutic methods. While Dollard and Miller's book has had limited impact on both theory and practice, Salter's strategy has made enduring contributions.

In lively, literate, and sometimes puckishly provocative prose, Salter courageously and successfully challenged the establishment and articulated a vision and a set of techniques that have become so widely accepted and applied that he is often not formally cited. This is especially true when contemporary writers in psychotherapy refer to "assertion training," "expressiveness training," and "getting in touch with one's feelings." These and related phrases refer to the expression of both the positive and negative emotion that people, to their detriment, are often reluctant to do under a mistaken belief that they will infringe on the rights and sensibilities of others.

The central thesis in the present volume is couched in Pavlovian terms, to wit, that the direct expression of both positive and negative emotion leads to improvement in a wide variety of psychological disorders via a disinhibition of excessive cortical inhibition. While the theorizing was open to question, the techniques Salter derived from the theory were effective for a wide variety of disorders. (This kind of "disconnect" between theory and technique is not uncommon in scientific and clinical applications. No lesser a figure than Sigmund Freud has been evaluated in this light, as well as other major figures in psychotherapy including Carl Rogers.) Throughout his application of the techniques, Salter's emphasis was on changing overt behavior rather than on changing thoughts and feelings. Changes in the latter would follow behavioral change, he cogently argued. This approach was in sharp contrast to the prevailing doctrines of the "insight-based" therapies, in particular psychoanalysis and its many offshoots. I believe Salter has been proven right, much to the benefit of many patients, their pocketbooks, and the financial resources of insurance companies.

Less generally known than Salter's "assertion training" is this avowed behaviorist's innovations in the use of imagery, specifically paired with positive affect, to reduce unwarranted anxiety. But it was this idea that helped to lay the foundation for Joseph Wolpe's pioneering work in systematic desensitization. (The degree to which an appeal to imagery is within the realm of behavioristic techniques has been argued for years, but Salter was always in good conceptual company with the likes of Clark Hull, Kenneth Spence, O.H. Mowrer, and Neal Miller.)

Though humanistic in his values and in his clinical approach to patients, Salter, like Pavlov and other Russian and later Soviet theoreticians of the time, remained a philosophical materialist in his theoretical conceptions of behavior and its therapeutic modification. In *Conditioned Reflex Therapy*, he wrote:

> ... we attain [behavior change] by what may be termed *verbal chemistry*. Words, spoken by the therapist, travel along appropriate nerve tracts in the person under treatment, and produce chemical modifications in his nervous system. These changes are associated with behavior changes, which in turn precipitate more biochemical modifications and more behavior changes. (Salter, 1949, p. 316)

Like other trail-blazing and creative thinkers, Salter's ongoing influence extends beyond behavior therapy and psychology generally. In the field of psychotherapy, he emphasized the importance of "I-talk" years before Fritz Perls pointed to its significance in Gestalt therapy. Assertion training has permeated our culture, especially in the feminist movement, a fact which made Salter very proud. Ironically, being an innovator does not guarantee that one's contribution will receive due visibility. So, just as references to "psychoanalysis" seldom cite Sigmund Freud, a similar scarcity of citations to Salter occurs in the literatures on "assertion training" and the origins of behavior therapy.

A wide variety of people beyond psychologists and other mental health professionals read and praised his writing. Who among us can say that our writing style is "captivating," as Thomas Mann said about Salter's prose? Who among us has written things that commanded the attention and approbation of people such as Aldous Huxley, Vladimir Nabokov, and H.G. Wells? And who, as a college student and writer of poetry, won an interview with the likes of Robert Frost? Finally, who among us has had a character in a book—and then a widely celebrated movie—modeled after us, as was the case with Salter in Richard Condon's *The Manchurian Candidate?*

Those of us who knew Salter personally appreciated his sheer brilliance, his wit, his warmth, decency, and consideration for others; his supportiveness, his keen intuitive grasp of human nature, his infectious zest for life, his love of art and literature, and his devotion to family and friends. These qualities come through in this classic book, which, though originally published in 1949, retains its importance for what it says about the human condition and the steps ordinary people can take to improve their lot and even have some fun out of life.

PREFACE TO THE FIRST EDITION

The human species, as well as all other animal types, has evolved gradually from earlier and less complex forms of life. For more than one hundred million years the ancestors of the human race had their spines situated horizontally. Only in the past half million years has that spine become erect. Man has been human only as of yesterday, and his behavior is inseparably rooted in his animal structure.

If we were to whip a playful dog repeatedly, he would soon become silent and submissive, and would acquire disturbances of digestion. We would not say there had been a conversion of symptoms. We would not say that the dog suffered from an inferiority complex. Nor would we say that the dog had an unconscious wish to retain his neurosis. We would simply say that the dog had been trained that way.

We recognize that we cannot apply these human abstractions to the dog. However, it might prove helpful to approach the articulate human animal in terms of the dog's behavior, for the way of science is to reduce the complex to its more rudimentary components.

Freud speaks of the id as the mind's "primitive" basis. Pareto speaks of the fundamental power of the "non-logical residues." Jung talks of the repressed "animal instincts," and Rank of the "fundamental irrationality of the human being."

These are all conceptualizations of an aspect of *Homo sapiens* which permits of more objective explanation. It is from the naturalistic viewpoint of Pavlov and Bechterev that this book will consider the development of human personality and will present techniques for its expeditious reconstruction in non-psychotic conditions.

I have devoted a great deal of effort to the arrangement of my material. The first two chapters [Editor's note: condensed in Chapter 1 in this edition] have been rewritten and expanded from my book *What Is Hypnosis*, and form the basis of all that follows. Chapter Fifteen appeared in part in the *Southwest Review*, and I offer my thanks to the editors for their permission to reprint.

Finally, it gives me pleasure to express my appreciation to Elizabeth Lassen and Jeannette Fahnestock, my secretaries, for their intelligent and devoted assistance.

Andrew Salter
New York City
1949

FOREWORD

William J. Salter, Ph.D.

This is the fourth edition of *Conditioned Reflex Therapy*. The first was published in 1949, to a vigorous mixture of criticism and acclaim; the second, in 1961, remained in print for almost a decade. The third edition was published in 2002, but has been unavailable since 2005, when Hurricane Katrina destroyed the facilities of The Wellness Press, including printed copies and associated electronic files. I want to thank Harold Dawley, publisher, for making that edition possible and helping to renew interest in Andrew Salter's work.

I write as a Ph.D. psychologist, but perhaps more importantly as one of Andrew Salter's two sons. Since 2005, I have received a number of phone calls and letters from therapists asking how to get copies of *CRT* or urging us to undertake a new edition. In mid-2018, Mark Davis, of The UK College of Hypnosis and Hypnotherapy in London, made one such call, stressing that the ideas in *CRT* were central both to his therapeutic work and in training other therapists. He connected me with Etan Jonathan Ilfeld of Watkins Media, who enthusiastically agreed to publish this fourth edition and whose support and encouragement have made it possible.

This edition includes this new Foreword and a new Afterword that provides more details about my father's background and intellectual history. The main text is identical to that of the 2002 edition, which differed from the 1949 and 1961 editions in two ways: The first three chapters were substantially condensed to Chapter 1 in the 2002 edition, and the chapter on homosexuality was omitted. Chapters 1 to 3 in the early editions justified the development of a Pavlovian approach to therapy, essentially as follows: Conditioning has been scientifically demonstrated repeatedly; emotional reactions, as well as physical ones, can be conditioned; therefore, by "building therapeutic methods on the scientific bedrock of Pavlov," psychotherapy "can be made much more effective more rapidly for more people." This lays the conceptual groundwork for the detailed material that follows. Developments in the seventy years since *CRT* was published have shown my father's basic argument to be sound, even obvious. But it was heretical when he made it, much criticized in some circles and strongly praised in others.

I have omitted material in those three original chapters devoted to a detailed review of the then current literature on hypnosis, to an attack on the Freudian concept of hypnosis, and to arguing that hypnosis is best conceptualized as a form of conditioning, content that largely recapitulates and extends material from *What Is Hypnosis* (Salter, 1944). Most of this early literature has been supplanted: the Freudian "far-fetched and impertinent" conception that "in hypnotism the hypnotist plays the role of the subject's parent of the opposite sex" (Salter, 1944, p. 21) has been emphatically rejected; the intimate relationship of hypnosis and conditioning has been established.

The chapter on homosexuality (Chapter 21 in the 1949 and 1961 editions) is grounded in a premise, virtually universally held at the time, that homosexuality was a disorder that could be treated. All of my father's homosexual patients in those years came to him to be "cured," as they saw it, of their condition. However, despite the now outdated premise in this chapter, *CRT* takes an amazingly modern stance on the origins of homosexuality: "Psychologically, homosexuality is as much a moral question as [is] a preference for strawberry ice cream" (Salter, 1961, p. 283). See the Afterword for additional discussion of his understanding of homosexuality.

Those interested in the omitted chapters can find an older edition in a library or hunt up a (surprisingly expensive) used copy. I have not otherwise edited the text to make it more "politically correct." It's pretty sound on that score, and such cosmetic edits would serve no useful purpose.

When *CRT* was published in 1949, the American Psychological Association had a few thousand members, of whom my father was never one. He was originally rejected because he lacked a Ph.D. Clinical psychology was almost exclusively Freudian (Freud had died only ten years before) and clinical training almost exclusively the province of psychoanalytic institutes. Once his ideas began to be broadly accepted, he was repeatedly invited to join; he repeatedly refused. He would have been gratified by the irony that this edition has blurbs from two former presidents of the APA, Alan Kazdin and Pat de Leon.

In 1949, America's postwar economic expansion was booming: unemployment was low, highways were being built, suburbs were starting to grow. Campuses were flooded with veterans going to college on the GI Bill. TV was a rare and expensive novelty, men still wore hats, and rare was the married woman who worked. Truman was president, Stalin was very much alive, and the Cold War was heating up. The first tenured Jewish faculty member at Yale had just been appointed, segregation was the law in the South, women's and men's roles were sharply defined, and homosexuals were deemed—and often felt themselves to be—mentally ill.

CRT is a product of that time, informed by a fundamentally optimistic and liberal—because emotionally liberating—orientation. It exemplifies the great energies released by the end of World War II, the optimism of American prosperity, the fruits of burgeoning science. But in an important respect it is an outsider's book, written by a man far from the mainstream, not only in terms of orientation but professionally as well. My father, with only a bachelor's degree, was never affiliated with an academic institution. *CRT* constituted a leap, in theory and in practice. When it was first published, behaviorists worked with dogs and rats, strictly within the Pavlovian experimental and theoretical paradigm, and those theories had no place for emotions. Years earlier, my father observed that upon graduating from college he "had no desire to spend the rest of my life studying the reactions of rats lost in labyrinths" (Wickware, 1941, p. 86).

Interest in behavior therapy continues to grow. Hundreds of books and articles, for both the lay public and professionals, now promote assertion, tell people how to "get in touch with their feelings" and how to change their thoughts and behaviors to thereby change how they feel. Behavior therapy has become part of the psychotherapeutic mainstream. Now there are probably as many journals devoted to behavior therapy, broadly defined, as there were practitioners when the 1961 edition of *CRT* was published. Subfields have proliferated, many with catchy names. A "third wave" of behavior therapy has emerged, "characterized by openness to older clinical traditions, a focus on second order and contextual change, an emphasis on function over form, and the construction of flexible and effective repertoires" (Hayes, 2004, p. 639; this article introduced the term "third wave behavior therapy" and has been cited more than 2,000 times). One could argue that the methods in *CRT* fulfill this definition. Indeed, Hayes provided a blurb for this new edition citing its "energy and boldness" and declaring it "of more than historical interest."

CRT introduced many of the foundational ideas on which behavior therapy and cognitive behavior therapy[1] are based, as well as many specific techniques widely applied today: brief therapy, assertion, relaxation, use of imagery, systematic desensitization, and a focus on behavior in the real world via homework and *in vivo* exposure.

Behavior therapy, in its many manifestations, is now entrenched in the mainstream. It has entered the phase of "normal science," a concept introduced by Thomas Kuhn (1962/2012) to refer to a field in which incremental progress is made by people sharing a common theoretical framework. Although my father never had much time for normal science, he would surely have welcomed this legitimization of a field that his rebellious approach helped to create. He drove a major paradigm shift, one that has unquestionably increased human happiness.[2]

My father is still rarely cited; indeed, I suspect that many of the authors, including academics, who fail to mention him have never heard of him. Yet the insights and techniques in *CRT* retain their relevance and in many cases still feel new, due in part to my father's "lively, literate, and sometimes puckishly provocative prose" (as Gerald Davison says in his Introduction to this edition).

The Association for the Advancement of Behavior Therapy, founded by my father and nine other practitioners in 1966, has become the Association for Behavioral and Cognitive Therapy, "a multidisciplinary organization committed to the enhancement of health and well-being by advancing the scientific understanding, assessment, prevention, and treatment of human problems through the global application of behavioral, cognitive, and biological evidence-based principles," as stated in its Mission Statement. It now has more than 5,000 members. And the APA has grown from a few thousand to more than 150,000 members.

CRT is of more than historical interest. It still has much to say directly to individuals seeking to help themselves. In addition to articulating my father's ideas and methods, it includes more than fifty case studies that illustrate how those ideas and methods can be put into practice both by therapists and by lay readers seeking to feel better. My father received, and treasured, hundreds

---

[1] See Ellis (2003).

[2] A paradigm shift occurs when a new theoretical framework emerges to account for accumulating "anomalies"—results that the existing paradigm cannot effectively account for. Indeed, Hayes (2004, p. 639) attributes the emergence of third-wave behavior therapy to "anomalies in the current literature." According to Kuhn, paradigm shifts are typically driven by younger researchers. My father was thirty-five when *CRT* was published.

of letters over the years from readers who said that *CRT* had enabled them to be more successful in their personal and professional lives, to overcome their fears and anxieties, to change bad habits, and to be happier.

In his focus on emotion, and the healthy expression of emotion as the key to happiness and mental health, my father was far ahead of his time. This focus is one of the fundamental contributions of *CRT*. Healthy expression of emotion was *excitatory* in his language—honest and open. This is now called *assertion*. He also argued that effective therapy must focus on what the patient *does*—on behavior in the world—as the path to changing how the patient *feels*. "In psychotherapy, it is not what the individual knows that counts. It is what he does" (p. 109)[3]: "To change the way a person feels and thinks about himself, we must change the way he acts toward others" (p. 75).

Over the years people have said, usually but not always approvingly, that changing behavior in order to change how one feels is equivalent to "Fake it till you make it." That's not wrong, but it doesn't capture my father's intent. I much prefer Dr. Frank-N-Furter's aspirational injunction in a song from *The Rocky Horror Picture Show* (Adler & White, 1975): "Don't dream it, be it." That sentiment guided all of my father's practice. He wanted people actually to *be* what they dreamt of being, not just to fake it. He spent more than fifty years, in tens of thousands of therapy hours with thousands of patients, trying to bring that about. I hope that this reissue of *CRT* will make it possible for more people to not only dream it but to be it, whatever it may be.

Bibliography for the Foreword

Adler, L., & White, M. (Producers); Sharman, J. Director (1975). *The Rocky Horror Picture Show* [Motion Picture]. United States; 20th Century Fox. Song by Richard O'Brien.

Davison, G. (1996). Andrew Salter (1914-1996): Founding Behavior Therapist. *APS Observer*, *9*(6), 30-31.

Ellis, A. (2003). Cognitive Restructuring of the Disputing of Irrational Beliefs. In W. O'Donohue, J. Fisher, & S. Hayes (Eds.); *Cognitive Behavior Therapy: Applying Empirically Supported Techniques in Your Practice* (pp. 79-83). Hoboken, NJ: John Wiley & Sons, Inc.

---

[3] Citations with only a page number, like this one, refer to this edition of *CRT* except where the context makes clear that they refer to a different publication.

Hayes, S. C. (2004). Acceptance and commitment therapy, relational frame theory, and the third wave of behavior therapy. *Behavior Therapy,* *35*, 639–665.

Kuhn, T. *The Structure of Scientific Revolutions* (1962/2012). Chicago, IL: University of Chicago Press.

Salter, A. *What Is Hypnosis* (1944). New York, NY: Richard R. Smith.

Salter, A. *Conditioned Reflex Therapy, 2nd Edition* (1961). New York, NY: Capricorn Books.

Wickware, F. S. Andrew Salter and Autohypnosis (1941). *Life Magazine,* vol. 11, no. 19, 83–92.

CHAPTER I
FUNDAMENTALS: HYPNOSIS AND WORD AND EMOTIONAL CONDITIONING

"... all the highest nervous activity, as it manifests itself in the conditioned reflex, consists of a continual change of these three fundamental processes— excitation, inhibition, and disinhibition"

Ivan P. Pavlov

It is high time that psychoanalysis, like the elephant of fable, dragged itself off to some distant jungle graveyard and died. Psychoanalysis has outlived its usefulness. Its methods are vague, its treatment is long drawn out, and more often than not, its results are insipid and unimpressive.

Every literate non-Freudian in our day knows these accusations to be true. But, we may ask ourselves, might it not be that psychotherapy, by its very nature, must always be difficult, time-consuming, and inefficient?

I do not think so. I say flatly that psychotherapy can be quite rapid and extremely efficacious. I know so because I have done so. And if the reader will bear with me I will show him how by building our therapeutic methods on the firm scientific bed rock of Pavlov, we can keep out of the Freudian metaphysical quicksands and help ten persons in the time that the Freudians are getting ready to "help" one. These are matters of the greatest importance, and I have written this book in order to explain the Pavlovian science of reflex therapy.

The scientific method is naturalistic. It denies the supernatural, and declares that all phenomena are traceable to natural causes. It uses as few concepts as possible. The simplest available explanation should be preferred, that is, the one which involves the fewest or least complexly related concepts that are adequate.

In order to develop these concepts we shall have to go into the laboratory. There, as we consider the extensive work that has been done with mice and men, and dogs and children, *under controlled conditions*, we will be able to edge a little closer to the truth. We will not be afraid to develop theories, but we will try to build them from the solid brick of laboratory fact, and not from the gas-inflated balloons of Freudian speculation that explode with a loud pop at the sharp needle of fact. Let us now take a look at some facts.

Pavlov's fundamental experiments with dogs are well established. (1) He found that when a hungry dog was given a piece of meat immediately after a bell was rung, and when this association of bell and meat was repeated often enough, before long the bell alone would produce a flow of saliva in the dog. It was as if the bell were acting as the meat. He called this a conditioned reflex, but "associative reflex" might be a more felicitous term. When the bell rang the dog did more than salivate. He pricked up his ears, turned his head toward the source of the food, and made anticipatory chewing movements. Pavlov, however, centered his work on a study of the salivary responses because they could be measured.

Conditioned reflexes in dogs—and what is more to the point, in all beings—do not involve volitional thinking. Once the conditioned reflex is trained into the subject of the experiment, he becomes a pure automaton to the non-genuine stimulus-the bell-that has been woven into the reflex.

It is possible to condition other neurological mechanisms besides the salivary reflex. We know that when a light shines into the pupil, it acts, and when the light is removed, it dilates. The pupillary reflex is completely involuntary. The subject has absolutely no control over it.

There is a very significant and splendidly constructed experiment by C.V. Hudgins, who followed Pavlov's method, except that he conditioned the human pupillary reflex. (2) Hudgins' procedure is worth following carefully.

The pupil was first conditioned to a bell with the light as the unconditioned stimulus. Each time the light was lit while the subject looked at it, the experimenter closed an electric circuit which rang a bell. Notice the parallel to Pavlov. The light made the pupil contract every time, and the meat made the dog salivate every time. The bell in each case was then tied to the genuine arouser of the reflex.

The subject was next taught to use his own hand-grip to close the bell and light circuits, for the more the organism is involved, the more conditioning is facilitated. The subject, then, through his own activity turned on both the light and the bell. When the subject relaxed his hand at the experimenter's command, "relax," the same circuits were broken, and the light would go out and the bell would stop ringing. Before long the bell and hand reactions were eliminated.

In several hours of training, Hudgins found that he could omit the bell, the hand-grip, and the light. *The sound of the word "contract," spoken by him, had acquired the "power" to force an involuntary and substantial contraction of the pupil.*

Let me repeat this. It is important. Hudgins, by merely saying the word "contract," could now produce a strong contraction of the subject's pupil. Further, this conditioning, with and without retraining, lasted from fifteen to ninety days.

Hudgins' work on pupillary conditioning is quite important, so let us consider it further. Some of his subjects said the word "contract" aloud as he went through the conditioning procedure. Before long, these subjects, by merely saying the word "contract," could produce pupillary contraction, without the light or the bell.

He conditioned other subjects to produce pupillary contraction by their *whispering* "contract" to themselves.

Finally, he conditioned five subjects to contract their pupils when they thought the word "contract," and to dilate them when they *thought* the word "relax." Light or bell was no longer needed. The subjects could auto-contract their pupils. Through conditioning it had been possible to build a control of that which was otherwise uncontrollable.

Words are the bells of associative reflexes. Such words as "splendid," "marvelous," and "magnificent" give us an unconscious lift because we have been conditioned to that feeling in them. The words "hot," "boiling," and "steam," have a warm quality because of their associativity. Inflection and gesture have been conditioned as intensifiers of word conditionings.

We can thus see that words are bound up with completely unconscious associative reflexes. Certain words in an appropriately trained person can produce actual bodily sensations, or more broadly, actual bodily reactions.

Many humans do not have a background of appropriate conditionings in which, as in physics, sympathetic vibrations can be produced. In psychotherapy, as we shall see later, we may proceed with such persons by training into them whatever conditionings are necessary to solve their problems.

An experiment by Diven gives some insight into the problem. (3) Subjects were asked to give their associations to lists of words that were read to them. For example, the word *barn* occurred six times on one of the lists, and was always preceded by the word *red* and followed by a painful electric shock. The shock caused emotional disturbances that produced fluctuations in a galvanometer attached to the subject.

When the experimenter finished a word list, the subjects were given a five minute rest, and again connected to the galvanometer. They were asked to recall as many of the words as possible, and their emotional responses were recorded, to determine how much of the electrically built-in emotions had remained. Then the experimenter repeated the stimulus words, but without any electric shock

Diven found that a "complex psychophysiological disturbance became associated" with the critical (shock) words. The conditioned disturbance to the critical word *barn* was transferred to all of the words on the list which were rural in meaning, such as *hay, cow; and pasture*. Significantly enough, words that were not on the original list but were also rural in meaning... *farm*, for example also produced emotional responses. Words on the list, that had preceded and followed the word *barn*, and were once neutral, in like manner became emotionally charged.

Subjects who could not remember the critical words retained more of the disturbance than those who were able to recall them. From a reflex point of view, it is clear that emotional conditioning exists without awareness, and becomes transferred to otherwise neutral persons, places, and situations.

Here is Pavlov's experiment again. Instead of a bell, there is a word. Instead of the meat, there is an electric shock. And instead of the saliva at the sound of the bell, there is the emotion at the sound of the word. Here is the linkage between word conditioning and emotional conditioning. The "subconscious" of hypnosis, and the so called "unconscious" of the emotions, may therapeutically be considered aspects of conditioning.

As we saw in Diven's experiment, whether an experience was recalled by the subject or not, its emotion remained present. Many people have tediously learned that "digging out" painful experiences from their "unconscious" does not cure, any more than a man is healed when we determine that he was hit by a southbound freight. And not by one going north.

Hypnosis, word conditioning, and emotional conditioning are thoroughly interwoven, They do not operate by different laws. They are aspects of the same laws. To understand those laws is to understand how to control human behavior.

The feelings of dignity of some persons will be revolted by my approach to human behavior. This is a short-sighted objection. Only knowledge can overcome ignorance, and provide a firm foundation for anything, including human dignity.

Science endeavors to reduce the complicated to rationally simple explanatory principles. To complain that this approach to personality is "too mechanistic" that "we are more than machines," and that man's personality is too deep and intricate to be so easily explained" is to stretch out pleasantly in the warm, soothing waters of ignorance, like a lobster being slowly boiled to death.

Herrick has estimated that the cerebral cortex contains about ten billion nerve cells. (4) "If a million cortical nerve cells were connected one with another in groups of only two neurons each in all possible combinations, the number of different patterns of interneuronic connection thus provided would be expressed by 102,783,000." Wolfle has shown that if we assume the human personality to involve twenty characteristics, each of which can be rated on a ten-point scale, over 100 trillion different descriptions of humans are possible. (5) All this should suffice for the production of a sufficient number of unique personalities. There is no conflict between mechanism and individuality.

Implicit in all the attacks on the reflex school is a resentment that the human being is composed of matter, and that, as the phrase goes, Darwin was right. Surely, the current state of the world casts serious doubts upon the importance of the higher mental processes in the determination of behavior. The application of science to the study of human personality needs no defense, not if we are interested in knowledge and its adaptation. It is only they who take refuge in pure reason and revelation that need apologize.

We have seen that conditioned emotions obey the same laws as conditioned words. And we have seen that the objections to conditioning from the theoretical and practical viewpoint are not well sustained.

In short, we have every reason to believe that from Pavlov's fundamental work in conditioning we can at last develop a true science of psychotherapy.

CHAPTER 2

INHIBITION AND EXCITATION

Everybody talks about heredity, but nobody does anything about it. It is immutable one second after conception. Consequently, let us concern ourselves with environment, for it is the only thing we can change after we're born. Physical traits, and these include intelligence, are inherited, but happiness is not based upon them. Happiness or misery is determined after the child is born.

Heredity provides the phonograph, but environment builds the record library of the brain. Not only is it impossible to choose your relatives, but you cannot even choose yourself.

Just as Pavlov's dog learned to salivate when the bell rang, so does the baby learn that certain behavior on his part brings certain responses from those around him, and he gets conditioned quite as involuntarily. If each act of the child is met with a motherly "don't," equivalent to punishing the dog when he salivates, the child will inhibit his emotions, and withdraw into himself. In Pavlovian terms, the flow of saliva, when the bell was rung to signal the appearance of meat, is an example of an *excitatory reflex*. But if the bell is rung again and again, and not followed by meat, or the dog is punished, the saliva stops flowing, and this is an *inhibitory reflex*.[1]

---

[1] The term "conditioned reflex" is more limited than "conditioned response." However, I prefer it because "reflex" emphasizes the involuntary side of the reaction, and because I am adhering to Pavlovian terminology.

The newborn infant's behavior is excitatory. It acts without restraint. If we were not to interfere in any way except to gratify its physical needs, it would continue in its excitatory path. But we begin early to inhibit the child, and that is how the trouble begins.

In this book we shall consider excitation and the expression of emotion[2] to be parallel, and we will study human nervous activity in terms of inhibition and excitation.

In Pavlov's words, "... all the highest nervous activity, as it manifests itself in the conditioned reflex, consists of a continual change of these three fundamental processes—*excitation, inhibition, and disinhibition.*" (2) And as we study these processes in human behavior, we shall be studying how neurotic reactions may be effectively and rapidly treated.

People are surprised that babies learn when so young. The question is, "Are babies stimulus receivers?" If they are, then learning has to take place. Children's psychology is a comment on their parents. Those whose children stutter should be ashamed to show their faces on the street, but they are all proud of their handiwork. Many a mother would call a policeman if she saw a horse being handled the way she treats her children.

The child is the megaphone of his training, and he never does anything to his parents that they didn't do to him in the first place. When I listen to mothers who have ruined their children's chances for happiness, and who talk confidently and determinedly of their methods, I think of Poe's line,

"Much I marvelled this ungainly fowl to hear discourse so plainly."

The basis of life is excitation. The creatures that survive in the jungle are those that slink and jump and kill. The polite and inhibited ones crouch behind a tree and are soon dead. The human species could never have survived if it were inhibited.

This is not palatable to most of us. Man, the talking primate, insists on clinging to his illusions despite overwhelming evidence to the contrary. We do not like to be reminded that, evolutionarily speaking, we are merely stomachs that grew more complicated.

The human animal, intelligent as he may be, can no more think his way out of an emotional problem than the monkey in the zoo. He can, only be trained out of it. We are no better than our equipment, and our equipment is primitive. There is nothing objective about an animal's reactions. The human being is bounded by the human body. We are

---

[2]   I am following the usage of Frolov, who worked with Pavlov. "... if looked at from the external aspect [when irradiation of excitation takes place], there occurs what is called an affective reaction." (I)

composed of jungle stuff, and ours is a monkey culture. Our troubles are caused by deviations into civilization, which is a fraud perpetrated on evolution. *Homo sapiens* has convinced himself that he is a dancing bear. Consequently, he can only lose his balance.

In the beginning was the gut, and the gut was law, and it is still so. It is the dog part of the human being that gets out of order, the part we keep telling ourselves we should be a little above, but we never are. The dog part runs by the dog rules. Everything is natural, under the circumstances. The twisted unhappy person is normal for what happened to him. No one does what he should. He only does what he can because that is what he has been conditioned to do. People are no more naturally one way, or another, than a piece of marble is naturally the Venus de Milo. Early environment is the sculptor's chisel.

Nothing is ever wrong in the individual's "should" department. It is the "able to" department that causes the difficulty. We live up to our conditioning, not our ideals.

I am always suspicious of the words "like to" or "don't like to." The inhibitory person does not "like" to talk, and the excitatory one does not "like" to keep quiet. An individual's philosophy of life is the product of his feeling-training. His philosophy changes with his emotional re-education.

"Correct and happy" thoughts do not cure, contrary to the inspirational pap found in popular books and magazines. Every issue carries a half dozen self-help articles. They are much like explaining to the eager reader how to make a million dollars. If one article can provide the answer, why read the others?

Only the drilling into the human tissues of healthy habits will yield "good" thinking and feeling. We are meat in which habits have taken up residence. We are a result of the way other people have acted to us. We are the reactions. Having conditioned reflexes means carrying about pieces of past realities.

We do not control ourselves. We are constantly being controlled by our habit patterns. What we deprecate as present irrelevancies are the imprints of past relevancies. We think with our habits, and our emotional training determines our thinking. Consciousness is like a moving picture. The emotional patterns of infancy are projected into awareness. We sit in the audience, and insist we're in the projection booth.

We have only the volition given by our habits. Where there is a conditioned reflex, there is no free will. Our "will power" is dependent on our previously learned reflexes. If they are inadequate, the individual will bemoan his lack of "guts", and deprecate himself, though he is not at all to blame. Everybody is a carpenter using the only tools he ever had.

We feel by doing, and we do by feeling. We do not act because of intellectual reasons. Our reasons grow from our emotional habits. The important point about conditioning is that it is not at all an intellectual process. Whether we like it or not, the brain case has been permeated by the viscera. Life would be impossible if we had to think in order to breathe, feel, digest, blink, and keep our hearts beating.

Personality is not a question of logic. It is a question of feeling. Many bright people are as dull as dishwater. It is their emotional training that makes the difference.

Children are interesting because they are emotionally outgoing. A childish childhood is a happy childhood. The baby is born free, but his parents soon put him in chains. The tragedy of the dawn of psychology is that all of the villains have friendly faces.

More men than women seek psychotherapy. In my own practice they outnumber the women two to one. For that matter, at all age levels they form the majority of first admissions to mental institutions. This has been explained by saying that men suffer more pressure from the world than women. This seems plausible, until we learn that among children, between the ages of five and twelve, before the "stress and strain" of life set in, at least two boys stutter to each girl. Some surveys show ten to one. Among adults the ratio is eight male stutterers to one woman.

The explanation is found in our original thesis. The basis of life is excitation. In popular terms, women are guided more by feeling and "intuition" than by logic, which is also true of girls as opposed to boys. Consequently, they stutter less.

In vino veritas runs the proverb. It would be more complete to say *in vino emotional veritas*. When the alcohol comes, the feelings flow out. In 1947 a total of 4.7 per cent of the entire national income of the United States of America went for alcoholic beverages. I cite this not as an argument for prohibition, to which I am opposed, but to illustrate how thoroughly humanity is inhibited.

Notice that I have not said that people drink to "escape" or to "lose" themselves. Such concepts are therapeutically sterile. I have simply said that alcohol is a chemical means of liberating emotion.

To return to our muttons. Excitation is a basic law of life, and neurosis is the result of the inhibition of natural impulses. I have also said, as can only be obvious in our daily life, that much of our activity is not logically motivated.

When we pause to consider what we have done when we felt happiest, we will recognize that we spoke without thinking. We expressed our innermost feelings. We did not waste time and energy percolating. We acted in an excitatory fashion.

People ask, "What are the roots of my troubles? How did I get this way?" They really mean, "How, in my childhood, was I robbed of my natural excitation? Where and how was this emotional component dwarfed, twisted, misdirected, or minimized?" *Hundreds of different causes produce the same fundamental deprivation of excitation.*

Causes like the following are easy enough to determine, but they do nothing except satisfy our intellectual curiosity. I take them at random from my files:

1 Excessively well-mannered English family.
2 Unhappily married parents. A drunken father.
3 "Both my parents are quiet and reserved."
4 A mother-bound only child.
5 A psychopathic father. Great love one moment, overwhelming rage the next.
6 A more able older brother.
7 Brought up in an orphanage.

Finding and exploring the situations that have caused the psychological difficulty does nothing to facilitate the cure. A judge is interested in who is to blame for an automobile accident. The physician is concerned with healing the wounds of the injured. Psychiatry and psychoanalysis play the part of the judge, although they insist they are cast for the role of the physician.

Man's physical and emotional equipment is the same as it was ages into obscurity. Yet modern man finds himself enmeshed in a web of constraining social forms with which he has more and more been required to conform, belying his essential nature, and denying that the human is, now as then, an animal—predatory, sadistic, craving, and emotional. From here springs conflict between artificial and natural, which overlooks the fact that man is a talking primate.

Living in society necessitates inhibition, but modern training goes too far when it teaches children to be polite at all times, not to contradict others, not to interrupt, not to be selfish, and always to consider other people's feelings. A well-adjusted person is like a housebroken dog. He has the basic inhibitions to permit him to live in society, but none extra to interfere with his happiness.

It will be objected that even the animals have their inhibitions. Doesn't the tiger crouch quietly before he leaps? If he went through underbrush in an excitatory fashion, wouldn't the other animals run away? True. Nevertheless, excitation is the meat of the jungle, while inhibition is the salt and pepper.

Following a set pattern, bowing to artificial vogue, conforming to a standardized mold, smothers excitation. This characterizes the inhibitory "types" -gentlemen-of-the-old school, chivalrous colonels, well-brought-up boys, "officers and gentlemen," stoics, and ascetics. Every chink in their emotional armor, with a few approved exceptions, is plugged with a socially originated inhibition.

At first thought it might appear that a return to excitation would produce a world inhabited by undisciplined brutes, yet nothing could be further from the truth. Only the predominantly inhibited person is selfish, since he is constantly preoccupied with himself. The inhibitory person's consideration for others is merely a burnt child's dread of the fire. He has no thought for others, because he does not have the ability to look outwardly upon those around him. He doesn't love, although he wants to be loved. There is no love without involvement, and he remains in his own shell. He has been conditioned against expressing the emotions of love. He is afraid of other people; he is afraid of responsibility; he is afraid to make decisions. His fears may express themselves in a show of aggression, egocentricity, and a lack of consideration. This type of inhibited person also worries constantly, and he is as maladjusted as his over-polite and shy brother. His suffering is equally intense.

A person has feelings of frustration and conflict when his psychological skills are inadequate to solve the problem that confronts him. It is as if he were trained to open doors, and it is not so much that the emotional lock before him is a new one, as that the keys of inhibition are made of putty.

CHAPTER 3

THE EXCITATORY PERSONALITY

As the human fish swim about at the bottom of their great ocean of atmosphere, they develop inhibitory injuries as they collide with each other. Most frequent of all are the wounds that the little minnows get from the parent fish.

Parents, and everyone else, are doing the best they know, but just as there is only one way for a wrist watch to run correctly, and hundreds of ways for it to get out of order, so is there only one way for children to be psychologically sound, and a multitude of ways for them to develop psychological troubles. Consequently, probability is against mental health, all of which is deplorable, but quite patent.

Nevertheless, some babies are fortunate, and are brought up in an atmosphere of sympathy, understanding, and responsibility. They are rare, and grow up to be happy children and happy adults.

An excellent illustration of a well-adjusted personality is General Eisenhower. Let us consider some of the symptoms of his healthy excitation as manifested in a press conference[1] on his triumphal return from Europe after VE Day. (1) The bracketed comments are mine.

Press: "Could you describe the ribbons you are wearing?"

General Eisenhower: "Well, this is one the President just gave me an hour ago. [Notice how he lets you into his confidence by telling you

---

[1] Reprinted by special permission of the Associated Press and *the New York Herald Tribune*.

of his personal doings. Notice also how his exuberance is boyish and unobjectionable.]

"This is a second Oak Leaf Cluster to my [not "the"] Distinguished Service Cross. The top ones are all American, and I think you know them all . . . [Notice the healthy naturalness.] The next one is a ribbon given by the King of England for having commanded two of his armies. He gave it to me personally. That was in Africa before we went into Europe. The next one is Russian.

"Captain Butcher [his Naval aide] reminds me that there are certain privileges that go with certain Russian decorations, among them, free train rides; you can commandeer taxis, [this is a witticism in wartime Washington, the scene of the interview] free rides on the subway, and certain other privileges that you can do just as long as they don't take them away from you." [The excitatory person is never a stuffed shirt.]

Press: "Do you think Hitler is dead? Are you convinced Hitler is dead?"

General Eisenhower: "Well, to tell you the truth, [frankness again] I wasn't. I was at first. [Note the unembarrassed use of "I".] I thought the evidence was quite clear. But when I actually got to talk to my Russian friends, I found they weren't convinced, and I found that it had been erroneously reported from Berlin. I don't know. [He is thinking out loud, and there is no barrier between him and the listener.]

"The only thing I am sure of is what I said in my Paris conference— [notice his emotionality] if he is not dead he must be leading a terrible life for a man that was the arrogant dictator of 250,000,000 people, to be hunted like a criminal and afraid of the next touch on his shoulder. He must be suffering the agonies of the damned if he is alive."

Press: "What units are going to Berlin? The 2nd or 82nd Airborne, or both?"

General Eisenhower: "It will be the approximate strength of one Division, but I have forgotten for the moment what unit we did set up. We changed it two or three times." [Note the key excitatory trait of improvisation and the absence of "infallibility."]

Press: "In your previous press conference you said the November landing in North Africa was the most worried night. What was your second most worried night?"

General Eisenhower: "As a matter of fact, I just guessed on that one. They put that question to me and it was one I had never thought about. It is pretty hard to go back over three years of a good many worried nights. Malta was pretty bad..."

In terms of platitudes for Babbitts, General Eisenhower illustrated courage, the ability to get along with people and to face them fearlessly, skill in thinking on his feet, and salesmanship of himself. This is true, but it provides no tenable course of action for the inhibitory person. It consigns him to unfulfilled hope and to cutting out coupons from magazines. From my point of view, what General Eisenhower illustrated was spontaneous, outgoing feeling. That is the basis of mental health. It is futile to talk of strength. Let us talk of freedom.

My cases want logic to guide their emotions. I want free outgoing emotion to guide their logic. The happy person does not waste time thinking. *Self-control comes from no control at all.*

The excitatory act, without thinking. The inhibitory think, without acting, and delude themselves into believing that they are highly civilized types. Civilization implies adjustment to a society, and the inhibitory are all anti-social.

Ability to absorb shocks comes from not being rigid. The excitatory person is relaxed and spontaneous, and takes things as they come. His snap judgments, and his whims and improvisations, are not manufactured from thin air. They are the expression of the full individual. They are the reflex action of experience and hunger. Environmental mastery is the only criterion of self-mastery. Anything else is frozen stoicism or asceticism.

To be human is to be juvenile. The important things of life are called childish, because the inhibitory are suspicious of emotional language they do not understand. Yet all the excitatory person wants is what is coming to him.

Emotionally honest excitatory people are not to be confused with the sycophants with asinine grins who surround us in all walks of life the products of their childhood, schooling, and their peregrinations in self-improvement literature. Who of us has not met the effusive prima donna, the energetic life-of-the-party, and the aggressive salesman with the false smile? Equally deficient are those who express dishonest emotions, and rationalize them as being "good business" or "how else can I keep my friends." As hypocritical are those inhibitory fly-fishers who cast lures chosen according to the human fish they aim to hook. Ninety per cent of the persons who consider themselves "extroverts" are really inhibitory.

Excitation is a matter of emotional freedom and has nothing to do with social participation. People with energetic drive and a liking for people are not necessarily excitatory. *The criteria of excitation are honesty of response and the content thereof.* The individual can withdraw while being active. At work, and at leisure, lawyers and engineers are factually noisy, but emotionally inarticulate. Lawyers in their probing for substance find only form, and engineers in their preoccupation with matter lose the essence.

The upper levels of commerce swarm with cold, competent, expressionless men who call themselves extroverts, but who are all inhibitory. They are bright for their work, but not for themselves, their coolness is the ice of inhibition.

They are undemonstrative and aloof. They are suspicious and seldom relaxed. Their friends, if they have any, consider these to be signs or genius, rather than of unhappiness. They may bombard you with personal questions, and tell you nothing about themselves.

They have a contempt for sincere praise and call it flattery. "Life," they will tell you, "is not a soap opera." They call the excitatory "sentimental, maudlin, and corny."

They regard their humble contributions with monumental seriousness. They lack a sense of humor, although they may pose to the contrary.

They are frequently satirical and cruel. They are the practical jokers. They consider their sarcasm brilliant, yet it is really sophomoric. I have never seen a satirical cat or dog. Animals express their emotions in a straightforward fashion, and the satirical human is unnatural and unhappy.

It is possible to be both inhibitory and successful, but at the price of happiness. Without emotional honesty there can be only discontent and misery, and the essential insecurity of these persons with dynamic aggression is shown in their predilection for "yes-men."

Excitation is possible at any social level. Here is a fine description from Dickens' *Pickwick Papers* of the excitatory Sam Weller. In this scene, Sam has unexpectedly encountered Job Trotter, an unctuous thief for whom he has been looking for some time. Trotter tries to contort his face "into the most fearful and astounding grimaces that ever were beheld" in order to avoid being recognized by Sam. Notice how Sam, in his rude and uneducated way, bears the same stamp of excitation as do all other well-adjusted personalities.

"Hallo, you sir!" shouted Sam, fiercely.

The stranger stopped.

"Hallo!" repeated Sam, still more gruffly.

The man with the horrible face, looked, with the greatest surprise, up the court, down the court, and in at the windows of the houses— everywhere but at Sam Weller—and took another step forward, when he was brought to again, by another shout.

"Hallo, you sir!" said Sam, for the third time.

There was no pretending to mistake where the voice came from now, so the stranger, having no other resource, at last looked Sam Weller full in the face.

"It won't do, Job Trotter," said Sam. "Come! None o' that 'ere nonsense. You ain't so wery 'andsome that you can afford to throw away [it's a Weller family trait to mix v's and w's] many o' your good looks. Bring them 'ere eyes o' your'n back into their proper places, or I'll knock 'em out of your head. D'ye hear?"

As Mr. Weller appeared fully disposed to act up to the spirit of this address, Mr. Trotter gradually allowed his face to resume its natural expression; and then giving a start of joy, exclaimed, "What do I see? Mr. Walker!"

"Ah," replied Sam. "You're wery glad to see me, ain't you?"

"Glad!" exclaimed Job Trotter. "Oh, Mr. Walker, if you had but known how I have looked forward to this meeting! It is too much. Mr. Walker; I cannot bear it, indeed I cannot." With these words, Mr. Trotter burst into a regular inundation of tears, and, flinging his arms around those of Mr. Weller, embraced him closely, in an ecstasy of joy.

"Get off!" cried Sam, indignant at this process, and vainly endeavouring to extricate himself from the grasp of his enthusiastic acquaintance. "Get off, I tell you. What are you crying over me for, you portable ingine?" [Engine.]

"Because I am so glad to see you," replied Job Trotter, gradually releasing Mr. Weller, as the first symptoms of his pugnacity disappeared. "Oh, Mr. Walker, this is too much."

"Too much!" echoed Sam. "I think it is too much—rayther! Now what have you got to say to me, eh?"

Mr. Trotter made no reply; for the little pink pocket handkerchief was in full force.

"What have you got to say to me, afore I knock your head off!" repeated Mr. Weller, in a threatening manner.

"Eh!" said Mr. Trotter, with a look of virtuous surprise.

"What have you got to say to me?"

"I, Mr. Walker!"

"Don't call me Valker; my name's Veller; you know that well enough. What have you got to say to me?"

"Bless you, Mr. Walker—Weller, I mean—a great many things, it you will come away somewhere, where we can talk comfortably. If you knew how I have looked for you, Mr. Weller

"Wery hard, indeed, I s'pose?" said Sam dryly.

"Very, very, sir," replied Mr. Trotter, without moving a muscle of his face. "But shake hands, Mr. Weller."

Sam eyed his companion for a few seconds, and then, as it actuated by a sudden impulse, complied with his request.

Unless a personality gives the total impression of the American general or the English cockney, it may be considered less than excitatory.

The excitatory person is direct. He responds outwardly to his environment. When he is confronted with a problem, he takes immediate constructive action. He is energetic, but there is nothing hyperthyroid about it. He sincerely likes people, yet he does not care what they may think. He talks of himself in an unaffected fashion, and is invariably underestimated by the inhibitory. He makes rapid decisions and likes responsibility. Above all, the excitatory person is free of anxiety. He is truly happy.

Unless the overwhelming proportion of humanity is freed from its shackles of inhibition, and made considerably more excitatory, the earth may be doomed to fear, hatred, hypocrisy, misery, war, and destruction. Only through excitation can we achieve mastery of ourselves. Only through excitation can we eliminate the fundamental unhappiness that haunts the entire earth.

CHAPTER 4

THE INHIBITORY
PERSONALITY

Most people are excessively inhibitory, and have elaborate rationalizations that match their conditioning. Many of them don't know enough to realize that the way they feel is called "unhappy" by the informed. At best, they find life a quietly worrisome chore. At worst, they are much bewildered and sore beset.

Fundamentally, the inhibitory person suffers from constipation of the emotions. Good physical condition requires that internal generatings be passed regularly from the body. Similar generatings in the feelings need to be vented continually, otherwise psychological accumulation, toxicity, and ulceration will result.

Childhood encounters, convention, manners, breeding, cliché—all contribute to this inner withholding, amounting to emotional hypocrisy. These conditioned patterns vitiate the stark fact that man is emotionally an animal who obeys the same laws and impulses as any primitive brute.

The inhibitory personality will feed on his adversity, and, unwittingly, or pridefully knowing, conceal true emotional impulses or distrust them; will be withdrawn or tied up inside and frustrated, condoning his behavior by his logic, yet feeling unsatisfied, finding relations with other humans irksome or not too comfortable, feeling no lust or joy in living, and quite unable to transfer fully his affections to a woman.

The inhibitory spend their days in mental acrobatics and their nights in insomnia. They find it difficult to get up in the morning because facing the world calls for excitation. They constantly go around with unfinished business. In their efforts to stay out of hot water they constantly fall into it. They keep roadblocks between the heart and the tongue. The code of the inhibitory personality is to suppress the gut and to inflate the brain.

They are simultaneously too selfish, being wrapped up in themselves and not selfish enough, because they do not fight for their emotional rights. They refuse to fight others, and end up by fighting themselves. Inhibition is a limitation. It is a disconnection from the outside. The inhibitory live in an ivory tower, although they will insist that they are quite sensitive to their surroundings. Theirs is not a sympathetic consciousness, because that comes from a true awareness of the world. The shut-in personality is really shut-out.

The inhibitory try to be everything to everybody, and end up by being nothing to themselves. As one of them said to me, "I'm the only man in Los Angeles with five hundred close friends. Or, "I'm a fine fellow. Everybody likes me, but no one seeks me out. They are the chameleons, trying to please the people they are with. They just "fall in line." They express everything except what they feel. They find it difficult to say "no." They are agreeable. They try to be friendly with everybody, and when they are rebuffed they know it is their own fault. They consider themselves open-minded, tolerant and democratic.

They are always doing things they do not want to do. Robert Louis Stevenson has spoken of "The pleasureless pleasures and imaginary duties in which we coin away our hearts and fritter invaluable years."

One of the rationalizations of the inhibitory personality is his desire for acceptance by his environment. In the past, usually as an infant, inhibition had survival value. He was punished if he expressed himself, and ran counter to his father's, mother's, brother's, nurse's petty societal structure.

The inhibitory are like flypaper. A harsh glance, an overlooked letter, an imagined slight, stick in their minds, and the more they try to shake them off ("Why should I let such little things bother me?") the more firmly stuck they become. They do not vomit forth nauseating emotional food. They try to digest it, and it makes them sick.

An incident that is casual to the excitatory personality, may be crucial and catastrophic to the inhibitory. He will tell you that he is sensitive, or shy and high strung. He is tense, and does not how to know relax. He is a smoker, a drinker, and a coffee lover. His hands tremble when he lifts a cup in company, or when he has to sign his name in front of strangers. He complains when he is criticized in the presence of others, yet he does not want to be criticized when he is alone. The person who fears crowds also fears individuals.

All self-consciousness is based on excessive consciousness of the other person. *Nobody is discontented with himself unless he is discontented with his relationships with others. The person who jumps out of a window wouldn't have done so if he had pushed someone else out.*

The inhibitory are no different in the little things of life than in the big ones. They're the last to enter, and the last to leave an elevator. They are always apologetic. They are the exploited, toiling at tedious tasks. They poison themselves with resentment for years before asking for a wage increase. They are pathetic with waiters, barbers, and salesmen, and they have as much difficulty with their mothers-in-law. They are the women who go into a dress shop and buy in order to get out. As one of them put it, "I've been refusing second portions all my life." They constantly fear that they are inconveniencing people and attracting attention. They fear they're taking up too much space, and breathing too much air.

They live on the see-saw of indecision. "Shall I wear the blue dress or the green one? Shall I call up John first or Jim? Or shall I call neither?" Everything is difficult to decide.

They waste their energies perpetuating inhibitory behavior. They try to negate one million years of evolution. The meek shall inherit the earth, because their faces are in the dust. Besides, modern scholarship has shown that the correct translation is, "The wise shall inherit the earth," which makes more sense.

The inhibitory person is intellectually honest, but emotionally a liar. His courtesy is a fraud. One never knows what is really on his mind, and this does not conduce to warmth in his social relationships.

An inhibitory person said, "A good deal of my conditioning has been self-imposed. In high school I read James Fenimore Cooper and decided to emulate the stoic Indian." This man had found a clothes tree on which to hang the inhibitory coat he always wore. We do not use volitional terms to explain the cringing of a dog in a corner. Only the dog, if he were articulate, would do so.

The inhibitory are secretive. They will not tell you what they had for lunch, whether the room is stuffy, or if their hearts are breaking.

"I don't have to tell my wife that I love her. I'm not a clinging little poodle. I'm the solid Newfoundland type." Most men will pat a dog on the head, but not their wives. A woman would rather be married to a man who doesn't love her, and always tells her he does, than to one who

26

loves her, but never tells her so. A woman wants a husband who is a cross between a gigolo and a longshoreman.

The inhibitory person will tell you that he suffers from too much foresight. He is always analyzing and planning. He worries about the future, and he worries about the past. The dog was kicked for acting on impulse, so he learns to distrust it. The inhibitory person interacts with his environment after deliberation, because he cannot act automatically. He is in a state of perpetual percolation. Some of his thinking is intelligent, but most of it is the foam of churning feelings. He is like a fighter who has overtrained for his bout. He cannot fight at his best.

Living by slide-rule, and figuring each move to four decimal places, is futile. When emotions are inhibited, the excitatory reflexes are unable to help the organism. Inhibition is paralysis. Life is excitation.

The inhibitory are detached, but not objective, and look at people as if they were insects mounted on pins. Affection is given to a man, and he emphasizes how much the woman gets from it. A daughter says of her father, "I never praise him, because it makes him conceited." A son says "Father was objective about me, except when he lost his temper." The inhibitory are well liked by those who are not close to them.

They are often colorless, dull, and boring. They avoid the word "I" as being in bad taste. Instead, they say, "shouldn't one," and "oughtn't one." They mean, "should I," and "ought I." They may look like caricatures of an undertaker, or an early case of Parkinson's disease. Study the faces of those over forty in the better restaurants, before they have had their liquor. They look serious, but they are pathetic. All people whose good manners are noticeable are excessively inhibited, but those who are inhibited are not necessarily well mannered.

Some have developed a fixed or easy smile, but there is no smile in it. Basically they are the same as the serious-faced. Only the frosting on the cake is different. But colorless and dull as they are, in the popular sense of the word the inhibitory may have a great deal of "personality," but it all remains inside of them.

The inhibitory person has been pushed in and equalized by life. That is why his opinions are neutral. He weighs every stimulus that enters his brain, and he continues to ponder over what took place fifty stimuli ago. If he tries to keep pace, nothing registers, because the stimuli cannot penetrate his inhibitory insulation. He cannot concentrate, and as a corollary, he is certain to be accident-prone.

The inhibitory will criticize themselves as being stupid. They may be degree and honor ridden, and highly successful, yet they will insist they are deceiving the world. Each one tries to be a new Erasmus. He thinks he needs a course in Spanish, in public speaking, in philosophy.

What is wrong with them is not a question of intelligence. It is a question of freedom. I tell them, "Never play another person's game. Play your own."

When parents well-meaningly make their child inhibitory, they are seriously reducing his chances for happiness, but they are annihilating it when they destroy his "self-sufficiency." It is difficult to explain this concept, except to say that it is an aspect of inhibition, and is akin to self-reliance.

The woman who is called a clinging vine is low in self-sufficiency, though she will tell you that she is simply being feminine. Berneuter says, "Apparently there are great individual differences in the extent to which various persons are dependent upon others in the ordinary affairs of life. Some individuals frequently need advice, some often need to receive expressions of sympathy, encouragement, or appreciation; others rarely require any such forms of stimulation. Again, some persons are unhappy when they are by themselves, others prefer to be alone. In a word, people differ in the extent to which they are 'self-sufficient.'" (1)

The person low in self-sufficiency (*B2-S* as Bemreuter abbreviates it) confides everything to everybody. He must always be prodded. He must always be encouraged. He depends on the environment for support. Although he has neither initiative nor persistence, he may be successful if there is an able wife or associate in the background. He works out nothing for himself. He likes to have someone else do it, and he rationalizes this as a "practical" seeking for advice. Actually he is looking for the spine his mother, or father, or brother, stole from him.

Those low in self-sufficiency are never their own Marines. They wait for someone to come to the rescue, and someone usually does. They are masochistic, and would rather be dominated than permitted to work alone.

They are slow in making decisions because they have nothing to make decisions with. They are the neurasthenics and the perpetually psychoanalyzed. They like company and dote on attention when they are ill. They can never receive enough praise, and a single harsh word throws them into the abyss of despair. The one who speaks to them last affects them most.

They often seem democratic. They will tell you that they want to know what people think, and that they like to be everybody's friend, yet their basic indecision makes them fundamentally undependable. This trait has been well labeled by Sheldon as "indiscriminate amiability and 'tolerance.'"(2)

Their emotional nourishment comes from the world without, and they are consequently always perplexed and harried. At restaurants they drive the other guests frantic as they try to decide what they want. They are like the horse that starved to death between two bundles of hay.

The problems of daily existence are almost insuperable. They constantly seek perfection, and never find it. They hesitate, fluctuate, and procrastinate through life. Despite their troubles, they are quite complacent. They would not cross the street if their lives depended on it.

Those with low self-sufficiency are emotional vampires, yet they always act sympathetic and interested in your welfare. They seem excitatory to the uninitiated because they are always talking about what they feel and what they believe. Yet all they are doing is trying to share their emotional load with others. They are not sure what feelings they have about anything. The persons with low self-sufficiency are passive, and want a masseur to massage their muscles. The ones high in self-sufficiency massage their own.

Although selected inhibitory personalities may be high in self-sufficiency, it will always be found that such persons had training in self-reliance as children. Low self-sufficiency, however, will not be found among the well-adjusted.

Watson was aware of the crushing effects of low self-reliance upon children. (3) He advised parents, "Let your behavior always be objective and kindly firm. Never hug and kiss [your children], never let them sit in your lap. If you must, kiss them once on the forehead when they say good night. Shake hands with them in the morning. Give them a pat on the head if they have made an extraordinarily good job of a difficult task." There is no doubt that this will teach the child self-reliance, independence from the family group, and ability at solving problems for himself. He will never become an inadequate Jellyfish. Nevertheless, this coldness may make him excessively inhibitory. Self-sufficiency is not equivalent to mental health. Many highly self-sufficient people are obviously tense and anxious.

The person low in self-sufficiency is a therapeutically discouraging problem, and unless he is treated with finesse and caution, is beyond redemption.

Inhibition is living death. The inhibitory person has been trained in habit-systems of inadequacy, which generate more inadequacy. The inhibitory personality works at what he knows best: frustration.

"I'm not always this way," he will tell you. "I loosen up with my wife." This is like the stutterer who says, "I don't stutter all of the time. Just with certain people." The objective of therapy is a satisfactory level of psychological well-being at all times. When I see a new case, I ask myself two questions: How did his natural freedom get lost? And more important, how can his natural freedom be restored?

The inhibitory have developed the brake habit. They have collided with too many automobiles on the highway of life, and have learned to drive with the brakes on. They do not suffer from a hundred different difficulties. They suffer from one related problem.

Bluntly put, the inhibitory personality is a type. Therapy consists of making him an individual.

CHAPTER 5

THE RATIONALIZATION OF CONDITIONING

Everybody today has serious psychological opinions of his own. He has learned about psychoanalysis from moving pictures and novels, and physiology from advertisements of laxatives, liniments, and headache powders.

The reasons given by inhibitory or even excitatory people for their behavior should never be taken seriously. I ask Mr. X, at the end of therapy, why he has stopped drinking. He answers, "Because I realize what a fool I've been." When I ask him if he hadn't realized it before, he says, "Yes. But now I *really* realize it." Like most people he adheres to the myth of rationality, and becomes prone to inaccurate cause-and-effecting. Actually, he has stopped drinking because his emotional patterns have been changed from inhibitory to excitatory. The shadow changes with the substance.

The Freudians conceive of rationalization[1] as having a self-protective function. People, they say, cannot face their true motives, and therefore tend to disguise and justify them. *The fact is that the excitatory rationalize precisely as much as the inhibitory.*

---

[1] This word was first introduced into psychoanalysis by Ernest Jones in 1908, but in its modern sense it dates back to the first half of the nineteenth century. See "rationalize" in Oxford English Dictionary, definition one.

The unhappy dog in the corner is no more silent because he decided barking was vulgar, than his brother is joyful because he decided it was mentally healthy. One is silent because he was punished. The other is joyful because he was patted. Dogs have only their reaction systems. They do not rationalize. We rationalize for them. Humans are the only members of the animal kingdom that tack on the word "because" to the emotional patterns that determine their behavior.

The head of a college department does not sanction the promotion of a young instructor "because" he hasn't enough experience. Although this is true, it is his brilliance that disturbs the professor. Professors rationalize as much as morons. The difference is that professors have more complicated and subtle rationalizations because they have accumulated more complicated and subtle reaction systems.

An inmate of a mental institution suffered from the delusion that his body had no blood at all. When his finger was pricked by a physician, and the blood came forth, he was asked, "Well, what do you say now?" He looked at the blood and said, "But it's very little, you must admit."

A man who was frightened by the "invasion from Mars" when H. G. Wells' "War of the Worlds" was broadcast, was asked, "What did you do to check up on it?" He answered, "I looked out of the window and everything looked the same as usual *so I thought it hadn't reached our section yet.*" (I)

There is no greater obscenity than an inhibitory psychiatrist, for he cannot help rationalizing his patients in terms of his own emotions. Nobody is exempt from the laws of the human nervous system. It may be objected that in order to examine a broken rib under the scan, it is immaterial whether the physician has ever personally sustained such an injury. This analogy is not well taken. In psychotherapy, the fluoroscopic screen is the therapist. That is his instrument for studying the patient.

We rationalize our conditioned reaction patterns. We think we are looking out of a window at our neighbors, but we are looking into a mirror at ourselves.

Knowing how rationalization works does not make us at all immune. There is no vaccination against it. If the reader smiles, and considers himself an exception, he is rationalizing once more. "Rationalization" is a word usually levied against someone else. "Objective" is a word we have a tendency to confine to ourselves. Our usage of the terms illustrates their subjective character. When a man calls his childhood "normal," I remind him that he had only one. If he answers, "I can analyze myself objectively," he is contending that his own brain is not measuring his own brain.

When we try to be objective, we must remember that the meat of our skin is us. It is futile to study our own emotions, because we are applying to them only the patterns that already exist. I always yawn when hear people say they are objective. No hair-splitter ever pleaded guilty to hair-splitting. Two recent illustrations are the reluctant reception given to Kettering's remarkable Diesel railroad engine, and to atabrine as a substitute for quinine. Atabrine has since been superseded by drugs that are much more effective. However, when it was first introduced, the unwarranted support of quinine by the most highly placed medical authorities was a serious threat to the success of large scale military operations. What was tragically amusing in all this was that it was the few supporters of atabrine who were accused of jeopardizing the nation's existence. The battles and libels of science, rationalized to the soothing strains of objectivity, belong in a comic opera.

Motion and change in the physical world generate heat, and human matter is no exception to this rule. Logical constructs are emotional. We never learn objectivity. We acquire different pairs of glasses. Conviction is irrational. People's biases and the front page of the newspaper illustrate the futility of proving anything. New data verify old prejudices. When we study objectivity objectively, it turns out to be subjective.

Ethics that were not conditioned through action have no serious effect on conduct. Everybody bemoans the backtracking of civilized people into primordial behavior. I marvel at any glimmerings of civilization.

Here the semanticists enter the scene. Rational behavior, they remind us, is permeated by the products of the lower brain centers. Feelings are fools. Let the cortex reason them away.

Korzybski, in a book well worth reading, advises that "we introduce a 'delay in action,' which is the physiological means for getting our 'emotions' under control and for engaging the fuller co-operation of the cortex.'(2)

This point of view is another disguise for inhibition and the rationalist fallacy. It is an anatomical impossibility to protect ourselves from our prejudices. To do so, we must vivisect the nervous system. Each person has his own conditioned language, and after a while there is a Babel. Conditioned feelings and organic needs permeate thinking, and it is impossible to cerebrate without them. The semanticists, distressed that human beings cannot think without their nervous systems, suggest counting to ten, and using your head. This is thin gruel. There is much more to thinking than thoughts. All thinking is value thinking. We think with our past.

The fact is, differentiating between reason and emotion is almost always a medieval relic. Morgan, reviewing the evidence on the anatomical localization of emotional integrations says, "no one nucleus or region can be said to constitute the neural center of ... emotional behavior." (3)

To point out rationalization in behavior is to pick out a particular series of threads in the thoroughly interwoven fabric of cortical-sympathetic behavior. The therapeutic utility of the concept *rationalization* lies in its emphasis on the idea that the real causes of behavior lie not in immediate circumstances, but in remote antecedent conditionings.

In a sense, reason and emotion are two nostrils of the same nose. We may talk of different levels of behavior, but whether we like it or not, the processes of emotion and reason go on side by side. At all times all of us cannot help using them together, because they are actually one neurological thing.

There was never any other kind of thinking since our reptilian ancestors left the swamp. This seems to leave us impaled on the horns of a dilemma. Yet the solution is simple. There is nothing wrong in being "guided" by our emotions. We cannot help it. The only question is, "What emotions?" Are they the sterile, stultifying, fearful emotions of inhibition, or are they the free, healthy, vigorous, and rewarding emotions of excitation?

CHAPTER 6

RECONDITIONING AND DISINHIBITION IN THERAPY

The principles of excitation apply to every psychological problem, no matter how remote they may first appear. It will be found that claustrophobia, for example, though presumably the imprint of a particular experience, is discarded when the individual develops greater excitation. This is an important principle, and I shall use three cases of claustrophobia to illustrate it.

Case I

Let us consider a stockbroker, aged 40, who has suffered from claustrophobia and fear of the dark since childhood. He is pleasant and somewhat dynamic, and speaks impersonally and to the point. His parents were always formal with him, and I soon realize that he is the classical inhibitory type that always seems calm. Fortunately, he is happily married, so that presents no problem. He works easily with mental abstractions, and is well-informed about psychology.

I tell him that he may expect results quickly because he has the learning attitude. It is not one of contradiction or dull acquiescence, but is rather that of a professional violinist, studying with a teacher, and trying to translate the instructions into muscular action with a violin. More cannot be expected of anybody.

I explain to him that his claustrophobia and fear of the dark are merely two aspects of his inability to liberate any emotion at all. "You're like flypaper. Every feeling sticks to you; and-the more so when you try to shake it off. Don't be so agreeable. Tell people what you think at all times, regardless of whether it's politic or impolitic. Down with Emily Post! Live with the shades up. Get the steam out! Be an emotional broadcaster, not a receiver. Don't degenerate into logic. Don't be so brainy in your work. Be more gutty. Practice these setting-up exercises for the emotions."

I showed him how to apply these principles with his wife, servants, office employees, and business associates, and after five hours of such therapy his claustrophobia and fear of the dark were gone. His sessions were helpful, but his psychological exercises outside of my office had been more important. He lost his phobia because he had become more emotionally free and had acquired greater ease with people.

The originally disturbing claustrophobic and darkness experiences were never elicited from him. To me, his symptoms were manifestations of his inability to shake off experiences of high emotional content. This is not symptom therapy, for it is the balance between inhibition and excitation that determines the extent to which an individual participates in life. That the success of this approach to claustrophobia is probably not a coincidence is shown in another case.

Case 2

The 45 year-old head of a huge advertising agency has had claustrophobia since childhood, and has also suffered from stomach cramps and gasping breathing for the past dozen years. This comes over him in his dealings with the men who decide whether or not to give their advertising to his agency, in short, with the men who have the power of life or death over his business.

As he sits before me, he is calmly puffing on a pipe, tweedy and looking like a young college professor. "My nervous ailment is getting so bad it is threatening to interfere with my work. I have been X-rayed and tested from head to toe, and nothing organically wrong has been found." These are the first steps that are usually taken upon any onset of a psychological disturbance. "My trouble seems to be a psychopathic disturbance of my breathing function. I seem to have a continual spasm of the muscles which control my breathing. About half the time I can't draw a deep breath, which is very frightening. I gel severe headaches during which I pant and fight for my breath, and gasp for hours. These attacks come on after meals, or when waiting in a theatre, or during important business conferences. It is hard for me to carry on a prolonged conversation because I seem to be unable to coordinate my breathing with my speaking."

He has seen "dozens" of psychiatrists, which is probably an exaggeration. Those who were psychoanalysts imply an Oedipus complex; the others counsel him not to "worry so much," and to "get a grip on yourself," and he bids them adieu and is a perambulating hypochondriac again.

He is unhappily married to a modern Xanthippe, and has read much, but not wisely, in psychology. He has the learning attitude, and any "psychological diet list" I give him will be followed implicitly. He owns a racing stable, and it is easy for him to see the importance of training healthy emotional habits in humans as well as in horses.

"Yes," he says. "You make sense. You're right when you say my emotional percolator is always perking, and I never pour a cup. Everybody thinks I'm cool, but I'm bursting inside. I'm always the first to pick up a dinner check, even if it's not my turn. I want everybody to love me."

"I see you have been reading a book."

He continues without a smile. "I suppose you want me to become a 'louse.'"

"I wouldn't put it that vigorously. Let us say that in this wicked world it is simply a question of fighting for your emotional rights. You never get your privileges anyway. You want nothing that isn't coming to you. The chances are," I continue, with superficial logic, "that if you do the opposite of what you have been doing all your life, you will probably feel the opposite of the way you do now."

He agrees that this seems plausible.

I speak to him much as did to Case 1. "Never be reasonable about anything. Get rid of your irritations. I don't care what you feel. I only want to know what you express. Don't keep your-real-feelings corked up, any more than you would your stomach. Yelling gets the knot out of your gut. Remember, they that spit shall inherit the earth."

We dispose of his childhood in a few minutes. This is the one with the over-protective mother, the uninterested father, the house full of children, and the selling of newspapers when he was ten. There is often no point in going into the background of the case. We see the malconditioned dog before us, and his problem tells us all that we need to know about the kennel from which he came.

At his next appointment, he told me that he had called at the office of one of his clients after leaving me last time, and was the sole passenger in an elevator operated by a young woman. The elevator stuck between floors, the nightmare of a claustrophobic. He said that he had been practicing by chatting with my secretary after he left, and with the cab driver riding to his account. "I was in a good mood when I entered the elevator."

"What happened when it jammed?"

"The girl was frightened and turned to me. She was pretty. "What am I supposed to do now?' she said. "How the hell do I know?' I told her. 'I'm not running this elevator.' She said, 'I just got the job this morning.' 'Well,' I said, 'damn it, let's see.' And we went over to the button panel and began pushing buttons. The elevator got going, and after a few wrong stops reached my floor."

I asked him how long he remained agitated after he left the elevator. He said not more than five minutes.

"Come now."

"That's exactly right," he answered.

"How would you have acted in the elevator if you hadn't seen me?"

"I would have told the girl, 'Keep calm, miss. There's no point in being excited', but I would probably have been ready to faint. After I left the elevator. I would have been dead to the world for the rest of the day, and most of the next one."

"You said the elevator operator was pretty. Don't you think you were showing off in front of her?"

"Maybe," he answered, "but I didn't give her the keep-cool routine. I exploded, like you told me."

He had a total of five hours of consultation, and now, two years later, his claustrophobia is still gone. He feels much freer, and his stomach symptoms occur rarely and with diminished severity. His business activity distresses him substantially less, and in general he is a much happier person. "I am greatly improved. I am advancing instead of going back."

Were the two cases of claustrophobia that I have so far presented really cured, or did they only get symptom relief? If the latter be so, was the relief temporary or permanent, or did the symptoms remain, but in a different form? Fundamental issues all, but answerable, I believe, to the satisfaction of persons with forbearance enough to follow the thread of my discussion.

Surely, these objections lose weight when they are voiced by those seldom able to provide their patients with temporary relief, to say nothing of permanent cure. But more fundamentally, the question of symptom relief versus root cure turns on *what happens to be denominated* as the roots of an individual's problem; and these will always reflect the school of psychology to which the critic or the therapist belongs.

"Know thyself." says the proverb. but with what? The individual has only himself to know himself with, so acquiring new knowledge is not easy. I realize it can only be difficult, for those whose conditioning in psychology is non-reflexological, to believe that claustrophobia can be solved as simply as I have explained. Nor should such persons be criticized when they find repugnant the thesis that the solution to personality difficulties lies in increasing the individual's level of excitation, whether the problem be claustrophobia, alcoholism, shyness, drug addiction, stuttering, or anything else.

To those of them who are endowed with the true scientific spirit, I commend Francis Bacon. "We find no new tools because we take some venerable but questionable proposition as an indubitable starting point. Now, if a man will begin with certainties, he shall end in doubts; but if he will be content to begin in doubts, he shall end in certainties."

Case 3

One man's symptoms are another man's roots. An understanding of this, as shown in yet another case of claustrophobia, will lead us deeper into the techniques of conditioned reflex therapy.

Dr. T. is a 55 year-old surgeon. He has suffered from claustrophobia since the age of seven or eight. His home looks like a medieval castle, and he has called in a procession of contractors to estimate the cost of putting windows through three feet of masonry, because he wants to feel closer to the outside world. Every door, including the bathroom, is kept open or ajar. Sleeping in the house makes him uneasy, but he sleeps comfortably in the open air. In summer he spends most of his time camping, so that he can sleep out-of-doors. He will not ride in an elevator, and he cannot ride on trains except near the door, and then he is uncomfortable. He has no recollection of the onset of the claustrophobia, but he recalls that when he was ten he had once slept in an attic at his aunt's house, and had felt oppressed by the confined space. The approach of cold weather always frightens him, but curiously, when winter comes, he rather enjoys it. He reports no other fears.

"Isn't this rather illogical?" he says.

I answer that by "illogical" we usually mean "emotional."

His marriage, I quickly see, is happy. Here, then, is a man with claustrophobia and fear of the onset of cold weather, who can recall neither of the original experiences, although he can think of times in his childhood when they disturbed him. I decide to consider the claustrophobia first, because it is probably a simpler problem than his fear of winter weather.

He has a strong scientific bent, and, quite unsuccessfully, has often tried to recall his original experience with claustrophobia that his reading tells him must have occurred. He has read my "Three Techniques of Autohypnosis" and is hypnotic minded.

"Well," I say, "first I will teach you to recapture the feeling of claustrophobia at will. Then the stimuli which originated it will come surging back to you." I explain how moods carry memories in their wake, and I direct the conversation so that he becomes completely retrospective toward his childhood. That is where his attention is directed, and that is all that occupies him. Then, with dramatic emphasis, I read the following passage from W. H. R. Rivers: (1)

> The incident which he remembered was a visit to an old rag-and-bone merchant who lived near the house which his parents then occupied. This old man was in the habit of giving boys a halfpenny when they took to him anything of value. The child had found something and had taken it alone to the house of the old man. He had been admitted through a dark narrow passage from which he entered the house by turning about half-way along the passage. At the end of the passage was a brown spaniel. Having received his reward, the child came out alone to find the door shut. He was too small to open the door, and the dog at the other end of the passage began to growl. The child was terrified. His state of terror came back to him vividly as the incident returned to his mind after all the years of oblivion in which it had lain. The influence which the incident made on his mind is shown by his recollection that ever afterwards he was afraid to pass the house of the old man, and if forced to do so, always kept to the opposite side of the street.

When I finished, he looked bewildered. "That's it! That trapped feeling." He repeated, "That trapped feeling! It's come back to me! When I was a child on my aunt's farm they were building a link to a reservoir across the property. They had big six-foot pipes lying next to each other before they dug a trench and covered them. It used to be fun to get in at one end of the pipes, and run through to the spot of light way down at the other end. One afternoon, I started to run through, and about half-way, something in the darkness grabbed me and held me. It was a man inside, fixing something. I was absolutely petrified, and I couldn't even scream. He let me go after a while, and I thought I'd never reach the other end.... Yes," he said, "it's odd how that thing comes back to me. I'm sure that's how I got the claustrophobia."

I said nothing. He continued, "Isn't it peculiar how I feel that frightened feeling right now? It's almost as if I'm back in the pipe again, but its less than the original feeling... You know, this is the first time I've thought of this in fifty years, and I have tried hard to recall it many times." Needless to say, knowing where a man got a bullet-wound does not stop the bleeding.

I found that he had tried self-suggestion, and had been able to induce feelings of lightness and heaviness in his limbs. This meant I would probably succeed in teaching him how to get his arms and legs warm or cold. I said, for example, "Your right arm is very light, extremely light, just as if there's a rope tied on your wrist, pulling it up, pulling it up. Your arm's just floating in the air, floating in the air ..." I then gave him suggestions of cold—his hand is frozen in a cake of ice, winter is here and it's very cold. And so on. I told him to seat himself in a comfortable chair in his living room at home, and to practice these exercises in sensory recall.

At his second visit, he reported that he could turn on the sensations with ease. He listened with interest to my explanation of verbal conditioning, and next I told him to practice turning his feeling of claustrophobia on and off, and conditioning relaxation to it. He was also to continue the sensory exercises, except that now they were to include vigorous statements that he was grown up, and that his nonsensical childish fears no longer plagued him. He was also to tell himself that the pipe broke open when the man grabbed him.

My plan was for him to establish a link between controlling his senses and feeling good. I also told him to take care not to make his claustrophobia stronger than his feelings of well-being, or the conditioning would increase his discomfort.

Before his third session he wrote, "No mental suffering today. Just a weak pair of legs which I can stand or stand on." He continued the exercises. When I next saw him I asked him to try to recall any distressing associations he may have had with cold weather, but he could think of none. Since he was somewhat plump, I told him, with a smile, that his fear of the cold did not seem to be physiologically determined. Shortly thereafter, pursuant to my instructions, he made his body feel relaxed and heavy at a living room self-suggestion session. He built up his fear of the coming of winter, and kept a retrospective attitude toward his childhood at the same time. He piled mood on mood, and another experience that he had completely forgotten returned to him.

On his aunt's farm was a lake, and in the winter ice was sawed from it, and stored in a big icehouse. One summer afternoon, when he was no more than ten, he was accidentally locked in among the cakes of ice, and only after becoming cold and frightened, and running hysterically back and forth in the icehouse, was he able to open the door and get out. This experience followed the one in the reservoir pipes, and no doubt reinforced his earlier claustrophobia. Without instructions from me, he worked on his experience in the icehouse as he had with his experience in the pipe. He told himself that such childish nonsense would not stress him any more, and besides, the doors of the icehouse had been wide open all the time. It was not possible to check the effect of these suggestions, because he was seeing me during the winter.

By this time, he was going about the house, giving himself what he called "those anti-claustrophobia vaccinations." On his fifth session, he reported a complete absence of any claustrophobic symptoms whatever, and he has remained free to this day, five years later. Gone also is his fear of the onset of winter. Further, although I grave him no direct therapy to facilitate relations with people, he reported a greater ease with them. We had one more session, in which we discussed the rationale of my therapy with him, and that is all there was to the case.

Please note that I devoted no attention to his basic personality, which was one of confidence in professional activity, and polite inhibition in personal relations. Although I treated him purely as a victim of specific claustrophobic conditioning, repercussions nevertheless soon occurred in his social relations.

Cases 1 and 2 received no specific conditioning against claustrophobia, and they seem to have been cured through an increase in excitation. A similar approach, I have found, is also successful with agoraphobia (fear of open spaces).

Apparently, it makes no difference which part of a "vicious" circle we start with, as long as we get a firm grip on any of its many radii. Conditioned patterns are an intermeshed set of gears, and it is not too important where we apply motive power. If we apply some force anywhere in the system, all of the other wheels will turn together. If we keep our eye on emotions and their conditioning, that is all that will be necessary.

In the case of the claustrophobic who feared the onset of winter, the amnesia surrounding the original experiences seemed to have been lifted, although I entertained some doubt as to the relevancy of the icehouse episode. In Cases 1 and 2, which were treated as problems in excitation, I made no effort to ascertain the original experiences, nor were they ever elicited. It is seldom the trauma that does it. It is the slow grind.

In terms of relief reported there seems to be no difference. Both approaches to claustrophobia seem equally fundamental, because substantial improvement occurred in areas that were neither probed nor treated. If it be contended that the relaxation techniques in Case 3 were also a form of excitation, it still would not affect my thesis. Let me recall my analogy of the gears. Turn one of them, and you turn them all.

Case 4

But what shall be done with the persons who do not let you turn the wheels? Often, they should be chased from the office with a broomstick, although they are not to be blamed for their personalities.

I explain to them that my appointment book is like a life raft. There is room for only a limited number of people, and I do not intend to waste my time trying to convince any of the bobbing heads around me to get on board. There are others drowning who are only too happy to cooperate in their rescue... Here, however, let us consider one of these recalcitrant cases, and implement our principles some more.

J. R. is the tall, handsome son of a millionaire. He is 25 years old, a post-graduate student in sociology, and talks vaguely of improving the welfare of humanity. He is convinced he is uninteresting. He is an alert, if too agreeable, young man, and acts somewhat mule-like when I disagree with him. Though he does not find his studies difficult, he cannot concentrate on them because his mind "wanders constantly." He tosses restlessly for hours before falling into a fitful sleep. He wants to learn how to hypnotize himself so that he may be rid of his insomnia. I test him for hypnosis, but his attention wanders as he compares my technique with what he has read about the subject, and with what he thinks I should do. Needless to say, nothing happens.

I then become stern, and tell him that I am utterly uninterested in the clap-trap that clutters up his mind. I am the authority, and he has come to consult me. He will do exactly as I say, if he wants to learn autohypnosis. All that he has to provide is the broken leg. I will decide the splints that are indicated. This approach is necessary with the spoiled-child type of adult, because our only means of communication with him (and with everybody else) is through his conditioned emotions.

He is interested in music and possesses absolute pitch. I decide to mold my technique accordingly, and tell him to listen intently.

I snap my fingers. "Can you still hear that pitch in your head, now that I have stopped snapping my fingers?"

"Yes."

I tap my desk with my pen. "Can you hear this sound in your head?"

"Yes."

"That's fine. I see the procedure necessary, and we'll take it from there when I see you next."

"Aren't you going to hypnotize me today?" he asks.

I smile blandly. "If you want me to help you, it will have to be in my way. I can't be bothered having you tell me what to do."

It might appear that such insulting disinterest would frighten him away permanently, but experience demonstrates that this is the only efficacious technique with persons who try to guide the therapy. This has to be tempered with judgment, but it involves a difference in tactics, not principles. If messages to people are not enciphered in their own peculiar emotional code there is no communication. To condition something new, we have to take advantage of something old.

Our young man is annoyed when he leaves, but he is very curious about what I have up my sleeve, which is precisely my intention.

When I next see him, I tell him that he simply has to listen to me and obey. He has my permission to waste his own time, but I resent his wasting mine, and unless he is completely and absolutely cooperative, he might as well leave right now.

"What have I done to deserve this tirade?" he asks.

"You are guilty of being you. That's all. The fact that you bought a ticket doesn't give you a license to tell the actors what to say."

He smiles.

"Very well," I say. I point to the glistening thermos jug on my desk. "I want you to look at the spot made by the reflection of the light. Do you see that spot?"

"Yes."

"Now, each time I snap my fingers, I want you to close your eyes in a docile, browbeaten way. For your sake, please, close them in a docile, browbeaten way. You will find this very interesting."

Many persons go through life in a constant flight from boredom, and their cooperation can be enlisted only by promising them relaxation and entertainment. Ringing these bells involves no hypocrisy. Our therapeutic duty to a human being in distress is all the validation we need.

He relaxes in the easy chair and stares at the jug. I snap my fingers. He closes his eyes. I wait about three seconds and then say quietly, "Open them." He opens his eyes, and continues looking at the spot. I snap my fingers again and he closes his eyes. I wait another three seconds, and then say, "Open them." He does so. "That's fine," I say. "From now on I want you to think thoughts of blankness, relaxation, and quietness in a vague day-dreaming way. At the same time, as I snap my fingers, close your eyes without thinking and keep them shut, until I tell you to open them. Think 'relax,' and try to feel blank in every part of your body. Do you understand?"

Yes, he says. I see that I have his complete attention, and that now, at least, he has no negativism toward me.

I snap my fingers. His eyes close. I wait three seconds and say, open them," and I snap my fingers again. He closes his eyes. I permit them to remain closed for three seconds and say, "Open them," and I repeat this ritual once more. After about forty times I stop. "How are your thoughts now?"

He is somewhat surprised. "I feel relaxed."

"That's fine," I say. "Now I'll tell you what," and without ado I snap my fingers, although he is not fixating the jug. He blinks. "What happened?" I ask,

"I blinked when you snapped your fingers."

"That's fine," I say, for this means that now his lid closure has become somewhat conditioned.

We resume the finger-snapping eye-closing exercises for another forty times, and then I stop. "Can you imagine my fingers snapping when I'm not snapping them?"

"Yes," he says.

"Can you hear them clearly in your mind?"

He nods.

"I'll tell you what I want you to do," I say. "Practice this ten minutes at a time, in the morning when you get up, and at night before you go to sleep. Imagine yourself looking at the shiny spot on the jug. Imagine the mood you're in now, and make believe you hear my fingers snapping. Think that relaxed feeling lightly, and then close your eyes. It sounds more complicated than it really is."

"I think I know what you mean. I'll do it, but what if I still can't sleep?"

"Just do the exercises," I say, "and if you continue tossing around, stop them. I don't want you to hitch bad conditioning to them. You'll fall asleep eventually. Maybe it will take some time. I'm only asking you to do the exercises. If you do that, forgive me if I sound cruel, the rest doesn't matter. Just do as I say."

On his next visit he reports that the exercises at night make him feel increasingly relaxed. Also, that his concentration has improved when he reads. He volunteers that a tension he has had in social relationships seems to diminish if he practices the exercises before going among people. In fact, he has been practicing the exercises as much as eight and ten times a day. He seems to get relaxed more thoroughly and quickly each time.

"Fine," I say. "I am not surprised that you violated my instructions and practiced more than I told you to, but this is one time when your being an *enfant terrible* has worked out well." He smiles beatifically. "Keep practicing those exercises," I say, "and particularly before any social activity. You do not even have to open and shut your eyes. Just keep them closed, and mentally go through the whole procedure."

"Yes," he says, "that's much the way I have been doing it."

My purpose in all this is to make life easier for him. He is a thoroughly spoiled, grown-up child, and any slight frustration of his wishes causes tension. I want to make him calmer, which will make him much more endurable, and in turn, will make him feel better. "The emotionally free animal has no trouble falling asleep, and as we get you more relaxed (that's what he wants, relaxation) you will be able to feel better through the day, and at night your tension will be less, so sleeping will come easier. Does this make any sense to you?"

"Yes," he answers. "I see what you mean."

I continued seeing him, and there was much chatter of pedagogy, hypnotism, and sociology, but now what intrigued him was that these relaxation exercises were making his relationships with women easier. At a night club, a semi-nude performer volunteered to dance with a member of the audience. Formerly, much as he wanted to, he would have lacked the courage to do so, but now, with very little prodding from his friends, he got up and rhumbaed, to the great acclaim of the audience. This he liked very much, and it made him a great believer in the importance of relaxation. He continued to pay little attention to excitation.

His interest in hypnosis became more marked, and he took great delight in demonstrating it upon such young women as he could snare. "Do you think you can hypnotize me now?" he asked one day.

"Let's try," I said. Nothing happened except that he felt more relaxed. His mind stopped wandering, and he became subdued. Meanwhile, I must add, he was tossing about in bed less and less. Instead of three hours each night, he now tossed around for about an hour and a half.

I then decided that the time was ripe for emphasis on the concept of excitation, which I tied up to greater social adequacy with women. I presented it as a laundry drier for social wet-blankets, which indeed it is.

"Come to think of it," he said, "I have the same inadequacies with everybody. I'm just a boy of good family. You say I'm bright, but that's about all. Really, I've never done anything of interest." This from someone who had spent a summer as an overseer on a rubber plantation in Africa, and during another vacation had hunted tigers in India, *pour le sport.*

He continued the exercises in auditory imagination. Once I jokingly snapped my fingers for him to check the pitch, but he said it only confused him. Before long, he had become more excitatory, and was sure that now people liked him. What is more, by thinking of the finger snapping exercises, he was able to go to sleep at night almost instantly.

At the end of our fifteenth hour, I said, "That seems to be that. You are now a social lion without insomnia."

"Yes," he said, "but frankly I'm disappointed because I haven't learned how to hypnotize myself."

I answered, "We acknowledge the fact that you are much less of a bore socially." He nodded with a wry smile. "And tell me," I said, "Let us suppose that you had told a friend that you had come to see that you had suffered from insomnia and would toss about for three or four hours before falling asleep. Now, after seeing me, by merely imagining that you're in my office, and that you hear me snapping my fingers, you fall asleep at night almost instantly. In fact, you almost go out like a light. You seem to have acquired a strange power over yourself. Don't you think that if your friend heard all this he would say that it was hypnotism?"

"Yes, he said, "but it still isn't hypnotism. It's just conditioning."

I was annoyed and amused. "Ho-hum. There isn't much else I can add. If you're not proud of the results, believe me, I am."

He left disgruntled, and that was the last I heard of him. Shakespeare could be rewritten to say, "Above all, only to thine own conditioning canst thou be true."

What is interesting about this case is that instead of tiptoeing around the young man's idiosyncrasies, I boldly took advantage of them. Since his language was emotional Greek, and it was the only one he understood, I spoke it.

Further, the therapy was successful, although his attitude showed that his basic recalcitrance had remained. Faith and belief are inadequate substitutes for science. As for gratitude, it is achievement enough to have helped such a person, without expecting the impossible. There will be others who will be grateful, and who will make therapy emotionally rewarding. Although I cannot expect to act without my nervous system, such things no longer disturb me—at least, for not more than a day.

CHAPTER 7

THE CONSTRUCTIVE USE OF PAST CONDITIONINGS

To arouse the feelings of an inhibitory person, for there is no communication without feeling-involvement, is almost as difficult as talking Beethoven to the tone-deaf. It is like the conception of resonance in physics. We can vibrate the established conditioned reflexes of personality only at their own frequency. We must talk to people in their private, personally conditioned language. Anything else is gibberish.

The first thing a person is loyal to is his own conditioned nervous system. How therapeutically wise, then, it is to work with the personality before us, rather than with a non-existent fiction. It is foolish to complain that a recording of *Three Blind Mice* does not sound like Beethoven's *Ninth Symphony*. People are faithful to the grooves in their emotional phonograph records, and rather than bemoaning us, it means that with a masochist we must be stern, with a clubman type we must be amusing, and with a scholarly person we must be as analytical as possible. As I have stressed, there is no communication except in terms of the person being treated.

This is illustrated in what I have called the "feedback method of hypnosis". It involves giving the subject a series of short verbal conditionings, after which he is asked to report his feelings. Some will say, "I felt as if the world went far away." Others will report the dominance of relaxed feelings. Some will confess to a "loss of control over me." When verbal conditionings are next administered to the subject, their motif is whatever predominant quality the subject had previously reported. In other words, rather than persistently ringing standard verbal bells, the subject's individual conditionings are found fed back to him.

The feedback is the basis of all successful publishing, advertising, motion pictures, and propaganda—of all communication. It has been termed, "Give them what they want. Tell them what they want to hear." Actually, it is possible to serve people almost anything, but if they are to be receptive, the fare can only be based on the feedback. The implications of this cannot fail to be unpleasant to the reflective. We have only the individual's past to work with in order to change his future, and if the past be twisted, it is nevertheless the only thing there is to put our teeth into.

Case 5

In the last chapter, when I discussed a case of claustrophobia, I mentioned recapturing feelings through thinking of previously established conditionings. Let us consider this more thoroughly with a discussion of the case of a submarine commander.

His first assignment was to induce feelings of heat, cold, heaviness, and lightness by recalling experiences which had previously induced them. "Think it with your arm," I told him.

His first and best results were with the feeling of lightness. He practiced this while lying in bed at night, before going to sleep. He imagined holding his arms limply over a spouting fountain, but he was unsuccessful. Finally, he pictured himself sitting at the edge of a pit, which in his mind took the image of ruins that had been excavated. From this position, he imagined himself bending backward from the waist, with his arms stretched out before him. After concentrating on this for about three minutes, he felt the muscles on the under side of his elbow twitch. He concentrated more deeply, and the twitching continued. Before long, he felt the touch of his fingertips on the sheet becoming lighter, and soon his hands left the bed completely. The rate of rise was rapid, and he hesitated diminishing his concentration for fear his hands would stop rising. Soon, however, he raised his head to see what was happening, and the lifting continued, which led him to try concentrating directly on raising his arms, without imagining himself at the edge of the pit. This direct approach was successful, and he could make his arms rise and fall at will, and change their direction without difficulty.

Practicing to feel cold was his next success. He had spent much time in stormy seas on the open deck of his submarine, and he found it easy to imagine feeling the chill of the deck plates after surfacing. By concentrating on the experiences of an especially cold day, he shivered, "with no small effect on the iron cot I am forced to call my bunk." First came a chill, then a shudder, and next a feeling of slight pain in his fingertips and toes, as if they were frostbitten. At his first effort to induce a feeling of cold he concentrated on goose pimples and cold feet, and nothing happened. When he concentrated on a cold day on the open deck of the submarine, it was comparatively easy for him to start shivering. This was true especially when he imagined himself standing there without warm clothes or with none at all. He never got goose pimples from this feeling of cold, and he explained this by saying that he started to shiver so quickly that he felt carrying it any further would be at the expense of his physical security. Whether or not this belief was justified, it well illustrated the subjective intensity of the cold.

Some persons are successful at inducing sensations of cold by picturing themselves taking a cold shower, not failing to imagine the minutiae of it, or making snowballs, or holding a hand under the cold water tap. Some mentally reach into the refrigerator, and picture themselves lifting out cold, green, frosty ginger-ale bottles, or imagine themselves holding a gleaming aluminum ice-tray, with their cold fingers stuck slightly to the sides.

A right-handed person can more readily focus impulses on his right hand, so it is desirable to start him off there. This is good strategy, because when both hands develop sensations simultaneously, the subject will often be uncertain as to whether he feels anything, and will engage in specious differentiation between "feeling it" and "thinking" he feels it. Before I learned this bit of technique, I would try to convince such persons by telling them of the experiment of Menzies in which he conditioned an actual physical drop in temperature to a light and to words spoken by the subject.

There is an experiment to be done with a hypnotized person suffering from a sinus condition. Would successful suggestions of wellbeing be accompanied by an actual vasomotor constriction of the nasal membranes, much as if ephedrine or neosynephrine had been introduced? Menzies' experiment gives us grounds for believing that this may well be the case. It is not mind over matter. Mind is matter.

To return to the process of inducing feelings of cold. One man was unsuccessful when he pictured himself holding a piece of ice, but when he imagined himself lifting it and putting it on the bureau, and involved his motor system, he was successful. It will be recalled that the experiments of

Menzies (1) and Hudgins (2) also indicated the importance of involving motor imagery.

Notice that the submarine commander used both actual experiences and imaginary ones. Mentally, he went from standing fully clad on the deck of his ship in the cold, to standing there without clothes. Notice also that he was unsuccessful when he concentrated on results, that is, on goose pimples and cold feet. The effects take care of themselves when the individual thinks back to the incidental minutiae of the original situation. For example, a man who told himself that he was carrying a heavy valise that was making his arm heavy, was unsuccessful. However, when I told him to recapture the feeling of arriving at the railroad station, of looking around and not being able to find a redcap, of bemoaning the heat of the city, of wiping the perspiration from his forehead, of cursing under his breath and picking up his valise, soon enough he felt his arm getting quite heavy.

The submarine commander then turned to sensations of heat. He had spent several summers in Hawaii, and passed many Saturday afternoons on the beach at Waikiki. By bringing this back to mind, along with a sunburn he had received, he felt a sense of warmth. He became aware of a pain on his shins and on his face, which had been badly sunburned, and he felt as if sunlight were coming through his eyelids.

He also imagined himself standing in front of a blast furnace that he once saw being used in the manufacture of steel. This brought warmth to his face, but not much to the rest of his body.

The imagined experiences may be of many years' standing, and still be effective. A woman imagined herself lying on the beach she had visited on her honeymoon thirty years ago, and she soon felt warm and relaxed. A man in his fifties imagined himself as a 14 year-old boy, back on his parents' farm. He had bought a mail-order pair of dumbbells to develop his muscles, and as he imagined himself waking up early one winter morning, and looking at the snow that had sifted in through the window sashes, and shivering at the thought of getting out of his warm bed into the cold room, and gritting his teeth and finally jumping out, and grasping the ice-cold iron dumbbells and tugging hard at them, and groaning that he had ever written away for the physical culture course. Here, in my office, 40 years later, he felt a distinct sensation of cold in his hands, and of tension in his arms and back—enough to make him shake his head incredulously and say, "I still don't believe it."

Which brings us to a discussion of heaviness. This feeling, the submarine commander found, was easy to induce.

Starting with the thought of a tired right arm from playing baseball, he developed a feeling of heaviness, and also the twinges of soreness he used to experience when active at that sport. This latter by-product was a surprise, but the association of his baseball playing with a sore arm was quite natural, since he had had one every spring for seven consecutive years during his high school and college days. (Cases of mine, who have imagined themselves playing tennis, have reported a similar twinge in the arm, and for analogous reasons.)

He made a constant practice of putting himself to sleep by inducing this heavy feeling, and before long he felt it so quickly that the first steps became quite remote. Soon he found that certain combinations of feelings were possible. He could combine heat or cold with the feeling of lightness. He could make one side of his body shiver, and the other side slightly warm, or he could leave it unaffected. However, he found it impossible to combine heaviness with any of the other feelings, although I have found that this does not hold for everybody.

One evening he was unsuccessfully trying to make his legs follow his orders as obediently as his hands. He concentrated on putting his body in a relaxed state, and on clearing his mind of all thoughts. This was poor practice, because he was trying this directly, rather than by doing the thinking that would produce the result. With amazement, he noticed a white spot developing in his mind's eye, and he concentrated on enlarging it. Before him came a picture of a white room with several doors. The doors faded, and he was in front of a blank white wall. He concentrated on this white wall until a feeling of dizziness came over him. He hesitated pursuing this further, because he thought it might lead to complications, and because I had warned him against building habits that might interfere with his training. Suddenly a violent shock went through the left side of his body, sufficient to move him an inch or two.

He concentrated on moving his left leg, and the response was immediate. He was aware of bending his knee a little, and his leg moved horizontally into the air, faster than his hands had risen. "I felt like a yogi," he said. He then shifted his thinking to his right leg, and then to both legs, and was successful each time. Then his arms were lifted into the air, and following that his head rose off the pillow and his back came along until he was bent over and touching his toes. He leaned back to a partly prone position, and then went forward again to his toes.

Now he could get results with great speed and ease, by merely thinking of them. His reactions seemed to occur as a direct result of concentration, and without any physical effort. "I lay for several minutes causing my leg to move one way and then the other, and during these minutes I gained great confidence that I would soon be able to gain control of my entire self, physically and mentally". All this took place between his first and second interviews with me...

When I saw him next, I told him to stop trying to erase thoughts from his mind. "Be oblique. The more you try, the less you succeed. The mind will free itself without any help from you. Easy does it." I asked him to relax his eyes, and then his tongue and throat, then his arms and chest, and finally his ears. "Shut yourself off from the world." I sat quietly and watched.

He followed instructions. In each case, he conjured up experiences or images that had previously brought about the desired results. For his eyes, it was a feeling of fatigue, and for his tongue it was lifting it from the bottom of his mouth and letting it fall as it would. For his arms, he concentrated on the heaviness he had been able to induce by direct thought. To make his chest feel heavy, he imagined someone sitting on it while he was wrestling, and to dull his hearing, he recalled the partial deafness brought on by the firing of large caliber guns.

He almost fell asleep as he did this, and when he practiced it after leaving me, he would often awake to find it morning. After a few days he worked out a method in which, by direct thought, he could attain a state that was neither waking nor sleeping. Cursory thoughts were enough to produce it. Originally, he had had to bring to mind the experiences that had tired his arms, but now he had only to concentrate on their being heavy, and they would respond readily. He spent little time on his chest.

He found it difficult to control his hearing. A busy corridor full of chatter and bustle was outside his door, and his room was bordered by the road used by sailors at his base to get to the next town, and by a railroad noisy with war transport. He had his best results when the room was quiet and he concentrated on relaxing his body. Then he could readily induce a stuffed-up feeling in his ears. Sometimes, his lips would part because of the weight of his lower jaw, and his breathing would become heavy and slow, as if in sleep. On some occasions he snored slightly, all the while being completely aware and awake.

At this point, he would forget about his body, and turn to directing his thoughts. It was as if he had made his mind a quiet pool, and was throwing rocks into it in order to make ripples where he wished. To mangle the metaphor, we might consider post-hypnotic suggestion as being equivalent to stopping a person's mill from threshing his wheat, and giving it our wheat instead.

I saw him several times thereafter, and have heard from him since. "Originally," he said, "I was a lazy lout, with no energy in a warm climate. Now, I am a man with a purpose and a routine which bids well to accomplish it ..." He developed an ability to utilize spare moments. He found himself able to read a book, or write a letter, picking it up or dropping it off wherever he happened to be. His tendency to daydream stopped, and he became effortlessly energetic. He was able to keep calm even when his submarine was depth-charged. This last is quite dramatic, but the details are not relevant here.

When he first saw me, he could hardly have been called maladjusted. However, he had always felt, and correctly too, that his mental and personal powers were above average. But they were being wasted, or at least not being utilized to the fullest.

After treatment, he no longer had to prod himself, but merely continued being constructive. Said he of the therapy, "It builds one, and the fundamentally important thing is that it breeds happiness. I like to work now, and I like doing what I am doing. I am not set for life, but I am getting everything out of it there is to be gotten, and I shall, in the future, transfer that knack to whatever I do ..." His postwar activity has shown this prediction to be well-founded.

It is possible to be mechanistic about this. The individual, whether he realizes it or not, has a multiplicity of bells, and reactions take place when we vibrate them. I shall not venture a neural explanation, but I shall content myself with saying that hypnosis is not so much a learning as a recall process.

A nonexistent bell cannot be vibrated. Consequently, if excitatory patterns are absent, they must first be built in, so that the individual may vibrate them later through hypnosis.

Case 6

The successful transmutation of past experiences extends to the production of anesthesia. Here is an interesting report by a woman, bearing upon novocaine and dental treatment.

Late one afternoon, having some spare time, I decided to experiment by recalling my last experience at the dentist in the removal of an impacted wisdom tooth. This had occurred about six months previously, and had been the only time I had novocaine in three years, which had also been in connection with a wisdom tooth.

I decided to use the later experience first, this one being in connection with the removal of an impacted wisdom tooth from the lower left jaw. I recalled the feeling of nervousness with which I had entered the dentist's office, not so much at the removal of the tooth itself, but at the possibility of having to undergo weeks of post-operative pain as had occurred with the other tooth.

I tried to recall the actual injection of the needle, but was unsuccessful. Then I remembered that the left side of my face had felt swollen when I tried to light a cigarette after the extraction. Actually, this wasn't the case, but the anesthesia made it feel that way. I recalled Dr. Day's preparation of the needle, and then the injection. This time I was more successful. Gradually, I felt a faint tingling of the left half of my tongue, and then the left half of the upper palate, the left half of my lips, the inner left half of my jaw, and the area around the space where my wisdom tooth had been. I then decided that this was enough for one session, but I had difficulty in making myself stop thinking of the dentist's office and its associations. This I found to be most annoying, until I deliberately forced myself to think of something else completely unconnected. Thinking of my husband, who was away on business, succeeded in making me forget my previous thoughts.

Later that same evening I practiced some more. This time results came much faster, and were more pronounced. The left part of my cheek, almost up to the eye itself, began to tingle, and the tip of my tongue felt almost numb. I found that the thought of the dentist's hammering at the tooth was strong enough to increase the sensation of numbness. At this point, I decided to use a code word which would become associated with the dental anesthesia, and I spent some time deciding upon a combination of syllables which would not be common enough to bring on the association, but which would be easily remembered by me. I decided on the combination, "Caine opia," by taking the last syllable of novocaine and combining it with opium, which in my mind has an association with novocaine.

I found I had better success by using mental verbalizations of each image, such as, "There's Dr. Day. He's hammering at the tooth. He's preparing the gut for stitches, etc." After my second session with myself, I discovered that I had been staring at one spot the entire time, and it seemed to me that I had been behaving exactly like a "hypnotic" subject. I remembered the feeling of complete focalization on the dental situation, trying to recall the various things that had been done, to the exclusion of every other thought, yet having complete power to control how long I wished to continue.

Two evenings later, while lying in bed, I decided once more to try the anesthesia. Almost instantly I had the tingling and numbness as strongly as it had been at my last anesthetic session, and then by recalling more of the images, I got the same numbness in my tongue and gum, but of very short duration. The tingling spread over my left cheek, but this time I decided that I had enough and was too sleepy, so I turned immediately to thoughts of my husband, who was still away, and fell asleep.

This report has a postscript. The woman developed an aversion to discussing her anesthesia, because merely mentioning it would involuntarily produce it. This illustrates its reflex basis. It is relevant that the anesthesia was never carefully checked, and that the woman was psychologically well-adjusted-and-well-informed and had never been hypnotized before.

Case 7

A writer of mystery stories and his wife suffered from insomnia, particularly the writer. Often it took him two or three hours before he could fall asleep as he wound and unwound his plots. He found that he could easily put his wife to sleep by jokingly saying, in a heavy voice, "You are very sleepy. You are very somniferous. You are very lethargic. You are very somnolent," repeated again and again. What is more to the point is that this procedure made him fall asleep in a few minutes, even when he did not wish to, paralleling the case of anesthesia above. Reflexes are will.

Case 8

I am often surprised at the associativities that lie dormant in the individual. Persons have read my "Three Techniques of Autohypnosis," and with no assistance, have successfully learned from them. The next two cases illustrate the awakening of these associativities.

A minister's sermons were pedantic and boring, because he was of a hairsplitting and analytical disposition. *Vox Dei* was not *vox populi*, and he wanted his preaching to become more emotional.

One morning, before a sermon, he sat down in his library, and thought himself into a blank, relaxed state of mind, and then gave himself suggestions of freedom and expressiveness. In the afternoon, he spoke with great fervor and assurance, and was highly praised by his congregation. He came to consult me because, although his preaching continued satisfactorily, his writing remained ineffective despite vigorous self-suggestion. I was not able to help him, because his plans made more than one consultation impossible. He has since written me that his sermons and lectures continue with great success, and that his increased prowess has brought him a larger pulpit.

I have found that such self-assistance is possible only for the bright and psychologically well informed persons who can implement abstractions. Others will fail, though they will probably not believe that these restrictions apply to them.

Case 9

Here, in impressive regalia, is a high-ranking staff officer of one of our more picturesque Pacific admirals, and one of the first Americans to enter Japan after the surrender. He is soft-spoken and alert, and easily underestimated. He is calm and completely confident, if somewhat mother-bound. His inner life had revolved almost entirely about my little book, *What Is Hypnosis*, and on his first visit he presented my secretary with a string of pearls, and me with a group of ivory figurines. Through all of his campaigns he had carried around my "Three Techniques." and had successfully applied them to himself in the direction of concentration and increased self-assurance.

Symptoms and roots form a thoroughly interwoven cable, and if we pull one thread, we are pulling all of the others.

CHAPTER 8

RECONDITIONING AS ROOT THERAPY

The ballet has been called the offspring of the dance, after it was raped by music. This analogy comes to mind in considering the hybrid of psychoanalysis and hypnotism known as hypnoanalysis. To mix psychoanalysis with hypnotism, or for that matter to construct a psychological system around a set of concepts, needs only the intent. Yet whatever else hypnoanalysis may be, it cannot honestly be called psychoanalytic.

The Freudian "Psychosomatic Medicine" of Weiss and English condemns hypnotism as "uncertain in its results and limited in its possibilities. At best it can cause a temporary shifting about of conflicts but it does not actually cure them. Furthermore it brings about a further dependence upon some outer authority (the hypnotist)."

"A therapy which *reveals* rather than *conceals* the emotional pathology has greater value!" (1)

Freud himself has declared that "the history of psychoanalysis proper, therefore, starts with the technical innovation of the rejection of hypnosis." (2) In this unequivocal statement, Freud chased the hypnotic money-changers from his temple. He made the use of hypnosis in psychoanalytic therapy structurally impossible. Persons are privileged to continue working in hypnoanalysis. However, from a Freudian point of view, it can only be considered an ersatz *Psychoanalyse*.

Psychology is concerned with two problems. First, how is personality formed, and secondly, how can it be reconstituted. The answers to these two questions form the different schools of psychology, with their different conceptions of the roots of human personality. The reflex psychologist is just as concerned with roots as the psychoanalyst. But rather than using vague terminology, the reflex approach is physiological and mechanistic, believing that the differences between the behavior of human beings and lower animals are to be explained by differences in neural structure.

Without reticence the psychoanalysts assert that they own the basic patents on psychological fundamentals, and that everybody else is a tinkerer with symptoms. They alone seek to extirpate neuroses by the very roots. This contention is scientifically childish.

To talk of the roots of a neurosis is merely to babble about the roots postulated by a school of psychology. To attack someone else's conception of roots is another way of saying, "You are going in the wrong direction because you do not use *my* compass."

I realize that this shoe can also be put on my foot in my criticism of psychoanalysis, but I shall let Pavlov provide the answer: (3)

> But I most emphatically object to what the author [the psychoanalyst Schilder] further says concerning the comparative study of these neuroses in man and in animals. He says, "The important experiments of Pavlov and his pupils on neuroses can be understood only if we look upon them in the light of our experiences in the neuroses. We cannot interpret the neurosis by means of the conditioned reflex, but by means of the psychic mechanism we have studied in the neurosis we can well explain what occurs in the conditioned reflex."
>
> [Pavlov continues] What is the meaning of the term "interpretation" or "understanding" of the phenomenon? The reduction of the more complex to the more elemental is a simple thing. Consequently the human neuroses should be explained, understood, i.e., analysed, by the help of the animal neuroses, as naturally the more simple, and not by the reverse procedure.

In the vulgate, Pavlov has said that a horse belongs in front of a cart, not in back of it, which is where psychoanalysts like to keep it.

To repair an automobile engine, it is necessary to determine its deviation from the behavior of smoothly-running motors. In parallel, it is impossible to have a sound conception of the repair of personalities without knowing what is normal in the first place. This is obvious indeed. Yet Alexander, one of the more rational psychoanalysts admits that they have neglected the study of the normal individual. (4) Glover even believes that the study of the neurotic character is a useful way of approaching the study of the normal individual. (5)

I am grateful to Carney Landis for the curtain line in the comedy of psychoanalysis and normality. (6) He asked a psychoanalyst who "was a close adherent of Freud and to the best of my knowledge I not deviate in the slightest from the orthodox Freudian method and theory... 'What is normality?' He replied, 'I don't know. I never deal with normal people.' I asked, 'But suppose a really normal person came to you.' He interrupted, 'Even though he were normal at the beginning of the analysis, the analytic procedure would create a neurosis.' "

Mental institutions are crowded with people who are normal for what happened to them, and so are psychoanalysts' couches. A person is his training.

Let us look at the psychoanalytic ten commandments from the reflex point of view.

1 *Infant experiences are determinants of adult behavior.*
   Of course. That is why Watson (not Freud, remember) experimented with children. We know that a burnt child dreads the fire, and a whipped dog fears the whip, and a boy with unhappy parental experiences is withdrawn. The song is over, but the melody lingers on. The meat is no longer there, but when the bell rings the dog still salivates.

   Psychotherapy is a problem in emotional relearning. Because psychoanalysis, with its vague re-educational procedures, is not concerned with learning and neural modification, it may not be considered a fundamental psychotherapy.

2 *Symbolism is the key to the cipher of human behavior.*
   To dog A, the bell is a "meat" symbol and he salivates simply because he has been conditioned that way. To dog B, it is an "acid on the right leg" symbol, and he scratches it. To dog C, it is an electric shock symbol, so he barks. The Freudian code book of sexual symbols, with its church spires and candles, and gardens and doors, is a non-individualized compendium of conditionings, which all too often becomes a Procrustean bed for the patient.

3   *Dreams are the short cut to the "unconscious."*

Night dreams are problems in personalized emotional conditioning, and so are day dreams, and they reveal nothing we can't find out otherwise. For that matter, it is as important to know what a person does after he has had a few drinks. All behavior is significant. The psychoanalytic interpretation of dreams is poker with everything wild.

4   *The patient's free association provides clues for the psychoanalyst, and presumably for himself.*

Propaganda may be defined as, "when you open your mouth." Obviously, the patient must talk in order to communicate with the psychoanalyst. Although I listen carefully to my cases' explanations, they do not know what they are talking about. If they did, they would not have to consult me.

There is no free association. It is all strait-jacketed association, determined by the individual's past conditioning.

5   *No therapy is possible without transference.*

If the psychoanalytically uninformed call this "falling in love" with the analyst, the Freudians have only their scripture to blame.

The ado about transference means that one human being cannot meet another, especially a psychoanalyst, without an emotional reaction. It also means that a dog barks joyfully on encountering a stimulus, or becomes disturbed, or is indifferent, depending on how he has been trained. Our past is always present, and determines our behavior.

Hollingworth has favored the term "redintegration"[1] for what occurs when an emotional response (say, fear) is aroused by one of the stimuli (red hair, for example) which in combination (with a stern kindergarten teacher) originally caused it. We might call it emotional parallelism. If the therapist parallels any of the pleasant conditionings of the patient, he may enlist his cooperation.

Conversely, there is the possibility of a negative reaction to the psychologist, as with Case 4, the post-graduate student with insomnia. Despite this, successful treatment was possible. Before the birth of "transference," the word "rapport" was satisfactory, and should suffice again.

6   *Beware of fixation,* say the analysts. Example: A girl may be so devoted

---

[1]   Literally, to make whole again.

to her father that she may fail to become interested in other men.
True. Each to his taste, but tastes are matters of conditioning.

7 *Beware of projection*, of which blaming others for our mistakes is an
   illustration.

   Projection means measuring everybody with our own yardstick, but
   what other yardstick have any of us? It is a truism that a person is his
   reaction systems.

8 The Freudians accuse the mentally disturbed of an *unconscious desire to
   retain their neurosis*. They have resistance to cure.

   It is a truism of epic proportions that habits have a tendency to
   remain habitual. The psychoanalysts do not like this formulation, so
   they have christened it "resistance."

   Habits have inertia, until they are changed. A body remains in
   one place until it is pushed. "Resistance" keeps it there. Thinking and
   feeling are physico-chemical processes, and to reverse them takes time.
   Psychoanalytic *censorship*, alleged as a method of repression, which
   forms resistance, is nothing but an involved way of talking about
   inhibition.

9 As we have seen, the significance attached to the *recapture of memories*
   is unjustified.

   The important thing is to stop them from interfering with
   the individual's relationships to the world, and to remove their
   uncomfortable emotional effect. To speak of forces of repression
   keeping them hidden, is to enter the realm of demonology.

   These repressions, we are told, may go through the process of
   sublimation–that is, those charged with inexpedient impulses may be
   diverted into more socially acceptable channels. The boy with incestuous
   love for his mother may learn to express it merely through affection.

   This re-routing of impulses means only that varied emotions, in
   varied degrees, get conditioned to varied persons and situations.

10 I devoted Chapter 5 to the phenomena of rationalization, which is an
   abstraction stemming from the false division of man's unitary behavior
   into reason and emotion.

The difference between the reflex approach and psychoanalysis is not a
matter of vocabulary. Words are instrumentalities used to express differences

in conceptual content. The few scientifically sound reflex conceptions codify, among other things, the elaborately unscientific Freudian laws and regulations. The psychic mechanisms of the analysts obscure the physiology of the nervous system. We do not want their concepts, and analysts would be well-advised to scrap their shopworn anachronisms.

Psychoanalysis is a witches' Sabbath of concepts that fades into air at the tolling of the Pavlovian bell. It is like a pretentious theology in its insistence that it has a monopoly on truth, and that all outside the church wander in the darkness of error. It uses its principles to prove its principles. Most of it will go the way of phlogiston, the hypothetical fluid in old chemistry that was supposed to be a constituent of all combustible substances.

Psychoanalysis is a concept-ridden form of instinctivism, based on Western culture, and with an undertow of associationalism. Freud, in discussing the associative aspect of dreams, once wrote, "The reflex act remains the type of every psychic activity as well." (7) But the history of psychoanalysis shows that he and his followers remained untouched by the fundamental and extensive work in reflexology except to damn it.[2]

I will never understand how Freud, who spoke of an "Oedipus" complex in which the son hates his father, and an "Electra" complex in which the daughter hates her mother, omitted a "Joseph" complex, in which the older brother has a hatred of his younger brother. I have found this pattern often, and I present it as a gift to psychoanalytic lore.

Some of the academic supporters of psychoanalysis declare, "The problems are highly complex, and extensive training in psychological matters is necessary to rule upon the issues." Training in psychologicalmatters is to be commended, but modern psychology is a thoroughly deductive science, much as it masquerades as inductive. Theories are no longer constructed from facts. As new data are accumulated, they are fitted snugly into old hypotheses. In a sense, therefore, research in psychology, for the clarification of theory, can be as futile as research in religion.

Sodium pentothal, one of the barbiturates, is the current philosopher's stone for psychiatrists who lack either the skill or the time to thaw out a patient in order to establish rapport. Whiskey, and I say this earnestly, could often be as effective, whether administered to the patient or to the

---

[2] Recently, however, many Freudians have begun to spice their jargon with Pavlovian terminology. This foreshadows the beginning of the end of psychoanalysis as a separate doctrine.

psychiatrist. However, I have nothing but praise for the use of pentothal with institutionalized psychotics. Then it becomes a highly important adjunct in the treatment of inaccessible patients.

There is nothing intrinsically curative in sodium pentothal. It is a chemical means of temporarily reducing inhibition, as was its proudly hailed predecessor scopolamine.

Insulin, the miracle drug for diabetes, has also become the harbinger of the psychiatric millennium. In a study of some 2,000 cases, the New York Temporary Commission on State Hospital Problems found that eight out of ten patients were discharged from the hospital after insulin shock, contrasted with six out of ten in a non-insulin control group. (8) They concluded that insulin shock therapy should be introduced for the treatment of dementia praecox in all New York State mental institutions.

The insulin cases were carefully selected, and were treated at a modern hospital where they also received intensive psychiatric and nursing care. The non-insulin group was comprised of patients at six different hospitals. Here are some details about three of them from a series of articles by Albert Deutsch.

Hospital A had one physician to each 450 inmates. (9) This is fifteen times as many patients per psychiatrist as in the insulin shock hospital. Such psychiatric care is a mockery.

The superintendent of Hospital B said, "The majority of [my] patients are receiving custodial care and little of the individual attention that formerly could be given them." (10)

Eleven years after the New York State Legislature ordered the abandonment of Hospital C, it was still functioning. (11) "The New York State Mental Hygiene Department requires that each patient be interviewed at least twice a year. Many cases had not been interviewed for as long as five years."

There is much to be said for insulin shock, but the widely acclaimed report of the New York Commission has not said it. Some experiments with rats, which we will consider later in this chapter, are much more impressive.

Many practitioners appropriate what they consider the best ingredients from each psychological school, and mix an eclectic cocktail. This is excused on the grounds that an attitude of systemic looseness toward contemporary psychology is a virtue. Whether or not this be true, by definition such persons are not shedding any light on psychology as a science.

In psychoanalytic literature, all mental mechanisms are malicious. There is always chicanery in the mental basement. The nervous system is an ectoplasmic chessboard for the weird moves of the psyche.

A moment's thought about evolution reveals the fallacy of this contention. The human nervous system, which has come to us from what Waldemar Kaempffert has called "a slimy, finny, furry past," is a remarkable heritage. It has kept the human race alive for a long time, and it could never have done so if it were not for its reflex structure. If we free it of its inhibitions, and let it work for us, it will know all the answers without ever having studied. We must not straitjacket our animal heritage. We must free it, for only then can we be happy.

The importance of this animal freedom has been verified by the results in electric shock therapy and in pre-frontal lobotomy—often called psychosurgery, in which nerve pathways in the brain are severed to reduce nervous tension.

Freeman and Watts, describing what happens after brain surgery, say:

[The individual] is freed from anxiety and from feelings of inferiority; he loses interest in himself, both as to his body and as to his relation with his environment, no longer caring whether his heart beats or his stomach chums, nor whether his remarks embarrass his associates. His interests turn outward, and obsessive thinking is abolished. He responds immediately and sometimes vividly to external impressions, showing something of an emotional incontinence that makes for ready laughter or petulance. The emotional responses may be vivid but they are lacking in depth and quickly evaporate. His mood is, on the whole, elevated, and the extraversion and ready response make for an apparently quick-witted enthusiastic individual who gets along superficially with everybody. There is something childish in the cheerful and unself-conscious behavior of the operated patient. (12)

The work with insulin and electric shock points in the same direction. Gellhorn, after considering the research on autonomic regulation, concluded that "It seems reasonable to assume that the alteration of the balance of the autonomic centers induced by various forms of so-called shock treatment results in a state of autonomic lability. ... We come, therefore, to the conclusion that the various therapeutic procedures used in the treatment of schizophrenia act primarily on the sympathetic centers. Due to the prolonged after-effect of these procedures on these centers, their excitability [which means excitation] is increased and the disturbed autonomic balance [between inhibition and excitation] is restored." (13)

Gellhorn conditioned rats to jump from one compartment to another at the sound of a bell, by simultaneously transmitting a shock through the grid on which the rat was standing. (14) After the conditioned reaction was built in, it was inhibited by repeatedly presenting the bell without the shock.

Gellhorn then found something with the profoundest implications for human psychotherapy. By subjecting the animals to metrazol convulsions, "electric shock therapy," or insulin shock, *the inhibitions were destroyed,* and the conditioned reactions were reestablished.

In later experiments, he found that a series of conditioned responses, although inhibited at different times, recovered simultaneously. (15) Insulin, or electric shock, disinhibited them, and *without disturbing the other conditioned responses in any way.*

The researches of Gellhorn, and the surgery of Freeman and Watts, strongly support the belief that human adjustment is a matter of balance between inhibition and excitation. And in psychotherapy, this always means increasing excitation.

Increasing excitation is a problem in learning, and learning is what happens to you. It is physico-chemical in nature. If I tell you that the fountain pen with which I am writing is a Christmas gift from one of my cases, as long as you remember:

1 The fountain pen is a gift, or
2 It is a Christmas gift, or
3 It is a gift from a case of mine,

I have succeeded in making a physico-chemical dent in your nervous system. There can be no other explanation of learning. As long as you remember any of these facts, tissues, of which your organism is composed, have been changed.

We are dealing with human behavior things, and even if we cannot yet determine their precise physico-chemical nature, in practice calling them matters of inhibition and excitation will be all that is necessary. Each person presents a different problem, but the purpose is always identical—to provide a free, outflowing personality in which true emotions are expressed in speech and action.

Attaining mental health is a matter of reconditioning the faulty, inhibitory patterns of earlier life in the direction of excitation. This can be done by a conscious process. In the words of Shakespeare, "How use doth breed a habit in a man!"

CHAPTER 9

CONDITIONING EXCITATORY RESPONSES

In this chapter I shall explain six techniques for increasing excitation. They are so interdependent and commingled, that by practicing any one of them, the subject, in effect, is learning all of the others. I shall discuss several of them only in passing, for despite their importance, they are only modulations of the basic theme.

The first discipline (for that is what it is) I have called *feeling-talk*. It means the deliberate utterance of spontaneously felt emotions. "Thank heavens, today is Friday and the weekend is here," illustrates feeling-talk. However, saying merely, "Today is Friday," would be dry fact-talk, and would do nothing to help emotional reconstruction.

Man is the word-using animal, and his basic means for excitation is through speech. In a sense, feeling-talk means only to be emotionally outspoken, and is an aspect of small talk. Here are some examples:

Animals also show emotion on their faces. The inhibitory person need not snarl like a tiger, nor grin like a Cheshire cat that has read Dale Carnegie. However, he should furrow his brow when he is vexed, and wear a long face. Be emotionally Gallic, is my counsel. I have named this second practice facial talk.

Our third rule of conduct is to *contradict and attack*. When you[1] differ with someone, do not simulate agreeability. Instead, externalize

---

[1]   I have retained some of my across-the-desk language.

Remark	Type of Feeling-Talk Like
1. I like the soup.	Like
2. I like that snow-scene. It makes me feel cool to look at it.	Like
3. I hate parsnips.	Dislike
4. I detest that man and everything he stands for.	Dislike
5. I don't like this pie.	Dislike
6. That shade of green is perfect for you.	Praise
7. You did a marvelous job, Miss Jones.	Praise
8. You're looking fine!	Praise
9. That hat really becomes you.	Praise
10. Today is Friday. I thought it would never get here.	Relief
11. I cried when he came home safely.	Relief
12. You can't do this to me!	Complaint
13. Excuse me, but I was here first.	Complaint
14. I'll wait, even if it kills me.	Determination
15. I can hardly wait until he gets here.	Impatience
16. My feet hurt.	Discomfort
17. What a wonderful time we had.	Enjoyment
18. The desk set was just what I needed.	Appreciation
19. I cleaned out the poker game.	Self-praise
20. I wonder what happens in the next installment.	Curiosity
21. It was the most extraordinary thing I had seen in a long time.	Amazement
22. You don't expect me to believe that, do you?	Skepticism
23. Say it again. I like it. approbation	Desire for
24. I'm not afraid of him. I don't care if he does his damnedest.	Courage
25. I'm just dying to meet him.	Anticipation
26. I'm going to keep punching until I win.	Determination
27. There's nothing to it. I'll take care of it right away.	Confidence
28. This meal feels fine.	Contentment
29. I think the dessert was a mistake.	Regret
30. Darling, I love you with all my heart.	Love
31. Good grief, I feel terrible about that!	Anguish
32. What kind of a place do you call this?	Annoyance
33. Today is Friday. The week went fast.	Surprise
34. Now, that was stupid of me!	Self-criticism

feeling, and contradict on an improvable emotional basis. At first blush, this would seem to obstruct intelligent controversy. Actually, it only means interspersing emotional content among bare facts.

The next, and fourth technique to keep in mind, is the deliberate use of the word I as much as possible. "I like this..." "I read that book and ..." "I want ..." "I heard ..."

This will not make you appear priggish, and will sound natural. Somebody told one of my cases, who was practicing this, "You know, you're conceited, but somehow I don't mind it from you."

The fifth discipline is to *express agreement when you are praised*.
When someone says, "That's a fine suit you're wearing," do not remain
expressionless. Do not shrug your shoulders and say, "It's nothing." Nor
be satirical and say, "Of course, I'm wonderful." Instead, if you believe the
compliment at all, say something like, "Thank you. It's my favorite suit.
Gives me big shoulders, doesn't it?"

When Dr. Smith congratulates me on my success with Jones, I answer,
"Thank you, Doctor. You know, he may consider himself fortunate that
you were wide awake enough to have sent him to see me." Notice that I
have praised not only myself, but also the physician. When you reflect
praise like a mirror, the giver of the compliment will not deny it.

The recipient, finding his self-praise accepted by the environment,
develops increased emotional freedom. This is excellent self-conditioning.
Praise of self should also be volunteered, and with straightforward naivete.

Improvisation is our sixth and last rule of conduct. Don't plan. Live
for the next minute, and that's fifty-nine seconds too long. This applies
to what you are going to buy, where you are going to visit, and what
you are going to say. Daydreaming is a sign of incomplete doing, and
improvisation stops it. In order to build this spontaneity do not waste
time Monday thinking about Tuesday and Wednesday. Live now, and
tomorrow will take care of itself, even though we need more foresight than
the grasshopper in the fable.

I am advocating a return to excitation, because psychology deals not with
the brain but with the heart. Thought is the smoke-screen of emotions. We
are honest with ourselves and with society when we follow our feelings.
Excitation is better than inhibition, because freedom is better than slavery.

People tell me what they think, but this does not concern me very
much. I want to know what they did, because it is what they do that gets
them into trouble, and what they will do that gets them out of it. To
change the way a person feels and thinks about himself, we must change
the way he acts toward others; and by constantly treating inhibition, we
will be constantly getting at the roots of his problem.

These emotional exercises may seem juvenile, boring, and unimportant,
but they are the very things that build a cure. The adult must develop
a healthy infantility. A case of mine said, "Since I realize that intellect
doesn't determine how you're going to react when you have to react, I have
become much wiser."

The emotionally paralyzed say that such exhibitionism is in poor taste,
and gets you into trouble. Besides, grown people don't act that way. This,
as we have seen, is rationalization.

My answer, to those who complain that excitation may be carried too far, is, "Yes, but not by you. You're like the person dying of thirst in the desert, and when you're brought to an oasis, you refuse water. 'No, thank you,' you say, 'I have heard of people drinking so much water that they have burst ...' Let's not worry about your practicing too much excitation now. We'll take that up later."

I am aware that only a fool would practice excitation at all times. Nevertheless, because it means environmental mastery, it is better than inhibition. You need a few stoplights, but not as many as you have now. Don't think before you speak. Speak before you think. Don't be sensible. Be emotional. Act as if you were constantly half-drunk.

Your dulled emotional razor cannot be cogitated into sharpness. You can only whet it on the stone of social experience, and this calls for constant effort.

Whatever will help you may seem unnatural at first, and you will often do the wrong thing before you can catch yourself. This need not be disturbing, if you take more care next time. You do not have to do much, but you must flex your feeling muscles at every opportunity. In the human gymnasium, emotional practice makes perfect. You do not have to become that frightful thing called a "mixer," but you must continually try to express your emotions.

You have been doing the wrong thing for years, so that now being psychologically correct simply means going against the grain. In truth, it is the grain your father or mother gave you, so it will not be your habits that you will discard. It will be theirs, and good riddance.

Changing habits always produces friction. The criminal who reforms is uncomfortable at first, and the carpenter knows that heat is produced when he planes a rough board. At first, your emotional exercises may make you uncomfortable, but that will pass.

I have found that as some people improve, they get a touch of melancholy, because they think back to their by-passed opportunities. "Whenever you feel depressed," I tell them, "you have forgotten to be nasty to someone." The human nervous system does not fight by the Marquis of Queensberry rules.

When the inhibitory find that they can catch more flies with vinegar than with honey, they express shock at the emotions they have discovered in themselves, and scold me gently. I remind them that they have found nothing in their pockets that had not been there originally. Suppression versus verbalization is the issue. There must be no invisible conflicts. The credo is externalization at all times.

The emotions that matter will be those that are present the moment before you speak. Do not say to yourself, "I think I ought to percolate." Rather, if you percolate, pour. Emotions are not to be manipulated; they are to be felt-out-loud. Ask questions. When a feeling or belief or expression comes to mind, propel it right out of your mouth. This is equivalent to giving vent to steam deliberately, and after a while, this will make your emotional safety valves automatic.

Meet people on your own terms, not on theirs, and beware of slipping into the old emotional role they expect you to play. They have been conditioned to expect certain responses on your part, and they too will have to readjust.

For some time, you will remain in the work stage of forming new habits, and then you will say, "I surprised myself, and did the right thing without even thinking." A woman went to a party and said, "I was afraid I was going to be afraid, and I was surprised when I wasn't." Her fears had no effect, because her excitation had become significantly more habitual.

When you reach this level, you must more than ever continue performing your new disciplines *deliberately,* for this will entrench them more thoroughly. Overlearning is important in retraining, for by constant repetition your newly acquired emotional habits are driven deeper into your nervous system. Practice conditioned reflexes when you have no particular use for them, and then you will have them when you need them. If you relax your practicing too early, although your emotional level will remain higher than before, it will be below the heights that lie within your reach. Resting on your laurels means you have stopped trying too soon.

It might appear that there is a paradox in my logic. To express emotion deliberately, it is necessary to think constantly about doing the correct thing. And such preoccupation can only breed introspection, the direct opposite of excitation.

This is a paradox in form, and not in content. To woolgather about inhibitory nonsense is one thing. It breeds frustration and misery. To keep excitatory procedures in mind and to carry them out, is something else again. It destroys introspection and produces healthy excitation.

In therapy the individual gets rid of:

1 Conditioned inhibitory emotional reflexes by practicing
2 Deliberate excitatory emotional reactions which become
3 Conditioned excitatory emotional reflexes.

Therapy consists of getting the individual to re-educate himself back to the healthy spontaneity of which his life experiences have deprived him. Inhibitory history stops repeating itself, and excitation regains its birthright. The objective of mental health is to "be me, not them," but the world is "them," and overwhelmingly bigger. Society is the sworn enemy of mental health.

Those who suffer from illusions about the human nervous system will find this point of view repugnant. With their pap about intellect, and their emphasis upon self-control, they unsuccessfully negate the human body. The reader who does not believe in the overwhelming importance of "emotion" in human behavior, might as well put this book aside, and continue to cherish his illusions. Claude Bernard said, "Science increases our power in proportion as it lowers our pride."

Man is the clothes-wearing animal, and "adjustment" often means maladjustment. We must adjust, not to society, but to ourselves; and all that I am trying to explain is how to live with our systems. Those who are disturbed about the world suffer from a delusion. They believe that people are civilized. Once we realize that humans are nothing but animals, everything becomes crystal clear and the world makes sense for the first time.

CHAPTER 10
SHYNESS AND THE WELL-BRED NEUROSIS

Most people believe in the spontaneous generation of psychological disorders. From nothing, or at best "hardly anything," they have suddenly become psychologically infected, and they seek a cure. How can they change, they want to know, and still remain the same, for the habit patterns that are present are more powerful than the desire to change—otherwise there would be no problem. To change the grain we must go against it. If there is no friction, there is no progress.

Curiously, it is unnecessary to be cautious in the matter of diagnosis. Robertson has shown that this can be true even in physical medicine. (1) He mentions a patient who "came from a physician notoriously deficient in diagnostic acumen and promptly the specialist covers every field except the one originally designated by the referring physician and this was the correct diagnosis." However, in psychotherapy we need have no fear. The diagnosis is always inhibition. The person who comes for help does not know what he wants. There is a blind spot in his reasoning and in his "rules of conduct," no matter how plausible they may seem. The customer is always wrong.

One of the simplest problems is the shyness pattern. This is the ailment that afflicts the people who look hurt and lonely, and who seem sad and uncomfortable even to the untutored eye. And fortunately, these are the people who are usually prepared to accept therapy. They are bothered by few rationalizations. They feel miserable and they want help.

Case 10

Mr. T. is a medium-built person of 45. He complains of chronic blushing. He and his younger brother are major stockholders in the manufacture of a patented specialty, and he is the salesman of the organization. Although they practically monopolize the field, meeting customers is extremely painful to him. It brings on palpitations of the heart, dizziness, and shaking of the knees. Often, he will avoid calling on someone, or he will walk around the block until he can muster the courage to do so. He finds that a few drinks help, but he would rather not sell than have to drink. He sweats, and he suffers from insomnia.

He feels inferior because he has had only a year of high school, and his work is mainly with college graduates. He is worried that his board of directors will soon offer him the secretaryship of the corporation. "I don't like people to make a big fuss over me. I suppose I'm too sensitive, but every time I face people I blush. It's getting terrible, and everybody is noticing it. What's more, whenever I have a lot of work to do, I want to run away."

As a child, he felt that his younger brother received more affection and appreciation than he did. This younger brother, I decided, had been the villain in the piece, and he had been abetted by their mother.

I began by discussing his blushing, since he was not prepared for anything deeper. I explained Dunlap's beta hypothesis. i.e., that "the occurrence of a response lessens the probability that on the recurrence of the same stimulus-pattern, the same response will recur." (2) An excellent illustration of the application of this principle occurs in D. H. Lawrence's *Women in Love*:

> "A very great doctor taught me ... that to cure oneself of a bad habit, one should force oneself to do it, when one would not do it—make oneself do it and then the habit would disappear."
>
> "How do you mean?" said Gerald.
>
> "If you bite your nails, for example. Then, when you don't want to bite your nails, bite them, make yourself bite them. And you would find the habit was broken."

I explained to Mr. T. that the human nervous system had, as it were, a logical battery and an emotional battery. Both were connected by wires to different parts of the body. "Your emotional battery, through what is called the autonomic nervous system, sends messages unconsciously to the blood vessels in your face, making you blush. Now, if we can use some power from the logic department instead, you will develop a deliberate hold on the blood vessels, and overcome the unconscious blush signals. The logical department of the brain will tell your face, 'You won't have to blush.' So I want you to *deliberately* practice blushing. Tell yourself to blush at all times: when you're alone, and when you're with people. Get practice in sending logical electricity to your face instead of emotional electricity, and that will put logic in charge of blushing. It will neutralize the involuntary emotional impulses, and condition, or train, a deliberate control over your blushing. When you control it, that will be the end of it." I emphasized that he must practice this vigorously, and it was my impression that he would.

When I saw him a week later, he was a bit perplexed. "You know," he said, "I find that I can't blush whether I want to or not. It's the darnedest thing."

"Fine," I said. I then went into his general behavior. "Through the years you have developed the habit of keeping your feelings to yourself, because your mother and brother beat you down to size. Just as you expressed your blushing, I want you to express your feelings. From now on I want you to express your emotions as much as you can, even if they get you into trouble. Don't worry, they won't. It's only your efforts to stay out of trouble that get you into it. Expressing this emotional electricity will make people like you and respect you, and they won't think you're a sweet, polite dishrag any more."

"Yes," he said, "I suppose that's what people think I am."

We discussed personal relations with his brother, employee problems, matters of factory procedure, and sales promotion. I instructed him to fight for his beliefs with all the emotional energy possible. I explained the key excitational exercises, and told him not to drink. Expressing himself when he took a drink would not make it any easier when he had none.

"But my brother is very fast on the trigger, and if we get into an argument, I'm sure to lose. What then?"

"Don't try to say anything clever. Simply stick to your emotional guns, and you will find that your answers will be effective. Set up your own issues and stick to them. You can't win on the battleground your brother chooses. If you follow his compass you're sure to lose. Follow your own compass. To change the results you must change your strategy."

After seven sessions, he told me that he felt better than he "can ever remember feeling," and that his wife thanked me. I saw him thereafter twice a year, and then once a year for a "general check-up." He has continued referring persons to me.

This case teaches us the following:

1 When resentment toward a relative is expressed (even if it may not be well-founded), it is good policy to climb aboard the bandwagon immediately, without hedging. This establishes excellent rapport. Once the responsibility for denting the fender has been established, it is possible to explain how to hammer it from underneath, in order to remove the dent. Excitation will even up the inhibition caused by environment.

2 It is important, except with masochists, who like to be blamed, to emphasize to cases their utter lack of responsibility for their condition. It is as foolish for them to blame themselves for being the way they are as for the wing of an airplane to scold itself because it is not a fuselage. If the aluminum of which the wing is composed had been worked on differently in the factory of life, in short, if the metal had different experiences, it would be shaped differently. Developing this analogy helps to get rid of some of the moralistic moonshine instilled in the individual.

3 The psychologist should go into great detail about the appropriate manner for the individual to conduct his personal and business life. If the psychologist is unable to do so, and is not broadly aware and sensitive, he can be more useful to society as an elevator operator.

4 In many instances, an excellent case can be made for the beta hypothesis as fundamental therapy, but successful results with it may sometimes preclude deeper treatment. I have always found it better policy to describe it as an adjunct to therapy, but I have no hesitation in saying that Dunlap's hypothesis, considered aspect of conditioning, is a highly stimulating concept.

Case 11

The following case illustrates an unusual use of the beta hypothesis. I think the reader will find it interesting, and I assure him is not overdrawn.

On a sweltering afternoon in July my, secretary came in and told me that my next appointment was outside. She was a new case, and was wearing a mink coat which she refused to hang in the closet.

"Well," I said, "it's probably not insured, and she feels that everyone is untrustworthy. Don't look so perplexed. You must remember that the people who come here are emotionally defective, and there is probably a story in that coat. Is she dressed underneath?"

"Yes," said my secretary.

I shrugged my shoulders, and poured myself a drink of ice-water. "Have her come in."

An extraordinarily beautiful blonde girl of twenty came in. Her face had classical features, and would draw the stares of men and women in the finest restaurants and theaters in the world. Her carriage was excellent, and she radiated refinement and sex. I had her take her coat off, and I put it down on a chair. She was dressed in a simple and attractive, but cheap, cotton dress. She asked if she might smoke. "Surely," I said, and she lit a cigarette. She puffed leisurely for a while.

"I'm waiting," I said.

She smiled. "Let me get right down to the point." She spoke clearly and distinctly, in a well-modulated voice. Simply put, the young woman had no control over herself, and constantly broke wind when with people. Needless to say, this made her feel wretched, and precluded social relationships. "I'd like to go out with men," she said, "but how can I?" Her life was thoroughly miserable.

She came of a wealthy family, and had been brought up in France. A stock market decline destroyed the family fortunes, and now she was living in a hall bedroom and working in a defense plant. Her mother lived in Philadelphia. The young woman herself lived in New York. Her father was dead, and she saw her mother frequently, and was favorably inclined toward her.

In an effort to mask any odors, she smoked constantly, and after working for several weeks at a job, she would be fired under some pretext. And so she went from one job to another. The poor child had taken her affliction to a series of physicians. Some prescribed charcoal and pepsin tablets, to absorb the gas in the stomach and to aid digestion. Others made intensive proctological examinations, and changed her diet and medication. One physician gave her large doses of phenobarbital, which kept her somewhat "dopey," but "seemed to help a bit, I think."

"Well," I said. "As you probably know, you are a very attractive young woman, and you carry yourself quite well." I paused. "Your speech is extremely dignified and cultured. And therein lies the trouble. These are precisely the things that are wrong with you."

She puffed at her cigarette. "What do you mean?" she asked.

I told her that she was nothing but a well-bred inhibited young woman. I explained inhibition and excitation, and how her good breeding had built up her tension. "Your mistake is to emphasize your stomach. Your back is just as tense, and your arms are just as tense. Your whole body is tense. One particular symptom happens to be disturbing, but you have other symptoms of equal importance. Your mental tension is the cause of your gut tension, and phenobarbital, by relaxing you, has a favorable effect."

"Yes, yes," she said. "I think you have hit the nail on the head."

I then explained conditioning and the basic disciplines for building excitation. I told her of the beta hypothesis. "What I want you to do is to practice the deliberate breaking of wind at all times. I want you to condition a control of your anal muscles!" I explained that there were voluntary and involuntary nerve cables all over the body. "So you see," I said, "our procedure is two-fold. First, I am going to have you live a life that will reduce tension by making you emotionally free. This will solve the problem. Now, regardless of whether we achieve the first objective, and you must work at it nevertheless, this yogi-like muscle control will also produce results. For all we know, it may simply be a poor muscle habit, but on the other hand, your cool and 'self-controlled personality, and your basic shyness, for you are shy, you know (she agreed), are probably the basic causes.

"Tell me," I asked. "Why the mink coat on a day like this:

"If your fees are more than I can afford, I'll leave the coat." It was the only valuable article remaining from the days of affluence, and her mother gave it to her to give to me if necessary.

I told her that I would charge her nominal fees, but I was careful not to tell her that I found her case technically interesting, for this is one of the easiest ways to lose a case. Life is based on hunger, and when the person on the other side of the desk feels that he has what you want, there is no hunger for what *you* have to offer.

Two weeks later, when I saw her next, she said, "My problem is ninety-nine percent gone! I'm sure you're right." I amplified what I had explained to her last time, and kept the spotlight on her basic personality difficulties, and away from her symptoms. I did not ask about her parental relationships. I blamed everything on "breeding."

I let a month go by, and then saw her again. Her problem was a thing of the past. "Oh," she said. "We can forget about it." Then we had an argument, much like a lovers' quarrel. Now that she was well, she insisted upon her right to enjoy herself. "I have been so starved that now I want to go out and have some fun."

I disagreed, for I was convinced that she would throw herself at the first plausible man who came along. It even appeared to me, she thought I might well qualify, for she spoke at length of my understanding and acumen. I smiled wryly.

She smiled back. "I feel like a bird that's left its cage. You can blame me for wanting to try my wings."

"No," I said. "I can't say I blame you. Very well, but whatever you do, please have some standards. That man is going to be lucky, and I don't want you to get hurt."

She thanked me, and left, and I could see she was a bit hurt by my rebuff. I told her to telephone me in a month, and to let me know how she was doing. A month later she telephoned, and was in high spirits.

"How are you?" I asked.

"Fine," she said. "Fine! Everything is wonderful!"

"Are you doing anything interesting?" I asked.

She laughed and said, "Everything's all right."

"Come now," I said. "You know what I mean. How are things?"

She laughed again. "Everything is all right. Thank you."

I saw that there was no point in pursuing the matter. "Very well," I said. "As long as you're happy, that's all that counts. If you ever find anything going wrong, and you need some help, don't forget to call me."

"Yes," she said, "I will. Thank you. I am very grateful." And that was the last I ever heard from her.

Notice that she held me at arm's length, and that I was no longer in her confidence. As people get better, they will tell you less about themselves. They may say that they have "grown away" from you lately. They are busy living, and have no need to lean—the shy person is at ease with people, the alcoholic stops drinking. These changes in symptoms mean success. But when there is a drying-up of confidences that is not accompanied by symptom improvement, therapy is at a standstill.

When there is a great deal of intellectual hair-splitting after therapy has continued for a while, there is no progress. But argumentation about concrete modes of conduct, after living patterns have improved, is quite satisfactory.

For the young woman above to have understood the causes of her problem, was not so important as her having worked on it. Insight need not be deep, but actions speak louder than rationalizations about feelings.

First and foremost, therapy is a practical matter. We are dealing with people who are wearing tight shoes. They do not care whether the softest leather comes from an old cow, or a young one, or from the rear of the hide or from the front. They are not interested in the chemistry of tanning, or the mechanics of sewing on a sole. They simply want their tight psychological shoes to be stretched and made to fit comfortably.

Case 12

Facts are stubborn things, says the adage, but in psychotherapy it is sometimes best to ignore them. Here is a girl who is almost six feet tall. She has heard well of me from her parents, whom I have treated. She is bright and pleasant, and extremely shy. She has two older sisters who are of average height, and as a child she wanted to be a boy, though she has no homosexual tendencies whatever. "If you're a boy and you're tall, it's all right," she said.

"Believe me," I assured her, "height is not the question. You can be tall and unhappy, or short and unhappy. Your height is just another alibi for your shyness. But be it as it may, we won't waste time discussing it. My contention is that as we make you less shy—yes, even though you remain tall-you will find that you just don't care about your height, and you will find life is fun, and the whole question of your height will fade away. You don't have to believe this at all. Let's simply work on your shyness." And that is what we did.

One day she went to an open air concert, and found that the marble seat was cold and uncomfortable. Instead of remaining silent, she told her escort that she was uncomfortable, and they left, although she had liked the music. On another occasion, when some friends wanted to go to a particular restaurant, she said that she did not feel like going there, and suggested another. To her surprise, they accepted. And when some girls wanted to go window shopping on Fifth Avenue, and she said "I hate it," they said, "All right. Let's go home." These incidents are not of cosmic magnitude, but therapeutic advancement is always based on minutiae.

After a while, her friends were telling her that she had "a lot of personality lately," and that she was "self-assured and frank." She developed a sincerely "So what!" attitude toward her tallness, and began to rationalize about it in a healthy fashion. "Of course I'm tall, but that's no reason for its bothering me." When I last heard from her she was doing well, and is happily married to a man who is three inches shorter than she.

Psychotherapy, in a way, must always be a reactionary profession, because it preaches adjustment to reality, whether it be to the tallness of an individual, or to the society in which she finds herself. A happy union organizer can do his work better than an unhappy one, and the same is true of a happy industrialist. In another sense, psychotherapy is revolutionary. It frees the individual from the shackles that culture and experience have put upon him since infancy.

Contemporary society is defective and breeds maladjustment. Change it, runs the cry, and mental health will blossom.

This is true only within the restrictions of the human body. Under the most felicitous social system there will be men who will be misshapen by ambition, there will be parents who overprotect their children, and destroy their chances for happiness, and there will be men (or women) who will covet their neighbors' wives (or husbands) and thus initiate an elaborate series of frustrations. Under the most felicitous social system, there will be men dissatisfied with their occupations, women dissatisfied with their faces, and people who cultivate the hypocrisy of social acceptance.

When the emotions are freed, environmental mastery proceeds apace. Only a few changes can sometimes initiate profound effects.

Case 13

Mr. B., aged 41, is a real estate broker, specializing in farm property. He complains of shyness, procrastination, and "a fear of seeming ridiculous. I get a good idea, and see the other side so perfectly, that I almost become the other fellow." He said that he was uninteresting until he knew people thoroughly, and then he loosened up. I explained the basic rules for developing excitation, and I taught him how to put himself into an autohypnotic condition.

On his fourth visit, he told me that he had called on a customer in New Hampshire, and following my instructions, he said whatever crossed his mind. When he was asked whether some farm buildings were solidly constructed, he answered, "Of course. You can use the chicken coop for an air raid shelter."

This does not sound funny now, but that year it had some point. "Not bad," said the man, who was the editor of the local paper. "Do you mind if I use it?" It appeared in a little box on the front page. The Associated Press picked it up and it was printed in several hundred newspapers throughout the country. The story included his name and address, and he received letters from childhood friends from whom he had not heard for years. When he called on persons to whom he had tried to sell property before, they said, "We read about you in the paper. That was some chicken coop."

Excitation became easier, and he felt better and sold more property. He wrote me several years later. "I was invited to join a small and exclusive poker club (incidentally, a game of which I know little). The stakes are higher than I can afford with my family, and before each game I have drilled the impossibility of losing while hypnotized, and never once have I lost." Apparently, this unique use of autohypnosis made him radiate confidence, and handicapped the other players.

Most of my cases feel deficient in the art of conversation. If they could just learn the technique of the *bon mot* ... If they could only think faster ... If they only had some skill at repartee ... What they really need is to open their mouths and to hurl forth whatever wild juxtaposition of ideas strikes them. *Go to the child, thou sluggard. Don't aim for cleverness. Let emotion be your guide. Practice feeling-talk and you'll become a wit.*

The lament of the inhibitory is that nobody likes them, and that this makes it difficult to obey my instructions. I reply, "Would you care for anyone who acted to you the way you act to them, giving them that faraway look in your eye as if you're in the fourth dimension?" People do not dislike the inhibitory. They simply do not warm up to them. The inhibitory are walking icebergs who deep-freeze everyone they meet.

Case 14

The inhibitory are particularly prone to complain about the difficulty of applying the principles of excitation with superiors. "After all, I can't answer *them* back." Here is the case of a major in the Army who had to kowtow, and what he was able to do about it.

Major W. is a physician, aged 42. His father is "bashful and always going into business with partners." His mother is an aggressive perfectionist. His wife knows that he is happy about their marriage, but she feels that he acts too cold to her. He is quite shy, has depressive spells, and cries when he is angry. He thinks little of the psychiatrists he knows.

Aside from some hypnosis I taught him, my advice was impossible, he said. After all, he had to take orders from people, and he had to get along with them. He came on a short furlough, and he left after four sessions, but he promised to try excitation.

He wrote me two weeks later. "I had a very good opportunity to test my improvement with a lady patient last week. She is the wife of one of our local generals, and a sister of Senator, whom she resembles somewhat. You can imagine how much she is toadied by those seeking advancement. I treated her as I would any other patient, telling her that she must follow my instructions. I really believe that she preferred the change. She resented the solicitous attitude of certain officers who phoned in order to ascertain whether or not she was being taken care of.

"My former fear of my commanding officer [a cold, cynical, egolating personality] is dwindling. I sit next to him at mess if no other chair is unoccupied, rather than go to another table. The Chief of Neuropsychiatry showed a twinkle in his eye when I did that one day. I interpreted it as a sign of encouragement on his part, as he has made no secret about his disapproval of the 'slave driver' tactics employed."

I heard from him four months later. "I am able to do a great deal more without feeling nearly as tired at the end of the day. ... I feel less tension about me, and don't put myself out if the request is at all unreasonable, this decision being made without unnecessary apologies.

"It may interest you to learn that I have attended several social functions along with more or less high ranking local army personnel, also visiting 'big shots.' Officers of field grade-majors and up-are expected to sit at the table with the Colonel, conversing and dancing with the ladies. I am a poor dancer, but I no longer apologize, but compliment my partners on their ability and formal attire. It certainly is more appreciated than an apology."

"Best of all, my immediate commander, who you may recall brought my deficiencies very much into the spotlight, no longer holds any terrors for me. He has done his utmost to have me transferred, and has failed to this date. ... Proof of my statement that I no longer fear him is that I don't hesitate to speak up for what I consider fair and rightfully my privilege. One instance, in particular, required a showdown. For months I had been driving over early each Sunday morning only to sit around awaiting patients that did not materialize. This, I decided, was contrary to the policy of the hospital. I took up the matter with the boss, and even though his first reaction was bitterly unfavorable, I stood my ground and insisted that I saw no real reason for being on duty each Sunday at that time. He finally agreed to my request. My family and I certainly appreciate the change."

Two months later I heard from him again. We had been corresponding about more appointments. "I feel that I have made considerable progress since last May. No better proof of this is possible in my mind than the fact that Colonel X. (his superior officer), whom I formerly feared, openly congratulated me when he learned that I refused to have my leave postponed by the machinations of another officer who wished to leave at the time I was promised. I know that he respects me more because I have not hesitated to stand for my rights and privileges. I have been able to obtain these at times by calling his attention to the matter. Whenever he barks at me I bark back at him. Much grief would have been avoided had I been more assertive a year ago. ... In attempting to follow out your suggestions for improvement of my personality, I have made use of autosuggestion in an elementary form. These suggestions have the same form of mental reminders of the necessary daily habits—little tasks that are to be performed at certain pre-determined times. Ordinarily I would either forget them completely or be guilty of procrastination ... I am acquiring the habit of paying my wife an honest compliment each day upon my return from the hospital. If I have a criticism to make, I try to temper it with a kind word. I know that she appreciates this. She would like me to tell her frequently that I love her, but I feel foolish and self-conscious while doing so. That may come more naturally later on."

Some months after this I saw him seven times, and we discussed excitation in more detail. He wrote me two months later. "You can conclude from the heading on this stationery that I now have a new job. I am the Acting Chief of Medicine in charge during the absence of our former chief. He is now hospitalized with a bad hypertension. He seems to think that he will be discharged from the Army before long. It is rather ironical that the one whom he tried so hard to get rid of is now acting in his place. His belief that I cannot make good is acting as an added incentive to me ... My opportunities of asserting myself have increased many times since I took over. I am making use of my various experiences while up to see you in helping me to overcome my obstacles."

Here he was referring to what I discussed in Chapter 7, "The constructive Use of Past Conditionings." He brought to autohypnotic sessions memories of successful excitation with cab drivers, bell-boys and waiters, and everybody else he met when he visited me. Those who come from a distance to see me are at a disadvantage if have no friends or relatives at hand for practice. Pursuing a hobby or some aspect of their business, and the associations that are an inevitable part of the daily life of a visitor, will give them the lake in which to practice their emotional swimming. It is easy to work this out, except with an invalid.

Case 15

We may ask whether therapy would have been as simple if the physician had not been a major, but was a mere private instead. Yes, is the answer, because he could have expressed himself to his equals. I must assure the reader that social position is irrelevant as long as there is someone around to be excitatory with Mr P, aged 41, illustrates this. He directs research for an advertising agency. When I received this letter from him, I felt that he would never again fear his superiors.

"After you, inspite of my reluctance, brushed me off last Friday, I had a more-than-momentary feeling of now-you're-on-your-own-can-you-do-anything-with-it. Then I decided I could and would.

"Washington has always awed me a little, not only because of its history, not only because of the austerity of its buildings, but also because of my consciousness that tremendous events are constantly taking shape there. . . So when I walked into Mr Big's anteroom you can imagine that I did not feel up to devouring the universe in a single gulp. As I sat there building up to the jitters (moist palms, tight throat, pounding heart, churning viscera) I remembered that all this combinations of symptoms had its origin 'above the ears'. Almost simultaneously I remembered your saying something like this: You are a perfect example of absolute self-control. Now being afraid has never bothered me half so much as the fear that someone would know about it. So—I thought to myself —Mr Big doesn't have a sporting chance of discovering that I am afraid. All he will see is this frozen mug of mine."

The facially expressionless always have this rationalization, and by praising it as an impenetrable armor it can be turned around to facilitate therapy.

"At any rate, when I walked into his office I did so with considerable assurance. I even managed a smile—and my face *didn't* crack after all. We talked for approximately fifteen minutes, and he was quite friendly throughout the conversation. I felt progressively more so as I told him what I thought

"Since that visit I have talked to no less than seven people who would ordinarily give me a real case of stage fright. I gain confidence as I go. Tomorrow I have further contacts to make and I am actually looking forward to them. I continue to practice with everyone who will give me half a chance, and sometimes whether they will or not. I'm having fun."

It had taken me three sessions to win rapport, for he had acted very distant. After that, therapy went easily, which shows why we should never give up too soon.

The question of superiors versus inferiors is an inhibitory rationalization. As I have said earlier, we must assume that reality is unimportant, as long as the individual practices his excitatory disciplines. In fact, only excitation can change reality.

Case 16

As shy men become emotionally free, their social relations become much more effective. This is particularly noticeable in their relations with women. A quiet young West Pointer, while on vacation in Canada, met a young woman and went out with her several times. She treated him as if he were dull and tedious, which, as he says, he was. Some years later, while seeing me, he got in touch with her again. This time she was the star of a Broadway musical comedy. He had some difficulty getting to her, but this time she was smitten by him. "Boy," he said. "It's sure easy to get them eating out of your hand if you know how." He did not go out with her again, because he was browsing elsewhere.

The same young man, after getting into a fracas at one of our better bars, and having two teeth knocked out, felt no self-consciousness at visiting the place next day, a thing he could never have done before. He was very proud of this, although most people might not consider it a worthy accomplishment. "It's hard to tell you what a caterpillar feels like when it becomes a butterfly," he said, "but it's good." Disinhibiting his social relations was the only thing I had done.

Sometimes the individual seeking therapy has sustained no particular psychological injury. He has simply been brought up in a rarefied atmosphere of culture and good breeding. He has become a well-bred automaton who has learned manners as a way of life. Nevertheless, he too has been driven into inhibition through his upbringing. However, inhibitory as those with the well-bred neurosis may be, they seem to navigate successfully, and usually even appear self-controlled.

Case 17

Mr. M., aged 45, was chief of the research division of a lumber corporation, and a lecturer on wood and paper. When World War II broke out in Europe, he was transferred from research to sales promotion, because his technical knowledge was necessary in dealing with Government bureaus and technical groups. He had little difficulty speaking informally, as long as he had no advance notice. I have to put myself over quickly with people," he said, "because of the nature of my work. I want to do the job I have now as well as I think I could do it." Each time he had to speak, he would drink a half-dozen whiskeys and soda, and this would stop his palpitations and give him a feeling of self-confidence. On weekends, he drank very little, but he felt that he was becoming an alcoholic.

He had been disfigured in an airplane crash three years ago, and had spent half a year in the hospital. His face had been completely remodeled, and bore no resemblance to the one he had originally. "It's embarrassing feeling when people you know don't recognize you." No scars were visible, and he looked pleasant and presentable. He reported one other symptom— an annoying twinge that had in his right leg since the accident.

He came of a landed English family. His father was a cool, well-bred country gentleman, and his mother had him in the hands of governesses and tutors at all times. He liked her quietly, but he said, "1 didn't get enough of her, I suppose. I was uncommonly shy as a child but I thought that's how life was supposed to be." He had a younger brother whose personality was much like his.

During World War I he had been in the Royal Engineers, but he found personal contacts so onerous that he had himself transferred an infantry battalion and assigned to the snipers. He qualified, and for two months, until the end of the war, he shot Germans as he had once shot grouse.

I explained the basic principles of excitation to him, and he agreed that they sounded "sensible." He promised to practice "feeling-talk" with great vigor, and he did so. The persons he met at his office, and in his travels, provided ample opportunity, and he found himself getting emotionally freer. A course in public speaking, which had done him little good, now seemed to have become more helpful. Before long he was convinced that excitation was the only way out.

I kept the conversation technical, as if we were discussing engineering. I compared the impression he made on people to the formula

$$\text{force} = \text{mass} \times \text{acceleration}$$

The force of impact is equal to the weight (or mass) multiplied by the acceleration with which it strikes. "Mass, for our purpose," I explained, "is intelligence, and is inborn. It also includes knowledge that has been acquired. Acceleration, however, is an emotional characteristic. When the large acceleration of the excitatory is multiplied by even an average-sized ability (mass), the resulting impact (or force) will be quite large. Of course, there are people whose basic ability is inconsequential, but multiplied as it is by a substantial acceleration, they make a dent in the world. Your ability is substantial," I said. "Let's increase the acceleration. Great ability times great acceleration equals a great force."

He disliked answering the telephone, because it made him uncomfortable, and he could not improvise readily. He would often have to call back, or if at all possible, write. He soon developed greater ease at the telephone, because he was practicing improvisation in everything he did. An explanation of conditioning and self-suggestion, followed by a few simple exercises, completely removed the twinge in his leg in two days.

He improved rapidly as he practiced the key disciplines discussed in Chapter 9, which I illustrated to him in terms of the people around him. He stopped drinking, and although it would not be fair to say that he began to look forward to his speeches, they were no longer ordeals. He said that life had become "pleasant for a change," and he later told me that he had never felt as happy in the last five or six years as he had after his first visit with me.

After a dozen sessions two things remained to be changed. First, although his worries about his face had subsided as he introspected less, he was still somewhat uncomfortable about his appearance. "You're not acting sadistically enough," I told him. "Cultivate more feeling-talk of the don't-give-a-damn variety. This will give you a greater feeling of power and acceptance, and put springs in your heels." At his next session he said, "People will take me as I am, and if they don't, I don't care."

His worries about his face seemed to disappear completely. He reported that he had answered impromptu questions before a large group, and only after he was through did he realize that he had not felt nervous, nor cared if any of the audience seemed uninterested.

His problem had a second aspect, which he considered unimportant and which had only partially improved. I have earlier referred to his unscheduled speeches as being easier than those of which he had ample notice. In the latter case he had time to magnify his worries. On reviewing his emotional exercises, I found that he had not been practicing enough improvisation. "Don't plan anything. I have told you this before, but please emphasize the discipline of improvisation for a while."

His speaking became quite satisfactory at all times, and he stopped drinking, except rarely, and then only socially. He began to cut a figure in professional circles, and was promoted in salary and status. He even became an amusing raconteur.

He was happily married, but felt that his wife had always "tolerated" him. This attitude toward her disappeared during treatment, and he relayed her thanks to me for making him happier and easier to live with. The wives of men I have treated have often thanked me, but the husbands of women I have helped are usually ungrateful. They resent another man's understanding their wives better than they do.

Emotional starvation is a frequent pattern in the childhood of the inhibitory who have been brought up in an atmosphere of good breeding.

This is especially true among the British middle and upper classes. In fact, in a broader sense, the English suffer from a national neurosis. Their traditional reserve is a rationalization for their inhibition.

Englishmen, especially of the upper class, refrain from expressing surprise, interest, or distaste. They seem secretly ashamed of their emotions, and their good breeding is a pose of poise. A gentleman does not brag. He speaks in understatement. A woman I treated had made a trip back home to England. When she arrived in London, and saw her parents, she wanted to run forward and embrace them, but instead she calmly shook hands. Later, talking with them about American mores, she learned that they too had wanted to run forward and embrace her, but they also had controlled themselves.

The Englishman drinks like a gentleman. The American drinks to get drunk. The Englishman drinks to unbend, and the American drinks to oblivion. We must not begrudge the British their whiskey and soda. It will have to do until some national psychotherapy comes along.

The well-mannered person is usually nothing but a stuffed shirt. Poise is too often paralysis. The well-bred neurosis...the English call it "character"...is nothing more than well-mannered inhibition, which results in the accumulation of tensions.

To listen to a joke that you have heard before is insulting to the narrator. It implies, "Talk on, fool. Waste your time and mine." I am not attacking courtesy and consideration. I am simply saying that much of it is a rationalization for inhibition.

The proof that the well-bred neurosis really has nothing to do with manners is that those who suffer from it often find it as difficult to praise someone as to be insulting. Honey is as difficult to express as vinegar. It is not a question of manners. The issue is freedom versus rationalized slavery. "Maybe it's just plain snobbishness. ... I was brought up to assume that it's bad taste to tell people of your personal interests." Or, "I always shuddered at people who went around sounding off about their likes and dislikes, and what they ate for breakfast. Stop the presses, and all that."

In working with the well-bred, it is often desirable to prescribe, as an additional discipline, the mere act of *talking more*. Of course, the talking should be excitational. Another point worth emphasizing is that they be decisive in judgment. They should not cultivate a fraudulent decisiveness, but when they feel certain about anything, they should speak and act with noticeable conviction.

Case 18

Here is the chairman of the board of a great corporation. He is a huge man of 48, and is in excellent health. He tells me that he wants to feel equal, or slightly superior, to whomever he's with. "I have as much to give people as they have to give me. I think I need more aggressiveness for my relations with others in the business world. Not that I can complain the way things are now. ... You have got to help me present myself better to the people I want, or have, to face. The larger the group, the more insignificantly I shine. I don't push myself forward if there's any celebrity around. Why should he want to meet me? I suppose I have a lack of interest, or a lack of concentration, or something. I don't dislike my work, nor do I like it, either. I want to develop more interest in it." He also complained of fatigue at the end of the day, for which his physician could find no reason.

His father, an active businessman, was "considerate," and his mother was a "pleasant person, always occupied with one thing and another." He had a younger sister with whom he got along well. He had spent his early life away at boarding school, preparatory school, and college. The only disturbing incident he could recall was that when he was twelve years old, and at school, he had been forced to "apologize" in front of his class.

He was intelligent, and could easily follow subtleties of reasoning. I explained the basic disciplines to him and he applied them. Soon, he developed more self-confidence. In addition, as in the case of the submarine commander, he learned to produce rapid relaxation at will, and at the end of the day he would be much less exhausted emotionally. And that is all there was to the matter.

Technically, there is not much to differentiate this case from the previous one. The engineer had developed the roots of his problem in England. The businessman had developed them in America. Both had suffered from the same quiet starvation of the emotions. On the surface, the symptom patterns seemed different, but fundamentally both had the same well-bred withdrawal from people.

A telling argument with the well-bred is that the emotional liberation you will teach them will be socially acceptable. True, at first they may sometimes seem self-centered, but if individual fulfillment equals selfishness, then hurrah for selfishness. Actually, the excitatory are not selfish. They want only what is coming to them. Sometimes occupations, friends-wives and husband will have to be changed, but if this sounds cruel, we must remember that environment makes personality:

To thine own self be true,
And it must follow, as the night the day,
Thou canst not then be false to any man.

Hamlet Act 1, scene 3, 78-80

Case 19

Mr A. is 44. He is a professor of English, and a skilled fund raiser for his university. He was sent to me by a former case of mine who had perceived that his calmness was a pose.

He is convinced that it is the height of poor taste to brag, though "I constantly have to be a polite salesman." He likes a few drinks each evening, but alcohol is not really a problem. He is "calm on the outside, but tense on the inside."

I thoroughly enjoyed treating him, because we talked on a highly abstract plane about literature, psychology, and philosophy. Although I realized that stratospheric discussion is always a method of avoiding therapy, I decided that it was necessary at the start in order to establish rapport.

"Yes," he said, in one of our early sessions, "I am a classicist at heart. I appreciate order, decorum, and good taste." Before long he agreed that finishing schools were well named, they finished the spirit permanently. He also decided that F.F.V., a popular abbreviation for First Families of Virginia, stood for Frozen-Faced Virginians.

Only after the individual changes his social behavior does he recognize that his defense of manners was merely rationalization. And as soon as he feels better, it is just as difficult to convince him that his new beliefs ("I decided not to waste time worrying") are also rationalizations. But then it doesn't matter.

As I listen to people talk, I carefully separate what they feel and do from the "why's" they give in explanation. The "what's" should be taken seriously, but for successful therapy we must completely forget the "why's," unless we are studying rationalization.

Case 20

It is often impossible to help the inhibitory who believe that changing their real situation is all that they need. Mr D., aged 22, has an Army psychiatric discharge, and calls himself a "high-powered bluffer." Actually, he is a gentle, dead-panned young man, and has come to see me only because a former case has asked him to.

"Really," he says, "It's just my stomach that's wrong with me." He suffers from biliousness, nausea, and indigestion. Medical examination shows no pathology. Faulty diet, he knows, is the cause of it all. He has only to drink sauerkraut juice, and his stomach is tip-top. You see, his spirits have been sapped by his physical difficulties, though lately sauerkraut juice doesn't seem to help. He nods his head constantly as if agreeing with everything I say.

He has an older brother, whom his father has always held forth as the model of excellence. His father is an aggressive businessman, with a twenty-year history of ulcers. Between his father and his brother he never had a chance, and his Bernreuter scores show high neuroticism and low self-sufficiency. "These scores are probably true," he says, "but you see, my stomach hasn't been acting so well lately, and when that happens it makes me feel blue," etc., etc. This latest stomach upset began immediately after his father told him that the time had come to learn the business, and to stop being a "playboy."

He grants that this may have been relevant, "but, you know, it might have been a coincidence." Each time I indicate that the problem may have psychological aspects, he defends the physical. When I obliquely suggest that he see a stomach specialist, he implies that his problem might well be psychological. You know, he's seen so many doctors. After two sessions he tells me what a pleasure it has been to meet me, and he leaves and I never see him again.

This case sharply illustrates the inaccessibility that often candy-coats the well-bred. Although they listen and nod their heads, they might as well be deaf.

The emotional relations of the well-bred with the universe are deficient, consequently why should their emotional relations with the psychologist be any different? For successful therapy, this barrier has to be penetrated, and at the start this can be done only by "agreeing" with them. If you wish to jump aboard a moving automobile, you must run along with it, keep even with it, and then jump on. The psychologist must first be a gentleman, and then, when he has an audience, become a brute. Otherwise, he will be convinced that he has carried all before him, but he will have been talking to himself and not have realized it.

Psychotherapy is both a science and an art. It is a science because it is coordinated and systematized knowledge. It is an art because the psychologist makes his own contribution, and handles problems with a dexterity born not only of knowledge, but also of the emotional patterns that he himself possesses. There is nothing sadder than the heavy-handed psychiatrist who tries to simulate a warm personality.

The well-bred, like most of the inhibitory, usually have erroneous conceptions of good adjustment. They may visualize an aggressive salesman who grabs people by the lapels as the ideal personality, and they must be quickly disabused of this belief. They will ask why they can't remain excessively well-bred and just develop some more "will-power." But will-power is a symptom of good mental health, just as indecisiveness is a symptom of a distressed state of mind. Destroy the inhibitory "bacteria," and you destroy the fever.

Well," they may say, "you agree that there is nothing fundamentally wrong with me." The answer is, "Nothing fundamentally wrong except that all of your life experiences have produced a state of inhibition, which means a state of being unhappy. Why did you come to see me in the first place?"

Then they may say, "If a person isn't born that way, or isn't naturally exuberant, isn't it difficult to cultivate that type of personality?" This question may indicate agreement that excitation is the goal, and in that event is a good sign. At worst, it is another form of, "I'm just naturally that way," and brings up a somewhat subtle point.

"I feel natural the way I am, even though I'm unhappy. You teach acting the way I feel. I say and do what I feel, yet you say I'm wrong." The answer is that the expression of free-flowing feeling is not the same as the expression of twisted inhibitory feelings that they "feel natural about."

I tell them, "As we change what you say and do, we will change what you feel and think. There is only one way to change character. We must change your conduct with people. You are lost in a forest of concepts, and there's no point in asking you for directions. You must follow me, because my compass will get you out."

CHAPTER 11

THE MERRY-GO-ROUND OF LOW SELF-SUFFICIENCY

Low self-sufficiency is the one psychological dimension most difficult to treat. It is even difficult to describe.

In Chapter 4 I explained that it was an aspect of inhibition, and meant dependency and immaturity. In this chapter I will fill in the details, and give some suggestions for treatment.

A writer, describing himself, said, "I dread the future, romanticize the past, and feel that the present is unreal." If persons low in self-sufficiency (B2-S on the Bernreuter scale) were given the key to paradise, they would say, "Yes, but are you sure this is the right key? How do you know it is? Maybe the lock won't work."

They will break their word when living up to it is inconvenient. "Yes, I may have promised I'd do that, but if I did, I had a mental reservation when I said it." If their promise had been more explicit, they will say, "Yes, but things have changed. When we spoke about this before ...," and they will be shocked if you call them unfair. Yet at worst, they are children, no matter how disconcerting their irresolution may be.

They mistrust themselves, and everybody else who does not beat them into submission. They will call you Master, and betray you for someone else's emotional silver. One of them, when I stood high in his graces, appropriately gave me an effusively inscribed book about Benedict Arnold's treason.

What causes low self-sufficiency? A child conditioned against shifting for himself is inadequate where the environment does not rush in to greet him. Where mother is responsible, the child is irresponsible. Where mother knows best, the child remains ignorant.

The over-protective mother accuses the good mother of neglecting her child, or rationalizes her own behavior as efficiency. "The dishes get done faster if Susan doesn't help." "Susan is cleaner if I wash her." These mothers do not realize that it is not a matter of efficiency. Susan's self-reliance and happiness are at stake.

Irresponsibility is also fostered by some of the parodies of progressive education. (I make no reference to the truly progressive and well-run schools.) This misconception is propped up by a pathetic aggregation of over-educated mothers. The child runs around like a madman. At age six he is permitted to scrawl with crayon on the walls of the living room, and to chop off the legs of the piano with his little hatchet. "We believe in letting Junior express himself. We want him to be free."

Surely, freedom is a commendable thing, but as used here it is meaningless. The child learns no techniques of environmental mastery. He expects the world to welcome his ill-advised intrusions and tantrums, and he becomes an egocentric *enfant terrible*. He is not free. He is the slave of special privilege. Those inhibitory mothers, who have mis-read a few books, are wrong, Only the self-reliant can be free. Irresponsibility hurts the child as much as over-protection, because both produce the same inability to accommodate to life.

Chronologically and intellectually, many a man is an adult, but still wears emotional diapers. If he marries a woman who also has low self-sufficiency, we have the makings of tragedy. They both think they have married giants they can lean on, but they find that they have married midgets who want to be carried. Their children may well be forgiven for being psychological derelicts.

To build a happy child parents need be guided by only two precepts:

1 Give the child a great deal of love. Not "smother" love, but a feeling of being appreciated and encouraged. The child who feels loved, i.e., accepted by his environment, will be well-adjusted.
2 Don't over-protect the child. Let him learn the hard way, through doing and through experience.

That is all that is necessary. It will be easy if the parents are excitational. If they are not, they will have to be on their best behavior.

There is some basis for the distress of those who fear the effects of governmental paternalism. But the only ones whose self-sufficiency it impairs are those whose self-sufficiency was faulty in the first place. Those who have always been self-sufficient, but have been the victims of circumstance, will remain unhurt by governmental assistance. We see once more that what matters is not the stimulus, but the kind of organism that receives it.

When the husband's self-sufficiency is high, and the wife's is low, we have the husband of whom people say, "John must be very much in love with Mary, because nobody else would tolerate her and the horrible house she keeps." Such a husband said to me, "If she'll go twenty-five per cent of the way, I'll go the other seventy-five, but I'll be damned if I'll go one hundred per cent of the way." Whenever a husband comes to brief me on his wife's problem before sending her on to me, I have always found her to be low in self-sufficiency. Such women want to buy therapy like a pair of shoes, only with less effort. Of course, we have a parallel situation when a highly self-sufficient woman, usually the driving executive type, marries a humble Milquetoast.

The qualities involved in self-sufficiency are made clearer by the following questions from the Bernreuter Personality Inventory.[1]* The answers indicate low B2-S.

1 Do you like to bear responsibilities alone? No.
2 Do you prefer traveling with someone who will make all the necessary arrangements to the adventure of traveling alone? Yes.
3 Can you usually understand a problem better by studying it out alone than by discussing it with others? No.
4 Do you find conversation more helpful in formulating your ideas than reading? Yes.
5 Do you find that people are more stimulating to you than anything else? Yes.
6 Do you want someone to be with you when you receive bad news? Yes.

---

[1] This psychological questionnaire was constructed after rigorous statistical analysis. It gives, as it were, a psychological electrocardiogram of the individual's personality. The test is composed of 125 questions, which are answered by encircling yes, no, or question mark, It measures six personality traits: neurotic tendency, introversion-extroversion, dominance-submission, and self-confidence, all of which are essentially similar, and self-sufficiency and sociability. Super's review of 133 published studies on the Bernreuter leaves no doubt that it is a definitely useful psychological instrument. (1)

7   When you are in low spirits do you try to find someone to cheer you up? Yes.
8   If you are spending an evening in the company of other people do you usually let someone else decide upon the entertainment? Yes.
9   Are you able to play your best in a game or contest against an opponent who is greatly superior to you? No.
10 Do you ever heckle or question a public speaker? No.

A low score in self-sufficiency means, "Caution, danger ahead." The proverb says, "Paddle your own canoe," but those with low self-sufficiency have nothing to paddle with. Persons who score about fifty will be found to teeter between adequacy and inadequacy, and their self-sufficiency must be increased if they are not to be in constant danger of losing their balance. In a way, they are to be pitied more than those with the low scores, for they have known what it is to be strong, and the others have always been weak.

I have said earlier that the person low in self-sufficiency has a fraudulent excitation. He will tell you that he is quite extroverted. "I like people. I like to be with them. I like to have a house full of company. I always like guests for dinner."

These are not the criteria of excitation. They are part of a widely held misconception of extroversion, fostered by many psychologists. An acute need for people is a sign of weakness, and the chatter of these self-styled extroverts is merely a method of seeking support. Under close questioning, they will grant that although they need people, they really don't care for them at all.

Their interest in people is not the interest of an equal. It is rooted in inferiority, and is an insatiable hunger for approval. Talking to them is like talking to a blotter. They absorb everything, and give nothing. Whether or not they successfully deceive others into thinking they are excitatory has nothing to do with the matter. The man with syphilis who says, "But nobody else knows it." suffers from it just the same.

Case 21

Here is a case which illustrates most of the principles involved in the treatment of low self-sufficiency. Mrs. T. is an attractive woman in her mid-thirties. Her husband has just been psychoanalyzed, and has been advised to do whatever he wants, whenever he feels like! He comes and goes as he pleases, and pays hardly any attention to my wife and two daughters. He is a cruel stranger in the house. He has always been charming, callous, and egocentric, and has used his "analysis" as a rationalization for his behavior. These details, together with his curious business history, lead me to conclude that he is a classical psychopath, a pattern we shall consider more fully in Chapter 19.

His wife, who now sits before me, is in an anxious state, and suffers from insomnia, loss of weight, and shortness of breath. Her doctor has told her that her troubles are "mental," and she has come to see me because I have been recommended by a friend of hers whose husband I once treated.

Her Bernreuter showed almost maximum neurotic, introvert, and non-confidence scores, and a self-sufficiency of 3.2 per cent. In her childhood she had over-protection and under-love, and a tremendous desire for affection, which of course she still had. "My parents," she said, "did more to me than for me." After our second session she wrote as follows:

"I do hope that soon, very soon, you will be able to see me again. As I told you, on the first day, I know that you will be able to 'make a man out of me,' and in my muddled state the sooner the better. I have the feeling that I'd like to take you home with me but then I know everyone else has that same thought. We all like to think we are different, but our reactions are very much the same." Notice the rapport. Successful rapport cannot be simulated. It must be truly felt, and only then will the person under treatment sense it and respond to it. Therapy is emotional both ways.

I saw her another half-dozen times, and through the disciplines I have described before, we worked at building excitation. At her ninth session she said, "I could live a normal and happy life with Tom [her husband] if you could only straighten him out."

"No," I answered. "Such characters are hopeless. You must believe me."

We discussed his psychopathy further, and then she said, "Perhaps all these things are true, but there's one difference between him and those other cases you told me about. Tom has remained faithful to me. I'm sure I satisfy him sexually."

I laughed. "That," I told her, "is the most ridiculous thing I have ever heard. I have never met your husband, but I have no doubt that my diagnosis is correct. And putting together the little details you have told me, I am sure he's as faithful as Casanova."

"No," she said. "I think you're right about everything else. I respect you very highly, but you are wrong about this."

"Well," I said, "keep your eyes open." She thought over my remarks, and then engaged a detective agency. In a day, she had the name and address and telephone number of her husband's mistress. She confronted him.

"Oh, that," he said. "It's nothing at all. Just something I ran into lately," which was not true. And more in the same vein.

This, she felt, proved that her husband really needed treatment by me. The lowly self-sufficient are masochistic, for pain has always been an integral part of their lives. I decided it was time to take matters into my own hands.

"Go to Reno," I said. "Get some rest and some sunshine. I'll see your husband, and if I can help him, you won't follow through with the divorce. If he's beyond my powers, get him out of your life."

"But you'll really try to help him, won't you? I know you will, but try extra hard."

The diagnosis of psychopath is best made on biography, and I had decided that her husband was one beyond doubt. Perhaps he might want help if I appealed to him on the basis of increasing his enjoyment of life.

He was cool and suave when I saw him. He was really well adjusted, he said, because he knew how to be free. There was nothing wrong with him. It was his wife who needed treatment. ...

"Then why were you psychoanalyzed?

"My wife insisted on it."

"What will you do if she divorces you?"

"If she can't take it, I feel sorry for her."

I nodded non-committally.

His analysis, he continued, though forced on him, had been a success. "Is there anything else you want to know about my wife?" he asked, closing the discussion.

"No," I said. "That covers it."

Several days after this his wife went to Reno. From there she wrote me as follows:

"I really feel Tom was sincere in wanting help, and I think if you told him you could help, he would have believed you and absorbed what you advocated. He listened and followed out Dr. X's theories and instructions, so why didn't he with you? Why can't you help him. If you can't, I feel I can never go back to him or be happy. I keep hoping we will get together again. I can't seem to get over him. My thoughts are ever on it, and I can't sleep because of it. The nights are really ghastly. I don't want to come back to New York for I fear I would never be strong enough to stay away from him, and that way I'll never get over him. I don't know what to do, and I feel like that rat you told me about that has to go crazy sooner or later.

...If only you could have found it possible to help him. You see, I'm still torturing myself, but then I wouldn't be me if I didn't."

Note how she was aware of her masochism, which after all is nothing but getting accustomed to misery. I wrote her that it was as possible to cure her, while she remained married to her husband, as was to cure a man of rheumatism who continued living in a rice swamp.

She answered me several days later. "Please let me thank you and tell you how appreciative I am of your special letter that came a little while ago. I have been waiting for this, but now that I read it, at least four times, I wonder why I was so impatient. Not that I didn't expect this, but it still is a shock because it comes from you, who I feel is the only person who knows enough to tell me.

"When your letter came I looked at it and started trembling. I could hear my heart beating and I was really afraid to open it, for knew what you would tell me. But I sat down and opened it. I got the same feeling I got when the doctor told me my baby died–and I am so afraid at this moment that I don't know what to do. I can't explain it, but you, in your wisdom, know what I mean. I am afraid to face life alone and bring up my girls alone. I feel if I were at your office you would tell me, if Tom were with me, I'd still be alone, and it's true, but it's different. Please believe me, I wouldn't want this past year again. The future I face is emptiness and loneliness. I haven't the assurance, confidence or self-reliance to face it alone."

She then expressed fear that I, who had been so understanding, would get a little impatient at her balkiness, and that her friends, the persons who had referred her to me, would also get tired of her. I answered, "Get one thing straight. Neither the Joneses nor I are the least bit 'fed up with you', and neither they nor I will quit, in any manner, shape, or form. So, if you must worry, please exclude that item from your worry department."

After a few more letters, she wrote: "I may be giving myself a shot in the arm–and I say this because I don't want to fool myself but I think I am much better in the mental department. I even feel that if I saw Tom it wouldn't bother me. He sent me flowers on my birthday, and I wasn't even excited or pleased. I sent him a most formal thank-you. Yesterday he phoned and I spoke to the children and then to him, and that too left me cold. In fact, I cut the talk short myself. Do you attribute this to being saner about the situation, or just the fact that I'm not near him? My intention all the way through has been to stay friendly, and see him whenever I could, and wait. But now I feel differently. I don't want to see him or even talk to him. I prefer to cut it clean, though this has never been my policy even with friends. I always hang on and on, but I have decided to bury my dead, for this is the only way I can get any relief. I think Tom is as good as buried in my mind. I am not saying these things in a positive vein, as I won't really be able to tell until after I see him again."

And so the mail continued reports of freedom from her, and messages of encouragement from me. Then her six weeks were over, and she had secured her divorce. Now she wrote that people were remarking how well she looked. She had gained weight, and she was sleeping well and feeling fine. She was very grateful.

In general, however, when persons with low self-sufficiency thank you, it is important to brush their praise gently aside. "Leopold Auer," I explain, "was a great violin teacher. It would be foolish for Jascha Heifetz, after each recital, to tell the audience, 'All that I am I owe to Leopold Auer.' No. I have been a good teacher, and you have been a good pupil. You have learned your lesson well. Thank you, and goodbye. I'm no further from you than the nearest telephone."

Appreciation is a good sign, if it does not indicate a hangover of low self-sufficiency. But when people continue to shower you with gifts, you have not treated them correctly. Successful therapy means destroying dependence.

Pavlov spoke of an inborn reflex of freedom and an inborn reflex of slavery. (2) Bechterev criticized this. (3) "... it is not possible to solve the problem of the innate character of a reflex merely on the basis of the inability of the usual methods to inhibit it (which was Pavlov's criterion), but it is necessary to turn in this case to an examination of the problem of its origin, for, only when we state the fact that the given reaction has originated independently of the animals life conditions and of the external activities which have influenced it, have we the right to regard it as an innate reflex."

As we saw earlier in this chapter, the slavery of low self-sufficiency makes sense only from Bechterev's viewpoint, i.e., we must study its origin to see if it is really innate. However, I assure the reader that my experience with humans inclines me to Pavlov's findings. It is extremely difficult to recondition the slavery of low self-sufficiency. Yet we know that today's impossibilities are tomorrow's platitudes.

What can we do at this stage of our knowledge? Everything we know about psychotherapy applies to the treatment of low self-sufficiency, only more so. The rule of the road is "Drive slowly, and exude confidence."

The low in self-sufficiency are blind believers in faith, because they are leaners to begin with. In fact, they will often lean on you so heavily that you will be hard put not to be crushed. They like to have the law laid down to them. They have no wish to participate in therapy, and the work and responsibility are all yours. To ring the personalized bells, you must exploit their weaknesses, and dominate them into self-sufficiency.

The way to establish rapport with an individual with low self-sufficiency is to tell him that you are taking charge. You are going to run his life— for a while. He will have neither worry nor responsibility. Those will be your province. This will buoy him up considerably, but it is not enough. Hope and inspiration are the stock in trade of the football coach and the psychiatrist who does not know any better.

Those with low self-sufficiency also need help in disentangling themselves from the uncomfortable realities in which their poor emotional habits have enmeshed them, and as we manage these real situations, we must show them what to do under parallel circumstances in the future. They ask:

Should I get a divorce?
Should I form a new company or stay with the old one?
Should I sell the big house or the small one?
What should I do about Mrs. Smythe's snubbing me?

They are the constant telephoners. "Shall I smoke three-quarters or seven-eighths of my cigarette?" "What does this dream mean ... and that one?"

These questions are amusing only to the strong. To the weak they are serious issues, and we must be patient and understanding. Our task is simultaneously to pet them and bully them into mental health. But we are on a merry-go-round. If we're too firm, they will leave. If we're not firm enough, they won't get better. Women, however, have known this for centuries: We must act cool, but not too cool. We must act warm, but not too warm.

Therapy is like an airplane ride. The take-off and the landing are most important. Rapport is important at the take-off. At the landing, when you shut off your motors, you must be careful that your passenger doesn't suddenly feel rebuffed. One-way love, taking without giving, is part of the illness of the low self-sufficient. If our therapy has been effective, they will not be angry when we leave them, because they will have learned how to fly for themselves.

Yet whatever we do, we may find that our therapy is like Penelope's web. What we laboriously weave at the office, is easily unraveled at home. Husbands, wives, and parents can destroy everything we do, for by definition, the individual with low self-sufficiency is prone to everyone's influence. But we must not be dismayed, for what applies to low self-sufficiency is true of every other psychological disorder as well: If we could control all of the stimuli that go into the hopper, we could remold anybody.

We can draw a few lessons about the treatment of low self-sufficiency from the case of Mrs. G. She was able to increase her excitation and self-sufficiency because:

1 She had to do something about her problem. Her husband's work kept her constantly in the public eye.
2 Her husband was a distinctly superior person, and cooperated thoroughly with the therapy.
3 Mrs. G. herself was alert, and applied herself vigorously to what she called her "homework."

But whether circumstances are favorable or not, and they usually are not, the therapist must be both a detective and a wrestler. He must be a detective, because he must find clues whose subtlety, or very blatancy, makes them difficult to detect. And he must be a wrestler, because he must break the holds of the persons under treatment, and apply the counterholds that will make them submit.

Hypnosis must be avoided with the lowly self-sufficient at the beginning of therapy, else they will have no interest in the basic techniques of excitation. They will practice the excitatory disciplines if you say, "How is it possible to ring hypnotic bells that you haven't got? To remedy this, you must first do the emotional deeds that mean cure, because only then will you be building in, however weakly, bells that we can later vibrate with hypnotic words."

We must remember our basic disciplines, for in a nutshell, the successful treatment of low self-sufficiency is based on conditioning excitation, with emphasis on the self-reliance that is part of it. We should never cope with anyone's deficiencies. We should take advantage of them, for they are all we have to work with.

The person who wants to build his self-sufficiency must hardly ask anything of anybody, even street-directions. He must follow his own impressions about everything, and avoid asking for advice, even though he may really need it. He must practice coming to decisions any decisions-as long as he makes them quickly. He must try to do everything for himself. It is kill or cure.

"But," he will object, "if I feel like asking somebody a question, and I inhibit it, isn't it wrong?" The answer again is, "We must not confuse the expression of twisted feelings with the liberation of healthy impulses. The same questions may be excitational for someone else, but for you they are inhibitory and cultivate weakness."

"Then what shall I do about my twisted feelings?"

"Nothing. Train the good feelings to come out, and the others will disappear."

Asking questions___"What do you think about...?" or, "How do you ... [something or other]?"-is often a leaning technique. Men who are called "charming," or women who are called "fetching," do this often, and may be defective in self-sufficiency. They can develop a community of interest with anyone. If it will not be about something they both like, it will be about something they both dislike.

Some of them, frequently with Continental backgrounds, are interminable metaphysicians. They will talk of everything except the issue, and insist that it is germane. For instance: "Surely I like friends, Why not? You get in a friend what money can't buy. Friendship, after all, is the most selfish thing in the world. Aren't you in favor of it?"

I answer, "Your other behavior patterns show that the desire for friendship, in you, is a rationalization of your low self-sufficiency.

In the report card of life nobody gets a mark for effort. The eagerness of the lowly self-sufficient to learn, and to take criticism, comes from their low opinion of themselves. It is not an intellectual mechanism, so it is a waste of time to explain the why's and wherefore's to them. They do not need insight. They need habits.

Almost all therapists, when asked for advice by a patient, will answer, "What do you think?" They do not consider this an evasion. They imagine that they are developing the patient's ability to cope with life. Under these circumstances I would as soon ask a case of mine "What do you think?" as I would ask a baboon what he thinks about Aristotle. We might re-word it to say, "With what do you think?" Then the answer becomes clear. He has nothing to think with but his past nonsensical habits.

To put it with brutal simplicity, low self-sufficiency is the leech sickness. Those who suffer from it leech onto everybody. We will consider low self-sufficiency later in its conjunction with other symptom patterns. Meanwhile, I need only remark that it is a subsidiary aspect of inhibition, and must be treated accordingly.

CHAPTER 12

PROBLEMS OF THE THERAPIST

Fundamentally, everybody has the same problem and the same cure.

Dr. A. is a dentist, and is afraid of blood.
Mr. B. has claustrophobia, and is afraid of elevators.
Miss C. is an actress, and finds it difficult to face an audience.
Mrs. D. is a writer who cannot concentrate on her work.
Mr. E. says that life isn't worth living.

Some of these people were brought up in the country, and some in the city. Some had kind fathers, some had stern ones. Some were indulged by their mothers, and some were frequently punished. Some were jealous of an older brother, and some were not. Some were only children, some were the youngest, and some were the oldest. In short, these people had entirely different histories, and presumably, entirely different problems.

After taking a phenobarbital pill, or a stiff drink,

Dr. A., the dentist, does not mind blood at all.
Mr. B. rides comfortably in his office elevator.
Miss C. finds it easy to appear before an audience.
Mrs. D. sits down at the typewriter and works for two hours.
Mr. E. decides that the world is a fairly interesting place after all,

To be sure, the problems return when the alcohol or phenobarbital wears off, but five different persons, with five different problems stemming from five different pasts, have been temporarily "cured" by one and the same thing. What other conclusion seems possible, save that all five suffer from the same disturbance—an excess of inhibition.

But penicillin, it may be argued, kills many different bacteria, and nobody contends that these bacteria are the same. Why then is the contention being made here that because the same excitation "cured" five different problems, the five different problems are necessarily the same?

The answer is that the analogy is not well taken. In bacteriology the differences among bacteria are thoroughly established. In psychotherapy the differences among psychological problems are highly debatable, and it is the specific contention of this book that the differences are immaterial. Practically, how the individual "gets that way" is of little therapeutic importance.

Our cardinal therapeutic principle is excitation, and we must use every art and stratagem to force the person under treatment to think of his problem solely in those terms. Of course, this is a difficult concept for the inhibitory individual to grasp, for his entire history has trained him to be opposed to it. His inhibitory training will present one obstacle after another, and we must overcome them all before we can consider him cured.

The usual obstacles form an unholy trinity: questioning, suicide-risk, and evasion. I shall discuss them separately.

For successful therapy, every question raised by the person under treatment must receive a clear answer. It need not be thorough, but it must satisfy him, no matter how foolish the question may appear.

"Don't you think that if I had the courage to do what I should, I wouldn't have my troubles?" The way to handle such philosophical flotsam is to explain that "should" and "ought" do not determine behavior. This is determined by training. When habits are far from ideals, unhappiness is the result. When habits are close to ideals, happiness is inevitable.

But we must not make the mistake of believing that people who achieve their ideals are happy. Excitation and freedom are the criteria of happiness, and when the inhibitory rationalize their twisted objectives, we must beat them into a figurative pulp. "How, we must ask them, "did you get into the state you're in except by that 'master strategy' of yours? Obviously there must be something wrong with it, so let us not take it too seriously." The "conscious ideal" of the individual is not the cause of his behavior, but is an incidental product of his conditioning.

And this applies as well to the threadbare question of reason versus emotion. "If I only followed my head instead of my heart. ... Even if I did, I don't think I have enough intelligence." In Chapter 5, in discussing rationalization, I made it clear that ours was a unitary nervous system, and that consequently every cortical act has its autonomic components.

The only thing wrong with the thinking of the inhibitory is their emotions. Although an engineer cannot build bridges with feeling-talk, he cannot build a happy life with anything else. In psychotherapy, it is not what the individual knows that counts. It is what he does. There is nothing like experience. We may read about it. We may talk about it. We may hear about it. But until it has happened to us, it hasn't happened. We must arrange for new emotional experiences if we want new emotional patterns.

Those who have been well primed by inspirational literature will talk of the importance of faith. It need not necessarily be in God. It may be faith in self, faith in others, faith in happiness, or simply faith in faith. Somehow, though, they have been unable to believe hard enough.

To consider faith as a problem of belief wraps it in an intuition that is neither provable nor disprovable. The entire matter of the acquisition of faith is subject to scientific inquiry, and a good case can be made for considering religion as a conditioned reflex. To put it bluntly, no one can "acquire" faith. It can only be re-acquired and only by those who have had the proper early conditionings.

Alas, these persons will tell you, they have an "unconscious desire to fail." If they could only lose their accompanying "fear of failure," all would be well. Here is Limburger to trap the hungry mouse. The "unconscious desire to fail" should be translated into the "inhibitory habits of inadequacy that mean failure."

"Well," comes the argument, "maybe I'm just naturally weak." If heredity is everything, therapy can only be nothing. True or not (and the hereditary viewpoint has deteriorated considerably in the past hundred years), we must assume that we can remove the individual's difficulties by changing his conditioned emotional patterns. It would appear needless to mention, save that the question often arises, that psychotherapy cannot do anything about structural defects of the body, or about germs, or about those who break the rules of hygiene.

"Very well," may be the answer. "Perhaps conditioning is everything, but after all, I am fifty-five years of age, and I have had 55 years of experience at doing the wrong thing. By now aren't my emotional habits firmly entrenched?"

The answer to this is simple. Let us assume that a chimpanzee had been confined in a cage for two years. Let us further assume that a small pedal-like device were introduced into the cage, and that the chimpanzee's paw was repeatedly forced down on it. This would throw open the cage door, and bring into view a bunch of bananas. Surely, it would not take even ten minutes for him to learn how to operate the pedal and to leave the cage—and this despite his two years of captivity.

And so it is with the human being who has had 55 years of bad habits. Our understanding of conditioning permits a centralized and effective attack on the problem. It is well-established in the psychology of learning that a simple way of doing an act is learned faster than a complicated one. Further, when the new way is mastered, its presence makes it difficult to relearn the old way, even if it has been of long standing. Technically, this is called retroactive inhibition. In emotional relearning, the new habits are the psychologically simple ones, and they soon overcome the old and unnatural inhibitions.

The question is often asked, "How can I learn to live with my husband (or wife)?" A woman is married to a man whose interests and aspirations are completely opposed to hers, and now she asks, how can she learn to accept her lot? After all, it is possible to recondition anything. And she launches into a description of her husband's virtues, although fundamentally she does not think he has any.

In essence, these women are asking, "How can I become a successful hypocrite?" This, of course, violates our fundamental principles of excitation, but they will declare that they are simply trying to find out how to adjust to their present realities. This sounds fair enough until we realize that what they are demanding is their own false conception of adjustment. These women need divorce and not psychotherapy.

When these women tell me, "My marriage is entitled to another chance," what they are really saying is, "I'm entitled to another chance to prove to my husband that I am what I really am not," which is nonsense on the face of it.

A more difficult situation that confronts the therapist is the problem of suicide-risk. Most persons who have contemplated suicide will not admit it when they first see us. They fear we may refuse to treat them. Unless they are psychopaths, or have irremediable defects in their real situation, this does not dissuade us from accepting them and acquiring a few headaches. Incidentally, all of them have low self-sufficiency.

My first professional fee, and my first letter of appreciation, came from a woman who drank a bottle of iodine, and was brought to the psychopathic ward of a hospital. The popular belief is false, i.e., if they talk about suicide they will never do anything about it. In truth, they may really commit suicide, or they may not. And in the long run, more people commit suicide with a fork than with a knife.

Case 22

A man told me that unless I changed his personality from "negative to positive." and thus made him interesting to his wife who had threatened to divorce him, he would put a bullet through his head. There was no mistaking his cool certainty. After some treatment, he called his wife, the woman he had admired, "a parlor whore," and he considered suicide the most foolish idea he had ever had. Now, several years after his divorce, he is still getting along splendidly. It is excitation that makes the difference.

Case 23

I once treated a psychopathic alcoholic with the understanding that it was an experiment and that I promised nothing. He had tried suicide twice before, and had been institutionalized repeatedly. He was mother-bound, and had guilt feelings at being a non-practicing Catholic. His wife felt I had made important progress, but that I was "doing the wrong thing in getting him to loosen up." He agreed. "I know we've gone a long way, but after all, your approach has been scientific. I don't think you pay enough attention to the soul. I heard a great deal about Alcoholics Anonymous, and if they help me to get more faith in God, I know my troubles will be over." I had planned to get him back to the Church after a half-dozen more sessions, and I tried to persuade him to continue, but to no avail. I asked his wife to remain in touch with me. Her husband kept himself busy with five inspirational meetings a week, and tried to get more faith. A year later he committed suicide. Let us render unto psychotherapy the things which are psychotherapy's; and unto faith the things that are faith's.

There is one particular pattern encountered in therapy that, no matter how it disguises itself, always has only one meaning. When therapy gets intellectual it is time to be careful. Intelligent conversation that is not concerned with concrete personal situations keeps therapy at arm's length. This is true no matter how intelligent the person under treatment may be. He will never understand what we mean until he starts practicing excitation, and until then, he will be full of keen irrelevancies.

"Wouldn't you admit that even the maladjusted are emotionally infantile? They are acting in the fashion in which they were trained as infants, and don't you advocate a return to childish behavior? This ingenious objection may be answered by breaking it into two parts. "Do people behave emotionally in the way they were conditioned as infants?" The answer is "Yes." However, "If people were conditioned to excessive inhibition in childhood, do you advocate their conducting themselves with inhibitory infantility?" To this, the answer is, "Definitely not." Often, if the person under treatment sounds intelligent, it is because he is a shyster lawyer of the emotions engaged in obfuscation.

Psychotherapy is an emotional process, and intellectual adaptation, without emotional involvement, prevents improvement. Those with the well-bred neurosis wreathe their fraudulent insight in smiles and sociability, yet they may be as inaccessible to therapy as the man who says he is Napoleon.

The simple-minded pose is another form of evasion or rationalization. "You know, these ideas you're explaining are somewhat complicated." As a businessman put it, "When anyone says 'I'm just a country boy who never went to college like you fellows,' I hold on to my pockets and run for the nearest exit." This is not possible in psychotherapy, at least for the therapist. What the therapist must do is to repeat his ideas in as many different ways as possible until he rings the right bell.

There will be persons who defend expediency-for which read hypocrisy and strangulation of honest impulse. They must stop being "expedient," if they want to be happy. By their present lights, the more inexpedient they become, the more excitation they will develop.

Persons who devote themselves to argument have a poor prognosis, unless the idea can be insinuated into their minds that the way for them to win, is to lose this particular argument. They constantly defend themselves. They are the aginers. If you blow hot, they will blow cold. If you blow cold they will blow hot. ... If they know anything about psychoanalysis they will call it ambivalence: Yes, but then again, no. I like him, yet somehow I dislike him. ... Their childhood always show extensive emotional laceration-orphanages, stepmothers, and an overpowering feeling of loneliness. They have always had to defend themselves, so we must be understanding.

Case 24

Satire and cynicism mean twisted belligerence and an absence of rapport. It will be found that those who act this way toward the therapist do so in all of their other personal relations.

Here is a man discussing spring planting with his two children. He knows that their favorite vegetable is corn. "No, we're not planting any this year. I don't believe in it. The bugs will get it anyway, so why bother?" He talks in this vein for almost an hour, and then, when his children are almost heartbroken, he laughs and says, "Of course, we're planting corn. You knew all the time we were going to." And he really loves his children very much. Therapy was quite successful, but it came too late to restore a contract that his inhibitory satire had lost him, and which would have netted him a quarter of a million dollars.

Skepticism, caused by experiences with unsuccessful therapy, is not an obstacle and is quite normal. The person under treatment should be told, "You're absolutely correct, I see no reason why you should feel any differently toward me, but let me explain my approach. ..."

The evasions and diversions we have been discussing are equivalent to the individual's saying, "I have not been doing the things you want me to, because I have been trained to do others." The practice of excitation will disperse his vaporings, because they are only the rationalizations of inhibition. Excitation is the difference between being happy and unhappy. The excitatory can be frustrated, but not as long nor as deeply as the inhibitory.

Particularly inaccessible to therapy are the people who are obsessed by hypnotism. They conceive of post-hypnotic suggestion as something that can be given to them easily, simply because they want it. Hypnotism, to them, means sitting in a chair and being talked to. They want to use hypnosis like aspirin to help them through the day. They usually have low self-sufficiency, and want reality to be germfree, because they themselves possess no psychological phagocytes.

They are the people who, when you hypnotize them, try to help you with all their might. They will tell you that they are "trying not to think about anything." They do not realize that this is tantamount to thinking of something. To them say, "Do nothing negatively", by which I mean that their doing nothing should be completely passive and non-active, unlike the vigorous methods of relaxation advocated in popular magazines. I once told such a person, "While I hypnotize you, you are de-hypnotizing yourself."

"But I have no conscious resistance to being hypnotized," he answered.

"I know," I said. "Your only resistance is caused by your being you."

A distinctly intelligent woman, to whom I explained that it was necessary to increase her level of excitation to create appropriate bells to vibrate, left me, superficially pleased. Several days later, she wrote me an angry letter. "I just want hypnotic therapy. I do not need psychotherapy. You know very well that I don't."

In a sense, the hypnotic state means that the individual is not doing any neural broadcasting, but is only receiving. Persons who come for treatment, and insist on broadcasting, are doomed to own static.

I have no objective data, but it has been my impression that the greater the excitation of my cases, the greater their hypnotizability, though there are frequent exceptions. It would not be surprising if this correlation turns out to be true, for the free-flowing individual is more accessible, and his mind is clear because it is really flexible. The inhibitory person is always thinking of so many things that he cannot provide a blank state of mind.

Through increasing the excitation of individuals, I have increased their hypnotizability. Once, when two lengthy attempts at hypnotizing a woman failed, I educated her into excitation for acting. After several months of training in emotional freedom, I suggested trying hypnosis again.

"Do you think it will work this time?" she asked.

"Why not try?" I answered. I was able to produce intensive cutaneous anesthesia with ease. Other factors probably underlie increases in hypnotizability, but I believe that building excitation is the most important

This seems to lead to the unfortunate conclusion that many of the persons who need hypnosis are the ones who are least amenable to it. This is true, but as I have said before, there are many exceptions. Besides, most important of all, these persons can be helped just as effectively through the excitational methods that I am explaining here. In short, as a hitherto unhypnotizable person learns excitation, his psychological problems disappear, and this in turn facilitates hypnosis, but then it no longer matters.

The hypnotic procedure makes use of what a person already has. In that sense, there are millions of hypnoses. These hypnoses are problems in verbal, social, and pictorial habit patterns.

When Pavlov was at work conditioning his dogs, there was no hypnotism involved. When reaction patterns had been inculcated, and a secondary stimulus, say, a bell, produced salivation, only then was hypnosis involved. Hypnotic responses occur in the later stages of the learning curve. This goes far beyond the conventional conception of hypnotism.

Propaganda and mass reactions are based on the multitude of verbal bells provided by modern literacy, and on the powerful emotional responses which they evoke. This presents a frightful picture, which becomes somewhat depressing as the conditioned human being jumps through the hoop when the bell rings, and insists that he has leaped through the air only after careful consideration.

Psychotherapy is a pedagogic process, and to know this is to have the key to successful therapy. Good pedagogy, of course, always begins with what is familiar to the pupil. Compare excitation to the time he was pleasantly drunk at a New Year's party. Tell the artist that it is much like the way he feels when he suddenly wants to use a particular shade of color. Tell the woman of leisure that expressing herself is fun, and more so than drinking. Point out friends or acquaintances who are psychologically free. Give rationalizations for excitation.

To one person, it may be better to say, "Don't reserve your emotion. Serve it." To another. "Be sincere." And to still another, "All I want to do is to make an honest woman out of you."

Tell those who are well-read in psychoanalysis that "Every time you open your mouth to anybody, I want you to practice emotional catharsis. This is no office confessional. It is a confessional every time you breathe."

For lovers of fact-talk, wrap the emotions in a technical package, but don't forget to include advice on specific personal behavior. Otherwise, the package will still be empty.

Persons who complain of light mood swings, of a watered down manic-depression, as it were, will invariably be found to be inhibitory. Their attention must be shifted from the question of moods and turned to the fundamental principles of excitation, with emphasis on acting sadistically. Depression means excessive inhibition.

Others will need emphasis on improvisation. Carefully planned remarks are futile, because if an idea is in the library of the mind, it will come forth when we open our mouths. If it isn't there, looking for it won't conjure it up. Our hearts keep beating, and our lungs keep breathing without any assistance from us. Thinking, which is nothing but brain chemistry, does not need any assistance either, unless we wish to confuse it. The purpose of habit is to stop us from wasting time using our brains. Don't work for your mind. Let it work for you. Planning guarantees frustration, because planning does not involve ourselves alone. It involves other people, and planning their actions is foolish indeed. It is always easier to look a thousand years back than a minute ahead.

Today's personality is the reflection of yesterday's reality, and today often needs changing. A person may have to change his occupation, or tell off his brother or his mother or father or solve any of the other problems that make up life. He may complain that all of his alternatives are unfortunate. When an individual is confronted by two poor alternatives, he should look for a third choice. If there isn't any, he should make a virtue of necessity and take the better one, no matter how poor it may be.

When a wife telephones or writes about a husband, or a father about a son, always to "help" with some confidential information, the person under treatment should be told about it. Details are not necessary. Something like, "Your wife called me yesterday at 3:30," will suffice.

"What did she say?"

"You can imagine what she said. Let's not go into it, but I just wanted to keep the record straight."

If the therapist has foolishly promised to keep the telephone call confidential, one fine day the wife who telephoned may say to her husband, as they argue, "You know, I've told that psychologist a few things about you," and if the psychologist hasn't prepared the ground for this, all will be lost. The "help" of relatives is almost always a hindrance. The therapist has little to lose by insulting them.

The person under treatment must be encouraged to become equally vinegary. He must discharge his belligerent impulses into the environment. There are limits, of course, but let us not concern ourselves with them now. He must spit, lest he be spit at. As a woman said to me, "All you are saying is 'Freedom through bitchery.' " We must liberate our vinegar, or it will become nitric acid and destroy us. Here are some precepts constructed by one of my cases in order to facilitate emotional liberation:

Be yourself! Don't be hesitant. Keep pushing yourself at all times, and demand anything that is coming to you.

If dining out, and the coffee is cold, or a cut of meat is not what you ordered, or there is no water on the table, or there is insufficient silverware for each course, speak up, man! Call it to the waiter's attention pronto.

If you are waiting for seats at the theater, and the usher asks who's next, speak up if it's your turn.

If you are shopping for a particular item, and the store is out of the color or brand, don't take a substitute if you think you can get it elsewhere. Even if women are waiting, speak up when your turn comes.

If you make reservations anywhere, and when you get there they try to put you somewhere else, demand that they give you what you reserved. In other words, demand what is coming to you first, and be a gentleman last.

This sounds like a code of rudeness, but please note that the individual demands only what he is entitled to. He wants nothing additional.

Another case of mine wrote to me as follows:

Every inhibitory person is a masochist. The antidote to this is deliberate sadism. This is outright sadism, and more than just firmness. I have found this idea to be probably the most effective of any others. It is a satisfying corrective to an old ailment. Ventilate your vinegar deliberately. An animal is essentially a sadistic creature, desiring what he wants, when he wants it, how he wants it. Make a conscious effort to return to the primitive. Don't abase yourself to women by holding chairs, lighting cigarettes, and opening doors for them. Too much of sophistication is really inhibition. Beware of pity. Don't be a shy, deferential, withdrawn, inhibitory character. Be sadistic in interrupting. Do it boldly, cuttingly, and constantly, especially at the start,

This must not be confused with the typical sadism of the inhibitory. That's a blind intellectual scratching that is not emotional excitation. In short, observe the amenities, but be nasty when you can. It will give you a feeling of elation. Never compensate for your deficient emotional stature with intellectuality in order to achieve superiority. Never mind the world. It's a mess of poor conditionings that interferes with feeling liberation. It means nothing to you.

The individual must learn that the only practical approach to his problem is in terms of habits of emotional response. These emotional habits are acquired through practice—just like learning to type, or to knot a necktie, or to tie a bow in a shoelace. Excitation can no more be learned without practicing it with people, than swimming can be learned without water. Consequently, the man who wishes to give up his job until he is emotionally "stronger," must be told to keep it. Those who are in positions of authority will have good occasion to be excitatory, and certainly everybody can practice on his equals.

The transfer of training applies to excitatory habits. The person who defends his rights with waiters, is strengthening himself for future encounters with his employer and with his mother-in-law. The person who stops being hypocritical with his barber, stops being hypocritical with his wife and with himself. And as the inhibitory person changes in one way, he will automatically change in many other important ways.

Here are specific situations, chosen from the Bernreuter Personality Inventory, and what the inhibitory individual is to do when they arise. Because the Bernreuter is a list of scientifically selected questions, this list reaches deep down into the behavior of the individual.

Do you day-dream frequently? Yes, says the inhibitory person. Day-dreaming is based on insufficient action. The person who does more, day-dreams less. You will stop percolating by solving your pretty emotional problems, to say nothing of your important ones.

Do you try to get your own way even if you have to fight for it? No says the inhibitory person. Fight for your emotional rights. You constantly want what is coming to you. You are rationalizing if you tell yourself, "it doesn't matter."

Do you usually object when a person steps in front of you in a line of people? No. The happy answer would be "yes." And do so on a personalized basis.

Are you very talkative at social gatherings? No. Try making it "yes," and when you talk, make it feeling-talk.

Do you very much mind taking back articles you have purchased at stores? Yes. Don't think too long about taking them back, lest you get yourself disturbed. Return the articles quickly, and be personal and emotional.

Do you usually try to avoid dictatorial or "bossy" people? Yes. You needn't seek them out, but if you encounter them and they are your equals, politely, or not so politely, chop them down to size.

Do jeers humiliate you even when you know you are right? Yes. If jeers humiliate you, be equally insulting and stick to your guns.

Do you ever rewrite your letters before mailing them? Yes. In writing to friends, cross out words if you have to, and mail the letters. You'll find out who your real friends are.

Do you make new friends easily? No. Don't try to draw out new people. If you give of yourself constantly, you will be able to make new friends... if you care.

Do you ever upbraid a workman who fails to have your work done on time? No. You needn't be disagreeable, but stop saying, "That's all right."

If you are spending an evening in the company of other people, do you usually let someone else decide upon the entertainment? Yes. Volunteer your suggestions, even if you happen to be a guest.

If you came late to a meeting would you rather stand than take a front seat? Yes. Take that front seat. You won't get heart failure, that is, if you have been following the other excitatory disciplines.

Do you ever take the lead to enliven a dull party? No. Why not? You are doing it for your own sake, not for anybody else's.

At a reception or tea do you feel reluctant to meet the most important person present? Yes. If the important person interests you, seek him out and tell him what is on your mind. If you say to yourself, "Who cares?" don't waste any time on him.

Do you have difficulty in starting a conversation with a stranger? Yes. If there's anything on your mind, talk up. You'll start a conversation without even realizing it.

Would you feel very self-conscious if you had to volunteer an idea to start a discussion among a group of people? Yes. Why not volunteer a feeling about a person, or at worst, about an idea?

The individual will often act in an inhibitory fashion before he realizes it, but this is to be expected. Training means practice, and practice means mistakes.

The therapist must be free of squeamish and moralistic attitudes. The alcoholic and the homosexual will detect them, and therapy will be impossible. Morality, and "right" and "wrong" confuse the issue. The individual is a reaction mechanism, with habits for which he is not responsible. Epictetus said, "One of the vulgar, in any ill that happens to him, blames others: a novice in philosophy blames himself; and a philosopher blames neither the one nor the other." The good psychologist is the philosopher. People do things not because they ought to, nor because they want to, but because they can't do anything else. Conditioned reactions are the reason for consistency in human behavior.

Therapy must be conducted in an atmosphere of optimism and good cheer. Even the long face of the earnest psychoanalyst is carefully kept out of sight of the patient, who lies stretched out much as in an undertaking parlor.

I must confess that I often neglect encouraging my cases, because reassurance and a synthetic optimism are the stock in trade of most psychiatrists. It is more important to remove the inhibitory blocks of the individual than to deafen him with platitudes like "Buck up. You're getting better. Don't worry." The individual's experiences condition him and his thoughts, and his thoughts again condition him, which makes the important thing his experiences in the first place.

"You been givin' me a lot of say-so and no do so." Thus does Moses accuse Pharaoh in Marc Connelly's Green Pastures, and thus would most individuals accuse their therapists. The individual needs "do so," and that means excitation.

How can we tell when the individual is getting better? Watching the fluctuations of his personality as he is gaining confidence, is as meaningless as taking too seriously the fluctuations of ticker tape in the machine that has chance soarings. This analogy was made by a case of mine, and is well taken. The alert therapist must not let the plausible reasoning of his cases persuade him to forget the basic strategy-always excitation. Yet he must not mistake the weather for the climate. What may seem like a setback may be just a tremor in the curve of progress. The graph line of improvement does not rise straight up like an elevator. It zigzags upwards. As the individual improves, he will find that more of his activity is reflex and excitatory and that his new "lows" will be actually higher than the "highs" he had formerly.

Some of the "downs" in the upward curve of progress would be there if the individual under treatment obeyed instructions. We must lead, but we cannot lead too fast. Bacon says, "Solon, being asked whether he had given the Athenians the best laws answered, 'The best of those that they would have received.'" We must not toady to the individual under treatment, but we can achieve our objectives by being firm about their smaller components. If we work hard at planting the acorn, we have only to wait for the oak tree. Despite my belief in directional therapy, my objective is to get the individual to do the correct thing by himself. As an ecclesiastical physician put it to me, "You teach them as though you taught them not. You lead them as though you led them not."

Pointing out tangible signs of improvement will help to keep the individual encouraged, but reassurance, even with those with low self-sufficiency, is not psychotherapy. When sedate businessmen wax poetic and compare themselves to budding flowers and cocoons, we may be sure that they have improved psychologically. They are forced to use these terms, and they feel embarrassed as they do so, because their vocabularies lack words for their new gut and feeling states.

A case of mine said, "I had something remarkable happen to me. I didn't realize how remarkable it was until afterwards. It's not what I expected it would be like, but it's good."

Another good sign is when they say, "It's been gradual, and I've hardly noticed it, but I'm feeling steadier now."

"What do you mean?" I may ask.

"Well, I'm feeling better. I'm feeling solider." Then comes the rationalization. "I've come to realize that the things that bothered me are really not so important after all."

"But didn't you realize this before?"

"Yes, but now I really realize it." And it will be impossible to show him that he is rationalizing his new emotional substance as much as he did the old.

Here is another form of improvement, this from a man who had been defending himself constantly and trying to improve everybody around him. "I don't fight all the time now. I enjoy myself each day as much as I can. I realize that it's no use offering alibis. I've given up the idea of doing things one hundred per cent."

An otherwise sedate woman reported that in a restaurant she had "unconsciously" volunteered information to some people at an adjoining table. She had told them that they did not have to order from the à la carte menu, because dinner was still being served. Therapy is going well when persons report that they find themselves acting emotionally free "without even thinking." Excitation is becoming reflex.

Daydreaming and nightdreaming become more cheerful as the individual improves. A woman dreams she is in Madison Square Garden, watching the pirouettes of a graceful ballerina. Confetti and streamers fill the air. The ballerina's dances are extraordinary, but she herself is quite ugly. When the performance is over, the ballerina removes a mask, and the audience sees that she is extremely beautiful. ... The dreamer is saying, in essence. "See how wonderful and attractive I really am." Dreams are a hash of the day's emotions and their associativities.

The person who says, "I'm getting a feeling of energy. I'm feeling more confident," is surely improving. "I don't hesitate. I react faster. I make up my mind and I act on it. I feel, 'You're somebody, as good as the next one, if not better.' I notice other people more. I have a feeling of release, or rhythm, if you want to call it that. I laugh more easily at the theater."

A man who resented the emotionally free begins to find them bearable, and even seeks them out. A woman who detested children begins to enjoy playing with them. A musician says, "I don't like people who are the way I once was. Also, I don't forget so many things now. Is there a connection?" A painter says, "I am enjoying me more. I am goddamned tired of these introverts hanging around. It's amazing how small all the problems are that bothered me. My objection to your work was really simple. When I think of the terrors of the past, and how simple your injunctions were, it seems difficult to believe that they could solve them."

The once prosaic woman who is told by a man who has no axe to grind, "You are vivid and colorful, and a woman of courage," knows she is getting better. Men will notice that strangers, including women, seem to be smiling at them more. "People's reactions change. They seek you out, and are interested in your advice. You feel magnetic."

One of my cases told some friends that he was feeling much better since he had seen me. "You wouldn't know," they said.

"Let's ask Helen [his wife] if she thinks you've changed." She answered, "I haven't noticed anything different. He only feels much happier now." And that, of course, is the objective of therapy.

We all live in the past, and our personality is its imprint on us. By practicing excitation, we create a new and healthy past, and this comes to determine our behavior. "But," I am frequently asked, "as I deliberately practice excitation, what becomes of my individuality? Won't I simply become an automaton that you have manufactured?" The individual who practices excitation makes it as much a sincere part of himself as were the accidental, misery-inducing, helter-skelter acquired experiences that originally distorted him. He remains an automaton, but now he is a happy one.

CHAPTER 13

THE WORK URGE: PROBLEMS OF THE CREATIVE

A reader seldom knows why he likes a book, or the author why it is a success or failure. Neither is aware of the psychological processes involved in writing. Words are merely symbols which communicate ideas and feelings. But everybody has feelings. A writer is a person who can impart them to his readers. Somerset Maugham has put it well: "The writer seeks release, the reader seeks communication."

Too many persons imagine they can write because they are sensitive," when all they mean is that they bruise easily. The sensitivity of an author is more like a microphone. He picks up feelings that are later transmitted to the reader in the form of words.

Contrary to Flaubert, he need not spend years in search of *le mot juste*. The right word will crystallize by itself when the feeling and thought are clear. Should the author's experiential feeling life be meager, he will have nothing to put on paper, for the person with a tawdry "subconscious" has nothing to release for writing or for anything else. The person whose nervous system is stocked with impressions and ideas has to organize and intensify them if he wishes to write. Anatole France has said, "It does not matter whether a man is writing about the eye of a fly or the life of Julius Caesar. He is always writing about himself."

It is important to have "lived." but it is not enough. The accumulated experiences must be channelized into words that have communicative value to the reader. A first novel is often easy. The author conducts a Cook's tour of his feelings, and their patent genuineness and great particularity insure his success.

Of course, there is more to writing than this, and though the almost infinite series of possible games of chess are embodied in a half-dozen rules, reading them is not enough to make a chess champion. Yet certain principles of playing chess, as well as of writing, are more efficacious than others. And what is more, they can be learned. "Genius" may be beyond learning, but it remains a rough diamond without it. Beethoven composed, and Leonardo da Vinci and Rembrandt painted by using their nervous systems and sensory accumulations. They used nothing mystical.

Some writers worry about their integrity, but we may quickly dispose of this issue. A writer, working on a plot with which he is not in sympathy, may be considered to have integrity as a writer if he tries to improve the story and to give it life and character to the best of his ability. He may be considered to have integrity as a citizen only if the theme of the story is worthy. What shall we think of Hollywood writers who prate of integrity and social uplift, yet who often work with only one-quarter of their brain at potboilers that set back the causes advocated by the authors themselves?

I have noticed that the writer who fears to prostitute his art usually can't even give it away. Writing is communication. Whatever communicates will reach people, and whatever reaches people will receive money or applause or laurel wreaths. This remains true, even though recognition came to writers like Melville and Stendahl only after they were dead.

Paradoxically, I do not believe that any communication ever takes place in the sense that a new message ever reaches the reader. The author merely sets up sympathetic vibrations in the reader's already established reaction systems. I first read *Point Counterpoint* when I was fifteen. Then I saw it as a series of humorous flashes. At twenty, it was an entirely different experience. It was the same book, but a different I.

A critic never reviews books. He reviews himself,[1] and sometimes tempers his remarks with a harsh word. One of my cases, who suffered from strong guilt feelings, told me that she had read Crime and Punishment three times, but had never been able to get beyond the part

---

[1] See the lack of understanding shown in many of the reviews of Aldous Huxley's Brave New World (1932), and B. F. Skinner's Walden Two (1948). Both books deal with a world of the future in which conditioning is everything.

where Raskolnikov, the murderer, walks across the square after hiding the loot. She felt his guilt so strongly that she could not continue reading.

A child has Pavlovian bells which can be rung by fairy tales. An unhappy adult has bells which can be rung by tales of murder, while a thoroughly happy and productive person lacks these emotional patterns, and has no interest in detective stories. People who want to reread a book or poem simply want to stimulate the same emotions again.

Readers do not care whether stories are true to life. They have merely to be true to their emotional and intellectual patterns. In Harper's and the little magazines, the hero introspects and experiences exquisite frustration. In the Saturday Evening Post he brings his employer home to dinner. Most of the popular women writers illustrate the case in point. Their books make the literate laugh, but in modern society there are millions of people who seek the feeling-clang of banal verbal stimulation, whether from the printed page or from radio serials.

Many books have emotional and intellectual implications beyond the grasp of the majority of people who read them. They may well understand all of the words; but they do not understand all of the emotions, and they react only to what they can, usually the sexual. *For Whom the Bell Tolls* is a fine example.

The reader is not interested in the author's reactions. He wants the author to paint verbal images so that he, the reader, can react according to his own conditioned emotional patterns. He does not want the author's saliva. He wants bells that will make him salivate himself. Sometimes a writer has difficulty bringing these bells to his readers. How to free him so that he can do so is what we shall now consider.

I doubt that a person who has never written while in high school or college will ever become a writer. He may have the potentiality, but developing it will take a long time. Chances are that his desire is just a superficial psychological quirk.

Many people go into writing not because they want to write but because they see in writing a chance to "get rich quick" and therefore solve all of their immediate exigencies. In itself, this motive is not an obstacle to success, but even in the intelligent it is usually associated with a poverty of ideas.

The hair-splitters and analyzers are something else again. They squeeze out a little writing, like frozen toothpaste from a tube. They are the perfectionists and the students of structure. A nuance is better than a thought. Their writing lacks what I can only call testicularity. Such a person is a famous contemporary playwright. His writing is like the universe, a great deal of space and very little matter.

There is nothing sadder than no endowment in conjunction with ambition. Then perseverance is a dangerous thing. It may guarantee your remaining a damn fool. Therapy cannot make a twelve cylinder mind out of a six cylinder motor, but it can make it work to full capacity. Most people do not use half of their potential, but they are all using whatever they have free at the moment.

The prognosis is excellent for the hard-working writers who lack skill but have something to say. They may have imagination and strength, but they need to learn excitation and more about writing. A case of mine wrote a 20,000 word preliminary synopsis of a novel. "I planned it out carefully, and have a step by step, chapter by chapter synopsis. I know every step I want every character to take, in every chapter. It is all planned in such detail that I shall easily be able to write 4,000 words a day of the main draft." But he did nothing of the sort. He was distinctly inhibitory. "I had deliberately schooled myself to withhold 'excitatory responses' for the sake of peace. I think my trouble starts from there."

The writer who seeks the work urge wants to be an artist without having the artistic temperament. He looks within and sees only his frozen self. He mopes and suffers at everything. He is excessively inhibitory, and his writing takes care of itself when he becomes more emotionally outgoing.

The inhibitory who wish to turn excitation on and off like a tap are particularly difficult to treat. A woman in her late forties, who had written a few fairly successful novels and travel books, came to see me. She considered herself well adjusted, but wanted her writing to come a bit easier. She was keen and fact-talking, and full of plausible psychological aphorisms. She did not realize it, but she had synthesized the unsynthesizable. Mutually exclusive psychological systems blossomed side by side. Not only did she have elaborate rationalizations, but they in turn had become thoroughly rationalized. I refused to treat her, because I felt that what I had to offer would merely join her library of intellectual constructs. We had some correspondence, and this verified my impression completely.

In another instance I accepted the case of an author who was just as emotionally ossified. Here rapport was simple. He was a non-practicing physician and I made what I said seem as scientifically logical as possible. He had an over-solicitous mother and a stern father. He complained that he found his writing difficult and he was not enjoying his children at all. I insisted that he practice "feeling-talk" and we made our slogan "toujours excitation." Seven sessions were all that were necessary. Excessive objectification presents no problem, if the individual is prepared to accept ideas rather than to collect them.

Case 25

The following report by a short-circuited author speaks for itself.

Past History. Ever since I could remember, I suffered from fears. Mostly I was put down as a neurotic, especially by those psychoanalysts I had seen. They have been three in number. By them I was led through a tangle of remembering dreams, hashing up infantile experiences and the like. I feel that what good came of it all was in the heart to heart talk and the consolation that was offered me in chaplainesque fashion.

The crisis was reached when I was ready to go into the Army. I broke pretty badly then and saw my last psychiatrist. At the beginning of this year I happened across your book. On the pretense of doing a magazine article, I approached you, finally coming out with what I wanted. My concept was that through self-hypnosis I could overcome my difficulties. Be, as you once said, "my own Svengali and Trilby."

At the time I came, I was in the clear, but had forebodings that trouble might come on the horizon and that I might need to meet it. It came in my job, and so far, it has been met. I really believe that I could not have done so if I hadn't undergone the personality changes I had.

Also of interest is the fact that I have a new interest in women. Heretofore, I always evaded them when they showed affection. Now, for the first time, I find myself responding to it. How warm I am is hard to say. But there is more feeling now than there has ever been, and no fear of being "trapped," as there has been before.

Results. To date I would say the greatest result has been a great lessening of fear, I am no longer as afraid as I used to be. I'm not worried about the future. I find that by daring I go further and do better. The terrible doesn't happen, either in my mind ... as it always did-or in fact.

So far as people's reactions to me are concerned, I haven't noticed any change. There have been six sessions at this writing [halfway through therapy) and probably that is too soon.

In many small things, such as catching trains, being late, hurting people's feelings, senses of guilt, worry, bossitis (fear of the boss) there has been a material decrease. I'm not completely cured of the last mentioned disease, but it no longer is as virulent.

The attitude toward myself has undergone an interesting change. Dissatisfaction there has always been. But I would say it was negative in its aspect before, whereas now it is positive. Instead of saying to myself, "Why haven't I been able to do this, why does Jones get what I don't?" I now find myself saying, "Listen you, what you should have done is this and so, and be sure to do it the next time." I am beginning to feel that I do something.

Concerning My Work. I feel that this is at present in a state of imbalance. I have at present no ideas for fiction. There are glimmering shots, but nothing that has "bite." However, I now begin to sense where, in what work along those lines that I did perpetrate, there was no real feeling or emotion.

In writing articles, there is now a hesitancy, where before there was more assurance. I simply went ahead and banged stuff out. I do not do so now. It is odd, but there is less confidence. Something is, at present, shaken. I am, however, not scared about this. I feel that it is a temporary state, from which something else should emerge. [This worked out perfectly.]

The neatly turned phrase, the trick adjective or adverb, the gag, they aren't coming forth. There is an intense desire to write simply and unaffectedly. This was partly there before we started. Now it is very strong. I want to eliminate myself from my work and stress whatever it is I have to tell. Rather than "I am writing," the feeling is "It is written."

Sometimes I even think that writing might leave and something else might come. Other times I feel very certain that it will come in a new form. This I feel more often. However, since I am happier, better adjusted, much less fearful, it seems all to the good; even though I do not relish the prospect of selling vacuum cleaners in tremendous quantities.

What I Have Got Out of the Sessions. At first I thought hypnosis would enter strongly in them. To date none has. At first, I felt somewhat disappointed. Now I don't. Whatever works is good enough for me. Results are what I want. The means I leave to you.

The three things firmly planted in my mind are 1) the Pavlovian dog as it relates to my childhood, 2) the release of inhibitory forces to outgoing ones (mainly by "Spitting"), 3) the use of healthy sadism.

These three have given me a rather new outlook on people and my own past. There has been a rather complete revaluation of the whole thing. My approach to problems and to people is changed. I feel quite sincerely much more confident, and that I have for a long time done myself a grievous injustice.

My Reaction to you. From my first revulsion of your self-praise I have now swung to almost a liking for it. While I can't say that I have blown any brassy notes on my own trumpet, I have at least taken out the mute I so long used in playing it. However, I tootle very softly.

Your tricks of emphasis, or crescendos and pianissimos, I probably ape feebly. However, none have noted them as you do. I would say that on my part, they are done unconsciously.

Also, I have confidence in you. I rather constantly catch myself when I do or think things wrongly, and urge myself to do them correctly. There is no longer the refuge of wrong rationalization. We are now on an open plain where there are no self-conceived bushes behind which I can conveniently and comfortably hide.

To throw in a final metaphor. The can of my emotions and feelings has definitely been pried open with a tool you thrust into my hands.

In eleven sessions his Bereuter score on neuroticism dropped from 69.6 to 42.8, and his self-sufficiency rose from 39 to 75. Now, three years later, he remains a happy and productive author.

Case 26

In psychotherapy, what you are sure is the wheat is often only the chaff. Mr. L. writes radio scripts. He is 31, handsome, and impeccably dressed. He has just given up a psychoanalyst who has been treating him for several months, and who, he is convinced, has made him more "neurotic." A former case of mine has referred him to me. I ask him to explain his problem, and he hands me this list:

Fear of women: premature ejaculation, social uneasiness in their presence.
Fear of authority: guilt feeling when passing a policeman. Lack of self-confidence in the presence of superiors.
Fear of homosexuality: shame and concern over small penis.
Compulsion to "bask in the glory" of people well-known in their fields

... desire to be subservient to them.

Lack of masculine aggressiveness. Lack of self-confidence in work, in general ability, and in thinking processes.

His father had deserted his mother when he was two and was never heard from again. His mother had worked as a servant in different households, and constantly scolded and beat him. After a particularly severe thrashing at the age of twelve he ran away from home. He had been seduced by homosexuals several times, and this, of course, had provided a field day for the psychoanalyst he had consulted.

I decided that this was unimportant. First of all, a severe and punitive mother is rarely part of the homosexual pattern. Secondly, homosexual experiences in themselves do not prove homosexuality, especially since in this case he described homosexual intercourse as "disgusting, boring but not unpleasant." Besides, he sought out women and had spasmodic success with them, and was nauseated al the thought of seeking out men.

I explained that his "fear of women" and "fear of authority added up to fear of the human race. He was repeating the same thing when he said that he had a "lack of masculine aggressiveness" and a "desire to be subservient." They were synonyms for inhibition and low self-sufficiency.

I hammered at his low self-sufficiency. "You'll do just what I say. Do you understand?" He agreed. I explained that he was inhibitory and lived too much inside himself. Consequently, he suffered from premature ejaculation because he had intensive sexual experience mentally before having it actually.

I saw him twice, and shortly thereafter he left for Hollywood. "On the train coming here," he wrote, "I met a girl and went to bed with her as easily as though I had been schooled in it as a life work. A tribute to your technique! However, that ole debbil erection failed to materialize. She telephoned me last night. Maybe that's why I feel uneasy today? I have more confidence in my work than I have had—but still not enough."

I answered that he needed to practice more feeling-talk and more living in the present. "You don't need any new instructions," I said. "You need more work on the old ones."

Three months later I saw him again. His problems had disappeared almost completely. I have since heard from him several times, and he is a thoroughly happy and successful writer.

Objection is sometimes made that increasing a writer's excitation may stop him from writing, since his reason for writing in the first place may be his "neurosis." This often occurs in psychoanalysis, and in my opinion is disgraceful.

I have found that increasing excitation has never stopped anyone from writing. On the contrary, it raises the sluice gates and for the first time the flow of ideas pours forth unimpeded. No longer do they have to emerge through an ill-constructed and ill-functioning spigot. True, the water that dripped from the old spigot may have been pure and distilled, and the water pouring out of the channelized conduit may be heavily laden with silt and mud dredged up by recently released excitation. But still, in the fantastically increased quantity, there will be more than enough to compensate the writer for his efforts. Some of his now facile writing may be trivial, but the thinking patterns and idea accumulations of a lifetime can never disappear. They will still manifest themselves in the out-pourings of the released writer.

The writer, formerly preoccupied with sordid and depressing matters, may begin to write more optimistically. Nevertheless, he is still expressing himself. His work is hailed as freer and better, even by the critics who are perplexed by the change.

Case 27

A bright and gifted young writer of 30 came to see me. He lacked confidence and ambition to write, and suffered from heavy depressions. "Never mind my writing," he said. "I just want people to care for me." He had strong guilt feelings, which had been brought on by his father who had been disbarred under spectacular circumstances. Other factors were involved in the genesis of his difficulties, but as we have seen, in psychotherapy cause is not seriously related to cure.

The first person on whom he practiced his excitatory disciplines was a friend with whom he shared an apartment. They were supposed to take turns at the household chores, but his friend was an accomplished "gold-bricker" who shirked his share of the responsibility. Some vigorous feeling-talk soon reformed him.

"Remember," I said, "I am not preaching 'salesmanship' of yourself. What is usually considered salesmanship is the projection of fraudulent emotions. The man that the world considers an obnoxious extrovert is really not excitatory at all."

In his low self-sufficiencied way he had been trying to be kind and agreeable to everybody. Said he, "I believe in speaking my opinion when it is well-supported by facts.

"I like to talk to people if I know I have something to say.

"Of course I want to feel sure inside, but I don't have to show it."

He rarely drank, but when he did he felt much better and wrote with ease.

"Look," I said. "I'm just running a psychological gin-mill. Whatever liquor does, I can do without the liquor and without the hangover."

"That's for me."

"From now on." I said, "I want you to be a no-man and not a yes-man. I want you to be emotional about facts, and to let your emotions run your mind as nature intended. Let everybody know about everything, because everything is important. All small talk is big talk to us. Don't be so cosmic."

A few sessions later he said. "It's quite disillusioning to realize that mental health lies in the direction of blah-blah."

Here is part of a diary he kept for me:

Tuesday. Left feeling good. Got into a cab, Was going to tip him ten cents. Decided he might not think it was enough. Pulled out another nickel. To hell with it. I said to me. If he doesn't like it he can lump it. Gave him a dime and said "Here" so strongly that I startled a "Thank you" out of him, (Obviously a new cab driver.) Perfect example of a noncosmic incident.

More noncosmic stuff. Had dinner in our room. The waiter usually leaves the food in the hot metal box and we have to serve ourselves, tonight I said: "How about serving the dinner?"

He said (rather wittily, I thought) "You want me to serve the dinner?"

"Sure," I said. "You've been getting away with murder, for Christ sakes." He said: "Are you complaining?"

"You're damned right I am. We're your boys. Take care of us!" He took out the soup and meat and put them on the table. "Better put meat back," I said. "It'll get cold. I'll take care of it myself." The whole point of this incident is that the dinner was lousy.

Wednesday. Just got back from lunch with my attorney, and am still a little shaken. I told him that I had decided to abrogate my trust fund. He argued very strongly that it was psychologically good for me to have a trust fund, etc. He said that he would send me a check out of it every week. I told him that I wanted the money, all of it. He offered to give me a thousand of it in cash. I held out against that. Then he offered to turn all the cash over to me and keep my bonds, so the trust would still remain. I told him that I felt like a poor man living in a great mansion. I was in no position to have a trust. Legally, the trust is set up for fifteen years, so he can refuse to close it if he chooses. He had many arguments, most of them sound. I really should have someone to look after my financial affairs. I will probably feel lost for a while. But, on the other hand, during the past year I have paid him a thousand dollars, and outside of banking my money he hasn't done a damned thing. (I did not tell him that; will discuss that phase of it in a minute.) Well, to wind up My Day As A Financier, in spite of all his arguments and all his concessions, I held fast to my original request. He told me I was wrong, but that if I were so insistent about it, he would turn my affairs back to me. It took over two hours, and I came out of it unhappy and shaken, but conscious of a victory. I remained polite, and was reluctant about some of my arguments. I didn't tell him that he hadn't done much for me in the last year. Part of this may have been because legally I knew he had me over a barrel; part of it was because I haven't taken enough psychological castor oil. (What the hell is a castor?) All in all, I came out of it all right, but not very proud of myself.

Some weeks later he sent me a telegram. "Dear Merlin: Happy as an idiot Do you have a magician's license?" While seeing me he began a book which became one of the biggest best sellers of the past decade. Elapsed therapeutic time: eight sessions.

It is not too much to say that the creative process, in general, is a problem in the psychology of learning. Nor is the explanation of inspiration and sudden flashes of "insight" anywhere as mysterious as the Gestaltists would like to believe. Learning is a trial and error process, and from a physiological point of view, an organism becomes aware of a sudden insight only when certain cerebral electro-chemical resistances have been overcome. Until the resistances are overcome, the flash of insight has been building up at levels below awareness.

Among the most frequently encountered creative problems are those of actors. There is something fascinating about being an actor—especially to the inhibitory personality. He wants to express something, though what it is, he doesn't quite know. And somehow, in front of an audience, that mysterious something gets liberated. What is that something? He will say that it is a desire to express himself, and to stir an audience into feeling the emotions of the character he is portraying. This will be true enough, but there is more to it than that.

An audience has no way of knowing whether the feelings expressed on the stage are at all genuine, as long as the accouterments of emotion are on display. Actors, who are chain-smokers in personal life, are transformed into papier-mâché Gibraltars before an audience; and comedians usually look like the muse of tragedy until they get on the stage. But even off the stage, actors hide behind a mask, and they often do this in a curious fashion. They go about unnaturally trying to act natural. The men do it with the folksy pose, and the women do it by affecting a toothy breathlessness.

People do not become actors in spite of their inhibitions; they are actors because of them. It may well be that a great actor or actress must originally be a frustrated, inhibitory person, else there would be no posturings and no juggling of fraudulent emotions.

Then why disinhibit the actor? For the same reason we disinhibit the author: to remove the sand from his emotional machinery. A disinhibited actor would no more lose his acting ability than a disinhibited musician would lose his musical ability. In therapy I do not break bad acting habits. I break the habits that get in the way of better acting.

Actors, who are convinced that the price of acting is the agony they suffer on the stage, are not much happier in their personal life, yet they may only need some light psychotherapy. An actor of about thirty-five quickly described himself as having "a mother complex." His parents were divorced before he was born, and he had an older brother who was "always bickering" with him. He was a solemn inhibitory type, but rapport was excellent. I explained the basic rules and saw him twice. His relations with people improved, he felt much more at ease, and his acting loosened up.

Actors or actresses with low self-sufficiency are a formidable problem. They must be mothered, fathered, loved, and pampered. And they are such amiable souls that before long the therapist will find himself thoroughly preoccupied with them. Treatment is complicated by the fact that like all those with low self-sufficiency they simulate excitatory responses, which in their case are especially convincing. Nevertheless, it is old-fashioned low self-sufficiency that confronts us, and it must be treated accordingly. I have a great feeling of Sympathy for the attractive but mediocre young women who are convinced they belong on the stage. Theirs is a life of hallway bedrooms and casting rumors. Many of them are so inhibitory that each audition robs them of a year of life.

I have always believed that it is possible to make a stage or screen star out of a good hypnotic subject, since self-consciousness can be broken completely. More generally, any therapist is distinctly negligent if he fails to utilize a person's hypnotizability. Hypnosis facilitates therapy, but we must be careful not to put all of our eggs into the hypnotic basket. Inhibition versus excitation remains the fundamental problem. In order to see how far I could carry inhibition and excitation as techniques, I must confess that for the past few years I have not used hypnosis as much as I might.

A case of mine told a Hollywood producer that I could make stars out of extras. "Hell," he answered. "Let him make actors out of stars!"

Case 28

Clara W, a young stage actress, wanted to play leads, but she was always type-cast as the home-wrecking "other woman." She complained that she lacked self-confidence, and was getting nowhere despite her impressive record. "I'm always acting," she said. "I think one thing and say another."

"You must stop living like a fugitive from *Strange Interlude,*" I told her, "and cultivate honest self-expression. You are not letting your unconscious watchman work for you."

Many people are afraid to lose control of their emotions, when that is all they have to do to be cured. They equate freedom with giddiness, and are therefore against it. "Grown people don't act that way."

Clara's self-sufficiency impressed me as above average, so the first thing I tried to do was to loosen her up somewhat. This was a constant battle, because she was reluctant to cope with her personal problems, which included the perennial one of marriage versus career. Her relative inaccessibility prompted me to shift to a more superficial approach.

We drew up three lists of screen actresses under the following headings:

1 The seriously emotional
2 The light comediennes
3 The sexy types, with and without delusions of acting.

She picked her favorite from each group, and I then proceeded to lecture her on their dominant traits. "Now." I said, "you are to synthesize these actresses into a new character for yourself by emulating one of them each day in your personal conduct." This she did enthusiastically, and after a few weeks I told her to under-play the "seriously emotional" actress, for it did not go with the stereotype she conveyed.

Clara went to a casting interview for the second lead of a play. She was chosen, and then she asked to audition for the main role. Her request was greeted with horror, for the part had already been assigned to what was euphemistically called the "girl friend" of the producer. She was insistent, (I had drilled a good deal of gall into her), and if only to silence her, they let her read for the part. The producer was so taken with her rendition that he gave her the part, and transferred the leading lady to the second role. The play closed after several performances, but Clara drew favorable notices and decided that she knew it all. Although I assured her that she needed more treatment, she stopped seeing me. Since then, she has been the lead in several shows, all failures, and now I no longer see her name in the newspapers. I do not know what has become of her.

Case 29

Contrast this with Vivian B. Today she is a movie star with carloads of fan mail and acres of space in the fan magazines, but it was not always thus. When I first saw her I wrote on her case card:

Actress, age 21. Has written poetry which was published. Lack of confidence in self, and tightening up. "I frequently have an uneasiness and anxiety in talking to people, for no reason whatsoever." Looks like a good, typical leading lady. Little education, but does not impress one as such. Good mind.

Her family had frequent rows, and her mother had a sharp temper. They lived on the wrong side of the tracks, and Vivian "had a feeling of separation from the right people that grew with age."

Friends flocked around her, for she was a charmer and with low self-sufficiency. She professed to be older than she really was, and cultivated a pose of bored wealth. Money was so vulgar. She would describe her stunning wardrobe, but would add nonchalantly that she didn't care for clothes, and that was why she wore "these old things." One day she came to school in a riding habit. She had saved a few dollars and rented it from a costumer. She told her friends that she was taking voice lessons and had operatic aspirations—fiction made out of the whole cloth. With all this, she genuinely liked her friends and was devoted to them. In her words, "I have tremendous vanity and tremendous inferiority at the same time."

Then came a few small roles on Broadway, summer stock, and acting the part of a housewife in a radio commercial which was widely satirized. She had a few minor love affairs which had nothing to do with advancing her career, and it was after one of these that she came to see me.

She was fascinated by hypnosis, but was a poor subject. Quit acting like a half-baked extrovert," I said. "Live your own life in your own way. Let other people muff their lines. You get yours right." She was not to utter a single feeling or opinion that she did not believe. "I'll make an honest woman out of you even if it kills you."

In stores, when she asked for change of a quarter for telephone calls, and got two dimes and a nickel, she would buy a package of chewing gum with a dime in order to get a nickel in change for another call. "Why not put the dime down and ask for two nickels?" I said. "Don't buy anything. If you haven't the courage to do a stupid thing like that, how do you expect to lose your self-consciousness on the stage?"

She followed instructions and soon showed improvement. "My acting is better at the microphone. I'm more spontaneous and less nervous. When I feel excited about things it's different. It's more stimulating and less neurotic."

"Remember the basic disciplines," I said. "Practice excitation all over the place."

She went on the road with a second-rate company, and wrote to me often. In one of her letters she said, "I walk into a room with more ease. I buckle down much faster, and don't have so many extraneous thoughts. I think more clearly and easily. I'm more relaxed in company. I nag less and blush much less. I have a live-and-let-live attitude. I'm more scheduled now...by which I mean I used to come too early or too late for appointments. Now, I come on time and don't worry."

Then she got a role in a Broadway hit. The critics praised her extraordinary ease and stage presence, and she was scooped up by Hollywood and started off as a full-fledged star.

Musicians have the same problems as actors and authors. How can we doubt what is wrong with Mr. W., the violinist at the Metropolitan? "I forget appointments easily. I'm always making up little stories about people, and about things I did or didn't do. When I'm in company, and use a glass or a cup, my hand shakes if people watch me."

And isn't it obvious what is wrong with the superb pianist who should be on top of the heap, but isn't, because he has a finger paralysis that moves from one hand to the other? Or the woman pianist who says, "I know I'm painfully shy. The only thing I want is a quick treatment for my recital tomorrow." All these people have extensive inhibitory histories. What they need is excitation.

Mr. R. is a professional pianist. At my request, he lists what he wants to achieve.

135

"As you said, I cannot expect to surpass my natural endowment or abilities, but I want to make the utmost of what I already possess. The factors that interest me are:

Mood and will
Memorizing and retention
Concentration assimilation
Reading-sight-reading music
Imagination
Sensitivity as to nuance in interpretation
Dexterity and accuracy
Immunity to self-consciousness by absorption in the work at hand."

He fills out a short questionnaire, and I learn that he constantly worries over humiliating experiences, that his feelings are easily hurt-that he keeps in the background on social occasions–that he feels very self-conscious— and that he has inferiority feelings. Once more the problem is inhibition. By teaching him the excitatory disciplines and how to relax, I successfully overcome his problems.

In the following instance, the dynamics are clearer, but they remained equally unimportant in the therapy. A 30 year-old pianist is losing her interest in the piano. She has become short-tempered with her pupils, and her playing is deteriorating. Night after night she dreams that she is playing in Carnegie Hall, but the keyboard is covered with broken peanut shells that cause her fingers to slide off the keys.

She is an only child. She lives with her parents and is their sole source of support. When she was young, she hated their constant bickering, and frequently ran away from home. Her father drinks and is always bellicose, and her mother, she says, is "highly neurotic and hysterical."

Her troubles brought her to a psychiatrist, who taught her how to live with her parents with as little friction as possible. This increased her inhibition, and when she came to see me, she couldn't practice the piano at all. Notice how her parents drove her within. Notice also that the psychiatric "You must control yourself" only aggravated the situation.

I told her that she was to reverse the process. She was to express herself. If she disliked anything her parents did, she was to say instantly. If she happened to like something about them, or about anybody else, she was also to speak out right away. One day, she washed her hands, and hung up her towel somewhat awry on the rack. Her mother followed her, and gave her a gentle reprimand. The girl turned on her, and shouted that she had enough on her mind without worrying about hanging up towels straight. She was fed up with being supervised.

In three sessions, and two and a half months, she disinhibited so much that the problems that had brought her to me disappeared completely. On the Bereuter, her neurotic score dropped from 77.6 to 29. What is more interesting is that the strain that had always existed between the girl and her parents, and that her parents had always felt with each other, loosened up perceptibly, and life in the household became much more comfortable. Excitation is like rain. It may wet everybody through and through, but it certainly clears the atmosphere.

Singers have the same problems as pianists. They want to learn how to concentrate harder, work better, and interpret with feeling. They are more interested in relaxation, though, because it improves breathing and tone, and helps to hit those high notes. Here, correct teaching in the formative years is important. Said one singer, "I took five lessons with the wrong man and they took me five years to unlearn."

Some inhibitory singers are as sensitive as a fresh sunburn. They are fluttery, and act in what they think is an excitatory fashion. It is best to leave them alone. Life is too short, and ten people can be helped in the time it takes to make a dent in one of them. They are low in self-sufficiency and are surrounded by a wall of rationalization that is almost impenetrable.

As usual, high self-sufficiency is something else again. An attractive young woman had no desire to be a serious musician, but was studying voice in order to become a nightclub singer. She sang well enough until she came before an audience, but then she would freeze up and her voice would come forth strained and tremulous. Her mother, a sweet and well-meaning little woman, had brought her up to be a lady—and that was the cause of the trouble.

When I finally disinhibited her, she got a job singing in a place nicknamed the "Broken Bottle." a rowdy barroom which her well-bred self would never have entered. From there she went to better places. In a half year, often with two weeks between sessions, her neurotic score dropped from 9.6 to 9.8.

She relayed her therapy to a cousin whom I had never met. Even at second hand the principles of excitation were beneficial.

I have had excellent results with two women painters by getting them to become more excitatory. They began to paint with increased freedom and imagination. One of them, instead of avoiding people, became eager to meet them and began to "have a good time and enjoy life." She even found the dentist less worrisome. The other entered eleven paintings in a large exhibition, and received six of the ten prizes that were awarded. When she asked me why the other artists were envious of her. I said, "The hungry have always envied the well-fed." In three months her neurotic score went down from 78.4 to 49.

A complete discussion of the creative personality must include some cases that at first glance seem unrelated. Inventors are an example. Beware of inventors! They are usually quite analytical and engineering-minded, and are solely concerned (they will tell you) with "facts." Experience has shown me that the more preoccupied they are with facts, the more tied up they are by emotion. They like interminable abstract discussions of psychology, when what they need is hard work on their own personal problems. Their passion for analysis must be penetrated, or therapy will be futile.

"But I'm just trying to get a scientific understanding of what you say!"

"Perhaps, but I'm running the show and I insist on your dropping the topic. Let's discuss (say) your wife ... Remember, intelligence is like the core of an electromagnet. Emotions are the wiring around it. If we change your emotions, your inventive power will become stronger, because it will become really free for the first time."

Case 30

I have included the following case in this chapter because although it is somewhat different, it really belongs here after all. A champion golfer once consulted me. "I have stopped having fun with golf," he said, "and have started to dislike it. Something has to be done. I don't want to play a better game. I simply want to play at my best more often." Golf had originally been a hobby, but it had now become a business. One or two extra strokes could mean the three-thousand-dollar difference between first and second prize.

We discussed golf for several sessions. The body, I explained, has a positional sense, which is as much a sense as sight or smell. Awareness of the position of head and body is regulated by the inner ear, and knowledge of the position of the limbs is mediated by nerve endings buried in the muscles, joints, and tendons.

The positional sense cannot be improved one iota by practice, and the great majority of golfers are doomed to be duffers, no matter how much time they waste trying to improve their game. The ability of a golf champion is based on an inborn gift, and he knows—rather, he feels—

with great precision how hard to hit the ball and where to aim it, and he readjusts his stroke accordingly. The less he uses his brain, the better he plays. His best game of golf is his easiest. I continued, "All this talk about correct stance is nonsense. One individual may find his muscle tension distributed better when he has one stance, and somebody else may find that another stance gives a better starting position. ... How's your home life?"

"Well," he said.

"Well, what?" He didn't want to discuss his family, and I couldn't persuade him to. "Very well," I said. "I can only help people as much as they permit themselves to be helped."

On our fourth session we went out to a golf course, and applied some of my principles to the game. Tournament golfers on a new course should practice as little as possible before teeing off. They should just get the vague feel of the grass and then stop. If they over-practice their first stroke, which is usually a long hard drive, their muscular adjustments get off edge for the strokes to follow. Watchmakers know this well. They repair all of their clocks on one day of the week. If they were to intersperse some watches with the clocks, they would keep on breaking delicate parts until their fingers had become readjusted to the lighter muscular tension necessary.

"Use as few clubs as possible, because you need different muscle adjustments for different clubs, no matter how carefully balanced they may be. Changing muscle adjustments as you change clubs will cost you strokes."

Next, through the methods I explained in Chapter 7, I taught him how to relax. He learned this easily, probably because professional athletes have well-traveled pathways between their brain and their body muscles.

"During a tournament," I said, "relax before each stroke, and then hit the ball. Most strokes of all can be saved in putting. Don't spend a great deal of time in lining up your shot. Simply look at the hole, look at the ball, visualize a line between the two, and hit the ball down the line without even thinking. It is especially pernicious to exchange shoptalk with other golfers. They have nothing to teach. Their secrets are matters of their own body structure."

The rest of the story is anti-climactic. His golf improved considerably and then relapsed to its earlier level. I am convinced that this wouldn't have happened if we had straightened out his personal problems.

Most tragic of all is the person with real gifts which could make him a success, but who remains a failure because he has never developed them. A handsome young man, who looked as if he had stepped out of a collar advertisement, once came to see me. He explained that he got one excellent sales position after another, but he never seemed to satisfy the expectations of his employers. After a short while he was always dismissed.

As I saw it, the problem was simple. He was a well-bred inhibitory young man who had always thought of himself as a salesman—as ridiculous an idea as a stuttering radio announcer. However, he possessed the gift of absolute pitch and could play any instrument without being taught.

I decided that the best thing for him would be to lead a popular orchestra, thus taking advantage of his appearance and his musical ability. But that might take a few years, and he had to augment his income immediately, "In that case." I said, "why not become a professional model and pose for magazine ads?"

He laughed. "I've always been a salesman, and this sounds ridiculous."

"You're not a salesman." I told him. "Not with the personality you have now. What you are is a very presentable chap, with nothing saccharine about your appearance. If you want to make money fast without becoming a gigolo or a burglar, become a model."

I gave him a few addresses, and soon I saw him in advertisements for shaving cream, cough medicine, and office stationery. "This is a nice racket," he said. "How long has this been going on?"

He was quite pleased, but I looked at it differently. He might have had an excellent future before a popular orchestra, and it might even have been a symphony orchestra—but he had never been trained. He could have been a success, but he was a failure. He could have been happy, but he had been conditioned into inhibition.

All too often the wrong things get done to the child early in life, and the right things never get done at all; that is, not until the therapist, with science and art, changes the whole sorry scheme.

CHAPTER 14

STUTTERING

What is wrong with the stutterer[1] is not his speech. It is his inhibitory personality. The non-stutterers I treat stutter in some other way. They are shy, they drink, they cannot concentrate, or they have other symptoms of inhibition.

Stutterers, according to Bender, are "more neurotic, more introverted, less dominant, less confident ... and less sociable" than non-stutterers. (1) He showed this in a study of 249 male stutterers and a slightly larger control group. But stutterers and non-stutterers averaged the same in self-sufficiency, which parallels our earlier observation that the inhibitory personality need not be deficient in self-sufficiency.

Which came first, the stutter or the inhibition? Did the stutterer's fear of speaking make him emotionally withdrawn, or was he that way to begin with and did he develop a stutter as a result? I have always found the stutterer to have a typically inhibitory childhood in no way different from the cases we have already considered. Nor have I ever encountered a single detailed case in the literature that is an exception. All stutterers are and were inhibitory personalities; and were it otherwise (which it is not), it would still be therapeutically unimportant, for inhibition, however caused, is inhibition, and need only be treated as such.

---

[1] *"Stuttering and stammering are sometimes distinguished in that the former is convulsive repetition, whereas the latter is blocking." Dictionary of Psychology, Warren. I am following current practice and using "stuttering" for both symptoms.*

Forcing left-handed children to use their right hands is not the reason for stuttering. Ballard (2) and Wallin (3) have shown this to be an old wives' tale. Their conclusions were based on a study of over 114,000 school children.

The physiology of the stutterer, his saliva (4), urine (5), blood chemistry (6, 7), pulse rate (8), and brain volume (9) have been elaborately reported as being different from the non-stutterer. These bodily changes are significant, but they are precisely those found in non-stutterers under emotional stress. (10) The stutterer's breathing apparatus is tense and disturbed, (11, 12) but this is only part of the picture. His back, his arms—his whole body, for that matter—are equally affected.

Give the stutterer a few drinks, or some phenobarbital, and his speech improves. Teach him relaxation, and his speech improves. If he talks to someone before whom he feels immensely superior, his speech improves. If he talks to himself, when he is alone, his speech improves. Distract him by having him walk on his hands and knees, and his speech improves.

The evidence makes one conclusion inevitable. The stuttering pattern is not a problem for the elocution teacher. Stuttering is a problem in the psychology of personality, and should be treated accordingly.

At one time or another, every stutterer has said, "If I weren't afraid to stutter when I speak, I could talk perfectly." It is true that the stutterer's fear of speaking tends to inhibit him, but actually he is just as inhibited in situations that do not involve speech or the imminence of speech. The stutterer who insists on regarding his problem purely as a speech defect is doomed.

He may have developed poor tongue habits, and conditions leading to a fear of certain sounds, but stuttering nevertheless is not fundamentally a matter of speech production. Excitation, however, is almost always verbal, and this puts the stutterer at a great disadvantage, and is the cause of most of the problems that arise in therapy.

The stutterer must talk excitationally. Even if he stutters when he does so, or develops a complete speech block, he must nevertheless constantly try to verbalize his excitatory impulses. Inhibition becomes excitation only through action.

The stutterer with average self-sufficiency, or better, can be made happier, more equable, and more relaxed. He can always achieve more frequent interludes of perfect speech, and sometimes almost perfect speech, or complete cure. I treated a young woman in her early twenties who had been a confirmed stutterer since childhood. Her B2-S score was

79.4 per cent. She married and found it difficult to convince her husband that she had ever stuttered.

Case 31

Talking to stutterers with low self-sufficiency is like swimming in an ocean of mush. It's difficult to get a grip anywhere, and it quietly overwhelms you. What the world thinks of their speech is too important to them. Here is a courteous and smiling woman of 40. In a pleasant southern drawl she says that she has "tried different psychiatrists and courses. You've heard of Dr. A. and Dr. B., haven't you?" Her slight stutter makes her unhappy, but after a few drinks her speech is perfect, which proves that she needs excitation, to say nothing of the "charming" husband who she is convinced would solve all of her problems. She is friendly and agreeable, and everybody does favors for her, but fundamentally she is infantile, squeamish, and dissatisfied and to boot, her mother dominates her by letter and telephone.

Many stutterers, even with high self-sufficiency, will not get better until they break with their parents. Therapy is often ninety per cent geography, and ten per cent psychology. What chance has a bright young man of sixteen whose mother is always dominating him, and whose father is always stuttering? It is no surprise that his speech is often perfect away from home. And what chance has the stuttering Italian beauty in her early twenties who is her parents' only unmarried daughter, and who wrangles with them constantly about their "Old Country" standards? ("Take off that lipstick. ... Be home by ten-thirty. ...") She supports herself, but she will not leave home because "it will break their hearts."

Pathetic indeed is the parent who says, "My child stutters. How can I help?"

"You can't," is my frank answer. "You did it to him in the first place, and you'll keep on doing it until you get some psychotherapy yourself."

Many stutterers choke up completely when they shout in anger. Pavlov's principle of negative induction explains this. In the cerebrum "an excitation arising in a certain place causes an inhibitory process around this region and ... the spread of the original excitation becomes limited." (13) It is robbing Peter to pay Paul. Yet some stutterers speak perfectly when they are angry. The prognosis for them is excellent, for emotional liberation when it becomes habitual does away with their stutter.

Relaxation is conducive to good speech. Most stutterers speak better on week ends than on week days, and in the morning than in the afternoon.

Autohypnosis is helpful in this connection, for it makes possible rapid relaxation. In turn, this facilitates excitation without speech blocks.

Words are the bells of conditioned reflexes, and it is no exaggeration to say with Watson "that in the neighborhood of 90% ... of our reactions are verbal." (14) It follows that when a person's training hammers him into inhibition, it dulls his sword of environmental interaction—speech.

Yet every inhibitory person does not stutter. Some develop ulcers or become alcoholics. Different causes produce different patterns, with the same common denominator of inhibition. What is wrong with the stutterer, as with every other inhibitory person, is not his speech. It is the things people have said to him when he was young. *Disinhibit the inhibitory* remains our guiding principle at all times.

CHAPTER 15
THE ADDICTIONS

It does not appear so at first sight, but the stutterer and the alcoholic are fundamentally the same. They are both inhibitory personalities whose childhood stresses are like those we have seen in the other inhibitory patterns. And similarly, just as we are not concerned with the speech of the stutterer, so are we not concerned with the drinking of the drinker. Our objective is the man behind the symptom. Of course, there is one big difference. Every person who stutters knows that he is a stutterer, but not every person who drinks considers himself an alcoholic.

Some men drink alone—a few quick ones at a bar after work, or at home in the pantry when no one is looking. Others like their liquor in company, and are always on the alert for parties, conventions, and college reunions. Some only have a few before dinner and rationalize it as a ritual. Others drink one after another throughout the day and know that they are far gone. Yet drinking a lot does not necessary make a man an alcoholic. That depends upon whether he needs and alcohol in order to endure himself or his environment. If

- he feels unhappy without alcohol, or
- he dreads giving it up, or
- he needs that first drink in the morning, or
- it puts his world in comfortable order,

he cannot take a drink or leave it alone. He is an *alcoholic*. This is a harsh word, but the drinker who wants therapy is not frightened by it, any more than he is made more cooperative by being called a "problem drinker" or an "alcohol addict."

Physically, alcohol dilates the blood vessels, allowing the blood to circulate more easily. This relaxes the heart and reduces the blood pressure-but it is silly to imagine that this explains why people drink. People drink because alcohol thaws their frozen emotional radiators and permits them to express their feelings. To watch a drinker (or a baby) is a sacred privilege, for we see revealed the deepest secrets of the human heart.

Curiously, alcohol is not a stimulant. Its action is narcotic, like ether or chloroform, depressing both the higher mental processes and the inhibitory centers of the nervous system. It is worth mentioning that in its early stages ether makes the individual articulate and excited, and in the 1820s and 1830s American medical students often held ether parties in which they tried to keep themselves in a state of euphoria short of unconsciousness. Too much ether, alcohol, or sodium pentothal, produces unconsciousness, but lesser doses produce a disinhibited, emotionally free state, which is why people drink and bartenders know more than psychoanalysts. Alcohol increases sexual desire by destroying inhibitory reserve. As the wit put it, "With liquor it's quicker"—but alcohol diminishes performance.

Alcohol is not a matter of sin or vice, as some would have it, and surely not of crime. It is simply a chemical method for reducing inhibition. Every inhibitory personality is an alcoholic in his heart, and what is more important, every alcoholic is an inhibitory personality here and now.

Some experiments of Masserman reveal a great deal about alcoholics, even though he worked with cats. (1) His conclusions will not be news to the millions of people who for years have been drinking heavily in order to face life.

Masserman gave nine cats a mixture of milk and alcohol, a cocktail as it were. He then subjected them to strong but harmless electric shocks around feeding time. He found that this caused only three of the cats to develop relatively mild behavior disorders.

He then repeated the procedure, but omitted the alcohol. This time the same three cats and five of the remaining six became markedly "neurotic." The alcohol had protected eight of the nine cats from psychological disturbances. This dovetails perfectly with our knowledge that the excitatory person can take emotional stress better than the inhibitory.

Another experiment of Masserman's illustrates a related point. (2) A group of cats were given a choice between plain milk and milk with 5 per cent alcohol. He found that the cats who had developed experimental neurosis tended increasingly to prefer the alcohol. What is more, he found that "neurotic animals, while mildly intoxicated, became sufficiently disinhibited to re-explore the problem situation ... and thus dissipate their neurotic phobias, aversions and aberrations. As relatively 'normal' behavior became re-established," *the cats lost their taste for alcohol.*

And so it is with human beings. When they work out their psychological problems, their desire for alcohol disappears. That is the key to the psychotherapy of alcoholism. There is no need for the disinhibition of alcohol when the individual has learned the disinhibition of excitatory living. It may be argued that alcoholism can remain as a pure habit after the personality patterns causing it have disappeared, but this contention is controverted by the experiments we have just considered, and by the experience of everyone who has ever worked with alcoholics.

Masserman's experiments also explain the futility of preaching self-control. Instead of wives saying, "If you had more will power you wouldn't get drunk," they ought to say, "If you had more excitation you wouldn't get drunk." Which also explains why threats of divorce, unemployment, or disinheritance have as much effect upon the drinker as saying "naughty, naughty" to intoxicated cats.

I realize the great number of lives that alcohol has ruined, and the number of homes that it has wrecked, yet I am firmly opposed to prohibition: It is a simple psychological fact that prohibition (of any-thing) does not reduce temptation. It increases it. The alcoholic will get his drink no matter how great the obstacle and prohibition will always breed crime. It is inhibition, and not liquor, that makes alcoholics. What we need is neither prohibition on the one hand, nor distillers' platitudes about moderation and social responsibility on the other. The consumption of alcohol will be reduced only by psychotherapy and better child care.

The pre-alcoholic personality is always distinctly inhibitory. Here are some typical examples:

Mrs. A. Youngest of eight children. Brought up to be polite. Mother paid little attention to her. Father quiet.

Miss B. Father deserted her mother when she was seven. Her mother always over-protected and under-loved her. Her brother is a drunken psychopath who to this day constantly beats his mother is then forgiven by her.

Miss C. Father a constant drinker who was never angry in his life. Mother "polite and cool."

Mr. D. Always told to "talk to the point. Don't beat around the bush." Mother dressed him girlishly until he was seven, which made him inhibitory though not at all homosexual.

Mrs. E. Just too well-bred, and married to the wrong man, which she knows. Brought up in a Philadelphia Main Line family. Stern mother.

It is interesting that Strecker and Chambers say that "at least 90 per cent of all abnormal drinkers are predominantly of the introverted type," and that in three years of clinical work with alcoholics they have had only one person consult them voluntarily who was markedly extroverted, and this was a case where the individual's environment completely blocked his extroversion. (3) Their remarks are well taken, although theirs is the usual conception of extroversion which, as we saw earlier, is not what we mean when we speak of excitation.

I wonder whether it is accurate to differentiate between "true" alcoholism and so-called situational alcoholism—the drinking brought on by the intolerable circumstances of heretofore well adjusted persons. These secondary alcoholics (as they have been called) manifest an inability to cope with their problem, but that is not enough to make the diagnosis. Before we decide to call anyone a situational drinker, we must first decide:

1 Whether he was confronted with a situation, which was insuperable by its very nature. A man who took to drink after losing his wife and family in an airplane crash would be a definite situational drinker.
2 Or was he confronted with a situation which his own nature has made insuperable, except by drink? Example: divorce, business reverses, and physical illness. The excitatory shake them off relatively easily, but it is the inhibitory who take to drink or commit suicide.

It is my belief that most persons who are considered situational drinkers have had inhibitory pre-alcoholic personalities. Almost invariably (there are exceptions) it is not the situation that makes the man an alcoholic. It is the personality of the man who is in the situation that makes him one.

Year after year the inhibitory repeat the same ineffectual emotional patterns, and they are always surprised to find that lightning strikes again and again in the same place, and it is their inhibitory lightning rods that always attract it. I once said to a case of mine, "You know, your troubles couldn't have happened to a more logical person."

Many women take to drink in order to relieve the boredom of an unsuccessful marriage and of a leisure which they do not know how to exploit. A drink is an oasis in their emotional desert, yet we will always find that their problem is not purely situational. They were inhibitory before they ever met their husbands, and they often have the well-bred neurosis.

Case 32

We can see this in the history Mrs. W., an alcoholic, age 46, wrote for me.

... After the children were born we lived in the suburbs. I found housekeeping and this type of life like the inside of a convent, only without coming in contact with anyone. In suburbs there are cliques. These groups of amoeba are interested only in their own swimming, and try to strike on to anything bigger than themselves and then try to grow and climb. Each group is oblivious to the ordinary surroundings. One could move to a suburb, establish a residence, exist and decay without the knowledge of anyone but the coroner.

The first years of married life I offered all acquaintances and so-called friends my heart, my time and energy, my talents, and the hospitalities of the fabled Southern home. These qualities were snapped up, used thoroughly as rags, and with a nod tossed back in my lap. If I believed my spontaneous offerings of golden-woven character fabrics would draw a host of friends, I was taught otherwise, for after these were returned thoroughly used and torn I had to stifle the unbidden droolings of the tear ducts, and squash the waves of hurt that simultaneously clutched the middle of my esophagus.

I cannot stand bridge for I cannot bear the inevitable accompaniment of family squabbles from other couples when he or she doesn't lead—God knows what. Yes, I know. Social climbers with clinging vines have climbed through this game. But it isn't worth it to me. The vines would probably be poison ivy. I do not like groups of women any more. They add to my uneasiness ...

It's all right to wish, isn't it? If I was the heroine of a fairy story I would do something special. I would become famous. I'd be the talk of the town. I'd make all of these formerly whispering small timers sit up and take notice! I'd have them wooing me!! I'd have them all proud to know me to say they had actually seen and talked to me. Would this "heah chicken" bask in the beams of glory? And how!

I reckon I should be classed as one of those neurotic women. Here I have an exceptionally attractive and affectionate husband–two beautiful children—unusual servants and the security of a home. Still

I pull a sour expression. Dissatisfaction personified. I'm a pampered, self-martyred old hen. It's hard to explain in so many words why one is bound in discontent. Especially when there is no reason for it.

Shall we say that this woman is a situational drinker simply because she is intelligent and has become bored with suburbia? Not necessarily. We can clearly see that she is inhibitory, for her story is permeated with low self-sufficiency ("The first years of married life I offered all acquaintances and so-called friends my heart, my time and energy, and my talents. . ."). We can also see that she is extremely sensitive ("I had to stifle the unbidden droolings of the tear ducts"). She also said that she was "bound in discontent," and that "there is no reason for it." But her childhood provides sufficient reason:

I was born with a silver spoon in my mouth, which became tarnished at the age of two. At ten it had become leaden—from which I contracted considerable poison. Let's skip the gangrenous growing pains. I will only state the fact that I craved to study music and painting (having shown exceptional talent from the age of four), the spring of which, however, dried up considerably as the years passed. I had an obsession to travel—for I was constantly running away from home as a child [where she was quite unhappy]. Adventure haunted my nightly dreams. All these so-called whimsical wishes were ground under the malicious spiked heel of Hard-Hearted Hannah, otherwise known as my stepmother ... I drew, by myself, a great deal, but had to dispose of these lest they be found, and when they were, they were immediately classed as lousy ... Well, up until I was married, as you know, I was nicely roasted and burned on all sides on Hard-Hearted Hannah's griddle, but strangely quite raw and very green on the inside.

We can conclude our consideration of situational alcoholism by saying that as a general rule, when the same problem confronts two individuals, one will take to drink and the other will not because of differences in their pre-situational personalities.

Periodic drinkers are extremely inhibitory and are difficult to treat. Sober, they are almost inaccessible beneath their lacquer of receptivity. On a spree, they are no more accessible and usually sadistic. Their prognosis is bad, unless excellent rapport is quickly established, and this is usually difficult because of the thickness of their inhibitory scar tissue.

Treating know-it-all's for alcoholism, or for anything else, is also difficult, nor are we interested in treating those whose constant refrain is "yes, but …" We must remember that "yes, but" means "No."

Businessmen, who are accustomed to their subordinates jumping through hoops, are good risks once they learn that they are undergoing psychotherapy, and that it is not they but the therapist who is giving the orders. I am quite abrupt with them. "Look," I say. "When it comes to the manufacture and sale of widgets I consider you a great authority, and I will listen to you with respect. But when it comes to psychology I want you to listen to me. I'm not the one who came here to consult me. It was you." At this they usually smile, sit back, and become cooperative.

The prognosis is unfavorable when wives drag in their husbands, or make an appointment for them under false pretenses. "He's a doctor and we'll just discuss your digestion." Sometimes they write in to ask if it is possible to teach them to implant suggestions into the minds of their sleeping husbands.

Women themselves, I must say, react as favorably to treatment as men, and sometimes more so. More than men, when they say they want to stop drinking, the chances are they really mean it.

When he is nursing a hangover, every alcoholic is full of firm resolutions; nevertheless this is no time for psychotherapy. He is too preoccupied with his miseries to give any significant attention to what we have to say. It would be just as bad a time for him to try to learn mathematics or Spanish. The treatment of alcoholism, or inhibition, is an educational process, and we must beg off treating the alcoholic when he is more interested in licking his wounds than in learning. He would be much better off with Vitamin B (to replace what the alcohol has depleted) and ice cream (for its soothing and slightly anesthetic effect).

It is not possible to get new livers for old nor a new nervous system for a wrecked one, but it is surprising how much alcohol the body can absorb without suffering any serious effects. Modesty has ruined more kidneys than liquor, runs the adage. A thorough examination by a good physician will usually put the alcoholic at ease.

The alcoholic we are interested in treating must have a sincere desire to cooperate, which simply means the intention to obey instructions. He must do exactly as he is told, and that calls for work. He must ignore the advice of well-meaning friends, or it will be the story of too many cooks. The best way he can help his wife and children is to get better for his own selfish sake.

Such an attitude means beginning therapy by trying to get him to stand on his own two feet. Encouragement is sometimes good therapy, but our goal is not a pleasant glow, but education.

Direct education, through painful association, is the basis of the "conditioned reflex method" of treating alcoholism. Lemere and Voegtlin are the key pioneers of this method. (4) Reflex aversion to the sight, smell, taste, and thought of alcoholic beverages is created by giving the patient an injection of emetine, which is a powerful regurgitant. Then the patient is offered a drink, at which time the emetine starts to work and the patient begins to retch. This need not be repeated very often for the patient to associate drinking with nausea and to "decide" to avoid alcohol.

Of 1194 patients followed up, 74.8 per cent who had been treated within two years of the study were abstinent. (5) Of those who were treated from two to four years ago, 52.5 per cent were abstinent, as were 51.5 per cent of those who had been treated over four years ago.

Granted that this technique stops people from drinking—is it fundamental therapy? Kant considers it "symptomatic treatment [which] does not eliminate the underlying causes of maladjustment. What it does is to frustrate a pseudoadjustment by the inadequate means of alcohol ..." (6) Carlson objects that "The conversation between physician and patient in the conditioning chamber is not always truthful. The patient is not always told that it is the hypodermic injection of emetine which produces the nausea and vomiting." (7) He also asks, "since the most successful doctors using this [conditioning] technique also employ psychotherapy and social therapy, is it accurate to ascribe all or in fact any part of the success to the conditioning therapy?"

I think it is fair to say that a study of the literature makes inevitable the conclusion that the conditioning therapy is responsible for much of the success of the method. It is true, however, that there was a selective factor involved in the choice of patients, but when was it ever otherwise? Experience shows that the conditioned aversion technique is an excellent mode of therapy with many persons, and a good beginning for further therapy with others.

I agree with Voegtlin and Lemere that "it would be advantageous to expose the alcoholic first to the well-tested methods of therapy that involve the expenditure of the least time, effort and expense and which are most readily adaptable to treatment of such patients in wholesale fashion. The need of treatment for alcoholism among the masses cannot be ignored. ..." (8)

I would like to see a before and after Bernreuter study made of alcoholics who had been cured by the conditioned aversion technique. If it were found, after they had stopped drinking, that their neurotic scores had decreased, that would indicate better psychological adjustment. If their scores would remain the same, it would indicate no fundamental psychological change, but they would not be drinking and would be functioning better. In the event that their neurotic scores increased, it would indicate that they had become more maladjusted.

My guess is that the neurotic scores would decrease—quantity to be determined. The cured alcoholics would look, act, and feel better in every sense of the word. But still there would remain those who would damn it as superficial therapy, and talk darkly of conversion of *symptoms*–the obscurantists of science who are more interested in words than in things.

The linkage of alcohol with emetine produces nausea in humans, just as the linkage of bells with meat produces saliva in dogs. Yet forming conditioned reflexes by direct association was only one aspect of Pavlov's monumental contributions, although it has received the greatest attention. Perhaps this is because it lends itself so readily to experiment. In any case, it is my conviction that it has paradoxically been responsible for stultifying the development of a system of reflex therapy. I say this because associationalism has blinded many excellent psychologists to the fact that correcting the *inhibition-excitation* balance is the key to the cure of psychological problems; while *associativity* is the key to the origin of psychological problems.

More concretely,

1 To understand cause—consider early conditioned associativities.
2 To produce cure-increase excitation.

More generally,

3 The basis of psychotherapy is Pavlov's concepts of inhibition and excitation translated into their human behavioral equivalents.
4 The scope of psychotherapy is the social relations of the individual.
5 The process of psychotherapy is disinhibition and re-linking, with the re-linking a correlate of the disinhibition.

An important question is in order at this point. "You are talking about inhibition and excitation. Just what are they physiologically?"

Said Pavlov, "The basic processes . . . are, on the one hand, the excitatory, and on the other hand, the inhibitory process—this latter a kind of opposite to the excitatory process. I say 'a kind of opposite,' because we do not know exactly the nature of either of these processes. We have only hypotheses concerning them, which have not led to definite results." (9) Pavlov said this in 1923, and we do not know much more today. It is true, for example, that we have since learned that it is the acetylcholine in the nervous system that allows excitatory impulses to flow across the tiny gaps between series of nerve cells. Nevertheless, the bio- and electro-chemistry of inhibition and excitation is in its most elementary stage. The future can only contain discoveries of the most critical nature.

For that matter, psychotherapy is a form of verbal chemistry. It is disinhibition produced by the verbalisms of the therapist and the person under treatment.

Alcohol is a chemical means of producing disinhibition. As the alcoholic follows instructions, and repeatedly acts excitationally without liquor, he recharges his excitatory batteries and the alcohol becomes unnecessary. It is not that he refrains from drinking. It is simply that he is so satisfied with psychological "drinks" that he no longer has any desire for liquor.

Our aim is the destruction of inhibitory habits. But those who say, "I have to break my habit of worrying," or "my habit of daydreaming," or insomnia, are referring to specific aspects of inhibition, which are only parts of the problem, and not the whole thing.

The alcoholic's bending his arm when he drinks has been called a muscle habit, but it is probably not more than five per cent of his problem. The other ninety-five per cent consists of his inadequate, inhibitory methods of grappling with his environment. It is those habits that we wish to break.

The alcoholic did not think himself into drinking. He was experienced into it and has to experience himself out of it. He learns by doing. He does not learn by thinking about doing, and he cannot think with imprints that he has not yet acquired. He thinks with his past experiences, and in sum they are inhibitory. As he practices his excitatory disciplines he will build up a library of useful experiences that will come to determine his behavior.

He will not be playing the hypocrite when he acts excitationally. On the contrary, it is inhibition that is hypocrisy. He must express *what he feels,* although at first he will be doing so because it is pursuant to instructions, and he will not feel like saying the truths that come out of his mouth. But before long it will be quite automatic, and he will realize how ironical it is that the same society that made him sick is the one that is curing him.

Mental health is a matter of balance between inhibition and excitation, although in therapy we emphasize the excitatory side of the picture. But we need have no fear that this will make the individual disturbingly expressive, for all too often he will be very cautious about speaking his mind—a rationalization for his excessive inhibition. Yet we may believe him when he objects that even before therapy he was excitatory at times, especially with friends. In that case he already has some green traffic lights, but he still needs more.

I believe in constant therapeutic intervention in order to show the alcoholic how to act in an excitatory fashion toward the problems that confront him. After all, a physical education instructor teaches his exercises by clearly demonstrating the movements to his pupils so that they may emulate them. This should be our practice in psychotherapy, for the more *concrete examples* we can provide of excitation in the daily life of the individual, the more excitatory he will become. This will make social workers out of us as we help our pupils to master their environments.

An important part of the alcoholic's environment is his wife, and the man who is married to the wrong one will usually continue to drink. Only when he is much improved should he think of divorce, and then he should always consider the children. My feeling is that children brought up in homes full of friction usually suffer no further deterioration if their parents divorce. They were confused enough to begin with. But divorce is a serious business, and should be weighed carefully before being recommended.

In some homes, the wife and children are united against the alcoholic father. This house divided is logical enough, but something must be done about it because it hinders therapy. Direct conversation between therapist and wife is seldom helpful, and the eager requests of the family— "What can we do to help?"- mean very little. They can try to act warmly, but usually they have forgotten how. When the alcoholic is a woman, her husband may be asked not to treat her like a "flannel-head," but he will rarely change his ways.

Basically, my belief is that it is just as futile to work with the family in alcoholism as it is in any other inhibitory pattern. The family has its ways and its rationalizations to match them. Tears and recrimination, and shouting and preaching can sometimes be reduced, yet nothing is lost if the family does not hold the therapist in high esteem. Consider the following:

Case 33

A young woman of about 30 saw me over her parents' strenuous objections, for they had spent a great deal of money on previously unsuccessful therapy. Among other things, she had been psychoanalyzed for twenty months, five times a week, and had considered it quite successful because, as she said, "I now say 'Thank you' when praised." However, she had continued drinking and felt as unhappy as ever. After I saw her for some time and her alcoholism was much improved, she went back to visit her parents. When they saw the changes that had taken place in her, her mother wrote me that it was "one of the happiest moments of [her] life."

When the young woman next saw me she admitted to a feeling of resentment toward me, and as we went into the matter we found that it was rooted in the fact that her parents had now become my supporters and were praising me lavishly. When I pointed out that she had always been opposed to whatever her parents approved, and when I took care both to dissociate myself from her parents and to heap a little invective upon them, her antagonism toward me disappeared and we have remained friendly ever since.

As a general rule, and with only the most infrequent exceptions. It is best to have nothing to do with the family, absolutely nothing.

As the alcoholic becomes more excitatory he will find that he can do with fewer drinks, and it is the rate of increase of his excitation that determines the rate at which he is able to taper off. In that event, a few relapses back into drink will not seriously affect the therapy. Alcoholism is the shadow, but inhibition is the substance. They grow and they shrink together.

I am always asked whether it is good policy for the alcoholic undergoing treatment to keep liquor around the house and to serve it to company. My answer is, "Yes. keep all the liquor you want at home and serve it to your friends as often as you wish. If they have psychological wounds, give them their alcoholic balm, and as long as you're working on your excitation you won't want to drink at all. In fact, you will probably feel smugly superior, and begin to bore your friends with denunciaitons of alcohol".

These well-meaning friends with their parties and cocktail hours constantly beset the alcoholic, and it is important to immunize him against their blandishments: "Come on. Be sociable." "Act grown-up. Have one." Or the usual, "One drink won't hurt you."

One drink won't hurt the man who is excitatory, but it makes the inhibitory tend to rely on alcohol for excitation instead of on themselves.

The excitatory do not need alcohol in the first place. I have often seen them get more elated on ginger ale than the inhibitory do on bourbon. The excitatory find it as easy to refuse a drink as to refuse a salesman or an invitation to a boring party. They know that to conform is not strong and manly, but rather to buck the social pressures of the inhibitory and to say, "No. Thank you," is what calls for character. As one of my cases put it, "I'm sick and tired of having people who need two cocktails to loosen up tell me how to live. What do they know anyway? I'd as soon listen to a tramp who lives on skid row tell me the secret of his financial success."

Refusing a drink should be automatic. "Don't cogitate," I explain. "Just say, 'No, thank you.' If they press you, as they usually will, you may stretch a point and say, 'Sorry, doctor's orders,' and keep on talking. You're simply refusing a somewhat forward salesman. You can be a bit aggressive if you have to, but don't be obnoxiously so."

There is much to be said for four o'clock tea for the alcoholic, for then his blood sugar is low and some nourishment (rather than a cocktail) is indicated. In general, he should try to take his meals at regular hours, and under no circumstances should he get up from the table feeling hungry. Substantial portions, a high liquid intake, and sweet desserts will overcome that hungry feeling that is too often followed by a drink. And for the same reason it is good to keep some candy conveniently near in desk or in pocket. A half hour nap before dinner, in order to relax the tension built up through the business day, is often helpful. But these are all mechanical details, and do not provide an answer to the fundamental question: How can the individual develop greater excitation? I would like to point out that my remarks apply not only to alcoholism but to all of the other inhibitory patterns as well.

We need only a few tools on our psychological journey. Inhibition, as far as we are concerned, is not strength. It is the scar tissue of experience, and has nothing in its favor. I know that this is an over-simplification, but it is nevertheless quite satisfactory in therapy. Nor are we especially concerned with the particular wind that bent the reeds. We know that the reeds were bent, and that they remained that way after they were removed from the influence of the wind.

In "The Hunting of the Snark" the Bellman said that whenever he said anything three times it was true. It is staggering to realize the number of times that the individual has been subjected to inhibitory pressures by his parents, his teachers, his older brothers and sisters, his younger brothers and sisters, his schoolmates, his friends, his cousins, his acquaintances—by the whole multitude of his psychological contemporaries. What we shall do is to counteract the inhibitions. Through repetition we will build in and reinforce excitatory patterns.

By doing what we do we become what we are, and as the alcoholic—the inhibitory person, if you will—flexes his healthy emotional muscles they become stronger and stronger. He must build in new patterns and that always means going against the grain, at least at the start. He must get rid of his false agreeability with people. He must express his honest opinions. He must break his habit patterns in the places he visits and with the people he sees. Fear is the literary expression for inhibition, and is banished only by exposure. Some inhibitions, of course, are healthy—the driver who waits for the light to turn green before he goes ahead; the child who is taught not to blow his nose in other people's faces; the conditioning given to children to make them housebroken—with these and related inhibitions we are not concerned.

If the alcoholic will give free play to his excitatory impulses wherever he can, they will not bother him so much where it is inexpedient to be free. Though excitation surely is not advisable on all occasions, there are many more opportunities for it than at first seems possible.

A hitherto shy dentist, whom I was treating, became fed up with an obnoxious ten year-old boy and called in his mother from the waiting room. "Take him to some other dentist," he said. "This boy needs to be hit over the head with a hammer." The mother protested that it is his professional duty to treat all and sundry, and he agreed that this was true. But, he explained, he was merely a dentist. He could not be a wet nurse and an acrobat simultaneously. The mother remained a patient of his, although she took her son elsewhere.

For excitation, a dog has merely to bite, but a human being finds it more complicated. For him it may involve extensive correspondence and many phone calls, but satisfy that excitatory impulse he must. Every social interchange is important, and there is nothing bigger than the little things. He must not only respond to situations but he must also initiate them at home, at work, among friends, with acquaintances, and in the most casual encounters.

If the alcoholic begins to feel irritable toward everybody, it may mean that he is not being excitatory where it matters. He may be practicing excitation in business when he needs it more in his personal life, or the opposite may be true. Some alcoholics, after a lifetime of being pleasant and agreeable, are quite disturbed when they find themselves becoming acid and a bit savage. This is temporary, and I remind them that it was not I who gave them their hatreds. They had them long before they ever met me.

It helps the excessively agreeable if they cultivate a seething and excitatory state of mind. "Damn everybody and everything. I'm going to do what I want to do when I want to do it. The hell with the world." This sounds cruel, but the "good Christian" pose often conceals nothing but inhibition.

The occasion will frequently arise when the alcoholic will realize, in retrospect (it may be three minutes or three days later), that he has violated some psychological precept. He should have told someone off and he didn't. He should have praised someone and he forgot to. He should not have been so dilatory in reading the restaurant menu; or he should not have acted with suspended judgment in solving a problem. All this should be no cause for distress. It simply means that the new habit patterns have not yet become firmly established. A human being can only do the best that he can do at a particular moment, and he must simply watch and try to do better the next time.

The inhibitory must cultivate emotional straightforwardness. It makes life so much simpler. I am thinking of a couple who had no children, and no affection for each other. After ten years they decided to get a separation, at which time they learned that they had both been contemplating divorce for the past nine years.

To be blindly outspoken is not sufficient. What matters is what we are outspoken about. The psychological liberation accomplished by the political chatter and intellectual analytics in our better circles is precisely zero. The world of intellect cannot bite back emotionally, and it is usually a futile exercise in rationalization. It is emotional small talk that is of the greatest psychological importance.

What I am advising is not so much being honest, as being emotionally basic. It is our original primitive reactions that count. Often, to keep quiet is to be a liar, and many people who realize this have a pose of sincerity. As one of them put it, "I was sincere being sincere." Honest communication of basic emotional impulses is one thing. An impression of sincerity based on fraud is another. It is good to say what you feel the moment you feel it. But chronic complainers are not excitatory because they express few sincere warm feelings, and because they are often critical even when their first impression is favorable. "Remember," I say. "No delay between stimulus and response."

When an inhibitory person walks into a room he should not look around and wonder. "What shall I say? The paintings ... mmhmm... the chairs ... I see." Rather he should wait until a feeling strikes him. For example, he suddenly realizes, "These pictures are relaxing," whereupon he should say to himself, "Well, this is something that I'm supposed to say," and open his mouth and say, "These pictures are very relaxing. I like them." There is to be no deliberate search for feeling, but at the start there should be deliberate utterance of it.

The question arises, what if the pictures are atrocious, what then? In that case he should say nothing, or at worst, if he is pressed, something vague. At no time should insincere feelings be uttered. As he becomes more excitatory he will learn how to liberate his steam without annoying the most sensitive listener.

Many of the inhibitory have lived a life of sterile intellect for so long that practicing deliberate sensory awareness is a good exercise. They should walk down the street and just practice feeling: how their feet feel in their shoes as they walk, how the air feels in their lungs, how the people look-a sort of emotional improvisation at the piano of the senses.

Our battle cry is "Down with the cortex!" The well-bred constantly mask their impulses, and they need scotch for themselves to tolerate them, and scotch in their guests to make them endurable. Alcohol is the great infantilizer, and the man who practices excitation does not need its help. At all times he must ask himself, "Are my guts showing?" If they are, he is becoming more excitatory. He does not have to be annoying. He must simply keep his eye on the target. excitation. He need not look down at people, he need not look up at them. He must simply look across at them.

In this matter of keeping the eye on the target and breaking the inhibitory habits, a schedule for the day is a help. This is a topic I approach with trepidation, for I am always suspicious of the tightly scheduled. The excitatory live on a vague schedule or without having any. The inhibitory either have a rigid schedule, and their relationships with humans are equally rigid, or they just mope around and do nothing. My policy is to suggest to my cases that in the few minutes in the morning, as they lie in bed before getting up, they should vaguely run through their plans for the day and then try to carry them out in as excitatory a manner as possible. Schedules are made to be broken, but they are useful to deviate from

It is silly to say that the alcoholic's life is interesting because it lacks the dull routine of the well-adjusted. It is true that the alcoholic's day is full of fireworks, but these are signs of tension, worry, and misery. Although the excitatory person lives with a vague schedule his life is interesting and happy because he is emotionally free.

There are few things as boring as an alcoholic's reminiscences of his drunken merrymaking. As he practices excitation without alcohol he will learn to have better times, and they will not be so rare that he will have to hark back to them. In the old days he had tenseness, worry, and fits of depression, but now they no longer plague him because he is free and spontaneous. He is rid of his frustrations because he follows his deepest yearnings.

But he dare not rest on his laurels. For the next few months he must continue to practice his excitatory disciplines deliberately, even though they are now automatic. This "overlearning," as it is called, is necessary in order to "rub in" thoroughly into his nervous system his new excitatory patterns. If we read a short poem ten times we will remember it for a day or two, but if we read it twenty or thirty times, we will remember it much longer. So it is with excitation. We must cut the grooves of retention deeply, so that transitory troubles will not wash the furrows away.

Overlearning is especially important because it brings up a critical point in the treatment of alcoholism. I call it the bitter pill, and I shall be blunt about it: The alcoholic who stops drinking must never touch liquor again in any form whatsoever. He must have no cocktails, no sherries, no beer, no wine, no cider-nothing alcoholic at all. He must not try slow drinking, fast drinking, infrequent drinking, or drinking with his food in an effort to ameliorate the effects of alcohol. He must not swallow a mouthful of butter or olive oil in order to line his stomach against it. It must be all or nothing. It is impossible for the ex-alcoholic ever to learn to drink moderately.

The usual explanation for this well-established observation, an explanation with which I do not at all agree, is to call it an allergy. Just as some people are allergic to strawberries or pineapple, and get rashes when they eat them, so are there others whose nervous systems cannot tolerate alcohol. This is plausible indeed, but it explains nothing.

I should like to give an explanation for the absolute necessity that the ex-alcoholic never again touch liquor in any manner, shape, or form. This explanation, while part of the psychology of learning, has never appeared anywhere before in quite this fashion.

I was talking earlier of the parallelism between memorizing a poem and overlearning a habit in order to make it last. If the reader will pause for a moment here is the way he will probably recall the beginning of "The Village Blacksmith."

Under a spreading chestnut tree the village smithy stands.
The smith, a mighty man is he, with large and sinewy hands;
And something, something, something are as strong as iron bands.

This is probably as much as the reader can recall. Yet if he were to pick up the poem, and read it through a dozen times, he would be surprised at the ease with which he could learn- or rather relearn—large snatches of it. The reason, of course, is that the old tracks made in the brain when the poem was originally memorized are still there, and can be deepened with ease. Old and seemingly extinct patterns can be easily resurrected without much practice, whether they be verbal habits in terms of a poem, motor habits in terms of swimming, or emotional habits in terms of inhibition. The old writings–the poor, inhibitory, alcoholic tracings—still linger in the brain of the ex-alcoholic. As on a palimpsest, the past has been erased, and the parchment written over, but the ancient writing still remains, however faint.

Each time the ex-alcoholic takes a drink, he is reinvigorating his old alcoholic habit systems. They are weak at first, but inhibitory behavior soon becomes more frequent and the next drink comes easier. A vicious circle has begun. There is none of the nonsense proclaimed at murder trials. "Suddenly everything went blank and the next thing I saw was a gun in my hand," or an empty whiskey glass. Nothing goes blank. The only reason for a relapse is negligence in practicing the excitatory techniques we have been considering.

All sorts of rationalizations beset the individual when he is weakening on his excitation:

"Just a small one. I'll try harder next time."

"One drink won't hurt a baby."

"Just one for a nightcap."

"Why shouldn't I be sociable? I'm getting to be a wet blanket."

"This is an emergency. I really need this one."

"I'm different." (He's no garden-variety ex-alcoholic. He's made of sterner stuff.)

With this last rationalization the individual is deluding himself that because he has had a mental reorganization, a drink won't hurt him. This is neurologically impossible, because each drink acts like a chemical that brings out the secret writing in the individual's brain. It starts the re-enforcement of the old and imperceptible memory traces, and the alcoholic inhibition patterns are soon fully activated. The laws of relearning apply to all habits that have become extinct, whether those habits be harmful, neutral, or helpful. No ex-alcoholic is an exception. Though he dreams of a time when he can take a drink or leave it alone, it is implicit in the laws of learning that such a time can never come. Yet when he has practiced excitation sufficiently, he will stop drinking completely, and will have *no feeling of deprivation.*

And why should he? His digestion and sleep will be excellent. His health and his appearance will have visibly improved, so much so that his friends will remark on it. He will have no feeling of guilt, which is worry about the past, nor any futile anxieties about the future. Some old friends will have become insufferable bores. Without his taste distorted by alcohol they will have no attraction. Other people and interests will have taken on added import. Just as many of our childhood friendships fade as we grow, so do many of the ex-alcoholic's cohorts begin to appear in their true colors when he quits drinking. He is growing, and they are standing still. He becomes a bit of a reformer. He enjoys expatiating on the "evils" of drink, which are rationalizations of his new habits. He feels happy, and he is certain that his worries are over. "At last," he says, "I am cured!"

But is he cured? What is cure anyway? Here are three different points of view, and each has much to commend it.

1 The alcoholic is cured when he stops drinking.
2 The alcoholic is cured when he stops drinking and has lost the "craving" and "need" for alcohol.
3 The alcoholic is cured only when his mental attitude is such that he does not wish to drink.

We are in a better position to decide the real meaning of cure if we take a look at our technique of treatment. We treat alcoholism by disinhibiting the alcoholic and making him more excitatory. He then finds that he has developed enough "will power," and he no longer drinks.

It is my belief that we may consider the alcoholic cured when all three statements set down in the list above are found to apply: That he no longer drinks, that he no longer has the craving, and all because he has the appropriate mental attitude. He will remain cured as long as he continues being excitatory, because being excitatory is what caused his lack of interest in alcohol in the first place.

Perhaps some day we will have an electric meter on which we can take a reading of the individual's mental health, and just as we check a battery, so will we be able to see when a human being's excitation is in the healthy range, the questionable one, or is down below the danger point. Until then, we will simply say that if therapy results in an individual's feeling happier, more useful, and more loved, we will consider therapy to have been worthwhile.

In the treatment of alcoholics who have low self-sufficiency,[1] the therapist must be quite opportunistic, for these persons must constantly be extricated from one quicksand after another. They will give the therapist his full share of headaches, many of which will be quite amusing—in retrospect. Like all the others low in self-sufficiency, they will be eager to lean, and will talk much about the importance of being "persistent" and "tough." But when they also have a desire for perfectionism, and at the same time are quick with moralistic platitudes, they will call for the therapist's greatest ingenuity.

I have been able to get selected low self-sufficiency alcoholics to stop drinking in from six to ten sessions, and to remain abstinent for months thereafter. But this does not mean very much, because they stay that way only as long as I permit them to see me once a week–and sometimes even two and three times when they have particularly distressing problems. Such results I do not at all consider cure, since making the alcoholic self-reliant is one of the goals of therapy. When I try to taper off my sessions with them, there are usually flare-ups and relapses, but not always. Low self-sufficiency remains a difficult problem.

Alcoholics Anonymous is the low self-sufficient drinkers' idea of salvation. Here at last, with their talk of "something bigger than the drinker," is something solid to lean on. What is there more omnipotent than God?

The cures of Alcoholics Anonymous are not religious miracles. They involve psychological principles which may be discussed without mysticism. Alcoholics Anonymous is evangelism with a scientific "gimmick." It is the old story of humble sinners getting religion.

Said Wilson Mizner, "I respect faith, but doubt is what gets you an education." Still, if people draw strength from religion, it is not only pernicious to rob them of it, but it is also bad therapy. As I have pointed out repeatedly, we can only work with the traits that the individual happens to have, and it is these traits—whatever they may be—that we must exploit in order to cure him. Alcoholics Anonymous, for therapeutic purposes, utilizes the religious beliefs in the minds of its members.

It is a unique kind of society. The disability of the individual is his credential for membership. There is always a meeting he can attend, and a

---

[1] See Chapter 11, "The Merry-Go-Round of Low Self-Sufficiency."

"sponsor" he can telephone at any hour of the day or night. Seldom before has he ever had a feeling of belongingness, and here, at last, among his fellow cripples, he finds sincere companionship and absolution for his sins.

He attains excellent rapport with the men who set out to help him, for he knows that they have all battled alcohol, and won. He is sure that they will understand, because he knows that they themselves have once had his problems. They give him as much religion as is expedient, and coddle his low self-sufficiency. They show him how to adjust his difficulties with his wife, his family, his employer, his business associates, his friends, and his acquaintances. He has little opportunity to think alcoholically, for at revival meetings night after night he is bombarded with anti-alcohol-propaganda (and kept away from bars and thirsty cronies). Soon he works up a lather against alcohol and becomes abstinent.

His next stage is to become a "do-gooder." Now, with missionary fervor, he will help others as he himself was helped. This is an important factor in maintaining his cure. As Bernard Shaw says, "A thing that nobody believes cannot be proved too often," and by constantly proving it to others the member of Alcoholics Anonymous is proving it to himself-thus helping himself and his "candidate" at the same time.

It is my belief that Alcoholics Anonymous emphasizes inhibition too much. There is a great deal to recommend in their efforts to make the alcoholic think of the other person instead of himself, but it results in a certain colorlessness in their cured members. Somehow, they always remind me of Christian Scientists and friendly YMCA secretaries. They are peaceful and kind, but their heartiness seems more cerebral than visceral. They are men of good will, but they have a bright eyed inaccessibility, and this despite their love for their fellow man.

Yet Alcoholics Anonymous does a great deal of good and merits our distinct approval. It might more appropriately be called "Inhibitories Anonymous, Alcoholic Chapter"...

More generally then, what of the prevention of alcoholism? I do not believe that a different economic system will solve the problem, any more than will new legislation against it. It is the nature of the human beast and of his social interrelations that are the basic causes of alcoholism.

I can put it in one sentence. The prevention of alcoholism is the prevention and reduction of excessive inhibition.

Very much like the alcoholic is the morphine addict. He too is an inhibitory personality, whose momentous problems become quite insignificant as he increases his excitation. But in the case of morphine the painful withdrawal symptoms must first be conquered before we can proceed with the personality revision that destroys the roots of the addiction.

I usually do not accept drug addicts because as a psychologist I am not empowered to supply narcotics. I have, however, treated several physicians[2] who have supervised their own physical treatment during the critical withdrawal period.

Case 34

Here are a doctor and his wife in their mid-forties. They take tour grains of morphine six times a day, enough to make them what the trade calls "hogs." They began with one eighth of a gram, and, as invariably happens, needed greater amounts of morphine to produce the pleasant, unruffled feeling they crave so much. They have been addicts for the past five years, and it has started to show in the doctor's serious neglect of his practice, whose pressure, he says, drove him to the drug originally.

The doctor has a bluff heartiness that is not at all excitatory, and his wife is soft spoken and polite. Both of them:

- worry over humiliating experiences,
- like to keep in the background on social occasions,
- are happy and sad by turns without knowing why,
- consider themselves shy,
- are hurt badly by criticism, and
- are "very self-conscious" before superiors, and "in general" adds the husband.

Clearly, they are inhibitory personalities, and what is more, they agree that their personalities were no different before they ever took the drug.

On three separate occasions they have isolated themselves in the mountains in a sustained but unsuccessful effort to break the addiction, and now they have gone to the trouble of a transcontinental trip to consult me. I see that their attitude is eager and cooperative, and everything considered I decide that they have a favorable prognosis.

"How are you fixed for morphine?" I ask.

---

[2] There is more morphine addiction among physicians, nurses, and druggists than among the general public, which does not have as easy access to the drug.

They look at each other. "Well," the husband explains, "we have enough for a month, and we have some codeine to taper off with. ..."

Toward the end of their ten day withdrawal period, when their symptoms were particularly acute, they remained in their hotel, and I would drop by to encourage them. The woman was an excellent hypnotic subject, and one day, while going through her withdrawal pains, went downstairs to the beauty parlor for a manicure. The operator told her that her hands were quite tense, whereupon she turned on her autohypnotic relaxation. After a few minutes the manicurist looked up in surprise: "Say, I never saw anyone before as relaxed as you."

When the withdrawal symptoms were at their height, and also several times earlier, she and her husband wanted to quit the struggle, but I persuaded them to hang on. It takes a great deal of fortitude to bear the agonies of morphine withdrawal-with its feelings of weakness and anxiety, goose pimples, perspiration, short breath, trembling, shooting pains, vomiting, and diarrhea. The flesh was weak, but they stayed strong in heart until the agony was over. Then they were exhausted, but they were free.

Now that they were off morphine, only the problem of disinhibition remained, and we devoted two weeks of daily sessions to the problem. (I saw them separately.) They returned home and wrote me from time to time about their happiness with their excitatory ways, and they remained off morphine for four years until the doctor was killed in the war. *Sic transit gloria mundi.* I have not heard from his wife since...

Rubenstein, in working with a tubercular addict, gently massaged his arm after injecting the hypodermic. (10) He gradually decreased the morphine dosage, but continued massage as a conditioned stimulus. Soon there was just sterile water in the injections, and the massage with its conditioned morphine association. He found that the treatment was rapid and effective, and did not produce the so-called withdrawal symptoms." He had the same results when, as the conditioned stimulus, he used a tuning fork held close to the ear, with the patient counting the vibrations until they ceased.

The massage approach strikes me as a good bit of technique. Except for the deception involved in using sterile water, it might well be applied to the treatment of morphine addiction. Perhaps it would even prove as effective if the patient were told the truth when he was receiving the sterile water, especially if he had been given a simple explanation of conditioning for its suggestive effect.

From morphine I should like to turn to something a little more innocuous—smoking. Here indeed is a subject difficult to discuss with any semblance of objectivity. E. H. Harriman, the railroad magnate, once said, "We might as well go to the insane asylum for our men as to employ cigarette smokers." And the smokers reverse the accusation. "We are suspicious of nonsmokers. People who have no vices are mentally twisted themselves." This bit of sophistry equates vices with good mental adjustment— a somewhat startling bit of news.

Just why do people smoke? To relax and feel at ease, say the smokers. To satisfy the craving for nicotine, say the nonsmokers. To exercise the sucking instinct, say the Freudians. All these statements are true, even including the importance of the sucking reflex, surely as far as cigars and pipes are concerned.

But another component in smoking, and at least as important, is a series of pure muscle habits. This includes reaching for the cigarette, tapping it, putting it into the mouth, fishing for matches on a lighter, lighting the cigarette, and then putting out the match or putting away the lighter. I have asked many smokers, "If just by willing it, a lighted cigarette could magically appear in your mouth, and you didn't have to puff at the cigarette at any time, or take it out of your mouth, or flick ashes and put it out–would you prefer this to the way you smoke now?" To this question, nine out of ten smokers answer "no." Regardless of why people start smoking (social pressure, poise, or the myth of masculinity), before long it becomes a conditioned neuro-muscular reflex, and what is more, a definite bodily craving for something in the cigarette, possibly the nicotine. Finnegan, Larson, and Haag have shown that subjects who did not know that they were receiving low nicotine cigarettes reported definite and prolonged lack of satisfaction with their cigarettes. (11)

By now everybody knows that the more you smoke the quicker you die—that is, everybody knows except the advertising agencies, the cigarette manufacturers, and certain paid researchers. Whenever truth has a fight with vested interest the victory is won by rationalization.

The most impressive figures about the effect of smoking were once those of Raymond Pearl. (12) He found, in studying 6,813 men, that "the smoking of tobacco was statistically associated with an impairment of life duration, and the amount or degree of this impairment increased as the habitual amount of smoking increased."

Pearl's findings have since been verified in a devastating study by the American Cancer Society. Drs. E. Cuyler Hammond and Daniel Horn wrote a now classic article called "Smoking and Death Rates—Report on Forty-Four Months of Follow-up of 187,783 Men." (13) Hammond and Horn found:

"The death rate of cigarette smokers increased with the amount of cigarette smoking" …

Consider the following:

Classification	The Death Rate Is
Smoke half a pack or less daily	34% higher than nonsmokers
Smoke between half a pack and a full pack daily	70% higher than nonsmokers
Smoke between one and two packs daily	96% higher than nonsmokers
Smoke two or more packs daily	123% higher than nonsmokers

"Many checks were made to determine the reliability of these findings, and no errors or biases were found that could have a serious effect on them.

"There is a high degree of association between total death rates and cigarette smoking...

"The following relationships with cigarette smoking are evident: an extremely high association for a few diseases, such as cancer of the lung, cancer of the larynx, cancer of the esophagus, and gastric ulcers; (2) a very high association for a few diseases, such as pneumonia and influenza, duodenal ulcer, aortic aneurysm, and cancer of the bladder; (3) a high association for a number of diseases, such as coronary artery disease, cirrhosis of the liver, and cancer of several sites; (4) a moderate association for cerebral vascular lesions. …"

And in a study of nothing less than 198,926 war veterans Dr. Harold F. Dorn (14) of the National Cancer Institute had results closely paralleling the above mentioned findings of Hammond and Horn.

There can be no question. The more you smoke, the quicker you die. Only the uninformed the cynical, or the corrupt can say otherwise. (15)

I think smoking is more chemistry and less habit than we usually realize. It is a chemical addiction, somewhat different from the other addictions, but an addiction nevertheless. In the words of Seale Harris, "If a physician does not believe that nicotine is a habit-forming narcotic, let him try to stop a woman from smoking." The alcoholic can be made happy with morphine, and the morphine addict can find temporary relief with alcohol, but only tobacco can satisfy the craving of the smoker. And conversely, a man can be a smoker, but he can also be an alcoholic or a morphine addict at the same time.

Anyone who has tried to help smokers knows that they are more difficult to cure than alcoholics or morphine addicts. With morphine and alcohol, once the withdrawal pains are over, and there is some personality reorganization, the craving disappears. But smokers, no matter how excitatory they become, remain smokers. Just as the morphine addict feels tense until he gets his hypodermic, so does the smoker feel uncomfortable until he lights his cigarette. His tension is a preliminary withdrawal symptom that the addictive drug quickly satisfies—which explains the origin of the contented, relaxed feeling that the smoker gets from a cigarette. Smoking is a friendly assassin. It inflicts a wound, which more smoking anesthetizes and keeps from healing.

Fortunate indeed is the smoker who is an excellent hypnotic subject. With him, the idea of tobacco needs only to be associated with nausea, and emphasized with vigorous posthypnotic suggestion. Tobacco must be made to taste horrible on the tongue, and even to burn. An elaborate series of rationalizations about the harmfulness of smoking, and whatever personality modifications may be necessary, will round out the treatment of these persons.

But those who are not excellent hypnotic subjects, and this includes the great majority of people, have a more difficult row to hoe. They must decide to stop smoking entirely, completely, and immediately.

"Very well," their body chemistry rationalizes. "I'll cut down. I'll practice moderation." Smoking moderately is the same thing as cutting your throat moderately.

Tapering off by rationing cigarettes throughout the day or shifting to pipes, only prolongs the agony. The break must be complete. As one of my cases put it, "Smoking is associated with so many things that unless you fight it constantly it overpowers you. When I feel tired, when I want to relax, when I read the paper, or just walk into the house, or I have a certain feeling of fullness after eating, these always call for a cigarette. The same goes for getting ready to make a phone call, or when there is company, or when I am sitting in my favorite chair, or whenever a guest comes into the living room."

Such persons as I have helped to stop smoking—and I wonder whether I am really entitled to any credit for it—tell me that it takes about two weeks to reach an early stage of improvement. Until then, they have an active gnawing craving for tobacco, and are somewhat irritable in their social relations.

Actually, as the distinguished Alton Ochsner has said, "The first day and a half after you have stopped smoking is the crucial period. Deny yourself tobacco that long and you've won half the battle. The pharmacological craving reaches its peak toward the end of the first 24 or 36 hours. After that it declines sharply and steadily. Remember that no matter how you feel, your withdrawal symptoms are actually signs of recovery from the disease of tobacco addiction. De-toxification is proceeding; that brings an improvement in mental and physical tone which is soon manifest." (16)

The irritability and craving remain for another two weeks, but at a lower and more endurable level. To chew gum at this time helps, but it is only of slight assistance earlier.

Thereafter, for three or four months, caution is still necessary, but after that the individual is fairly free, particularly if he keeps an anti-smoking attitude and does not try to smoke "moderately." Just like the ex-alcoholic, and for essentially the same reasons, the ex-smoker can easily become a smoker again. All he has to do is to smoke a few cigarettes, and the old addiction will have him by the throat once more.

Smoking, quite unlike alcohol, is thoroughly pernicious, but it can be extirpated much more easily. A far-reaching educational program against it, using all of the devices of modern propaganda, would improve the health of the nation to an extraordinary degree. It could surely immunize the new generation, and motivate most of the moderate smokers to quit. The heavy smokers, however, would need more help, though just what, I must admit, I do not know. The entire question of tobacco addiction still needs thorough investigation, for there is much to be explained.

Filter tips give the smoker peace of mind. They allow him to rationalize away his fear of cancer while he sucks in his shot of nicotine. But filtered tobacco smoke still contains carbon monoxide (as in automobile exhausts), hydrocyanic acid (the gas used to execute murderers), tars (used to produce cancer in the laboratory), nitric acid (used to test gold, and when mixed with hydrochloric acid to *dissolve* gold), ammonia (used for disinfecting garbage cans and toilet bowls) and formaldehyde (used by undertakers in embalming fluid).

Of course, by now the reader has guessed it. I do not smoke myself.

CHAPTER 16
ANXIETY

My case histories are like Hollywood westerns. The names are different, but the plot is always the same. The villains may be called alcoholism, shyness, or lack of the work urge, but behind their masks they are always inhibition. And the hero too is always the same—disinhibition, or excitation, if you will. This is an over-simplification, but it is the outline of all psychotherapy.

Inhibitory patterns are always accompanied by feelings of anxiety. They may vary from mild apprehension to intense jittery fear.

- I go around in a constant state of fright.
- I feel as if I'm nothing but a heart and I'll suddenly stop beating.
- I think they're going to catch on to me soon, and won't renew my contract. I have a feeling of impending doom.
- I don't know what it is, but I have a feeling something is going to happen.

To join the chorus and agree that anxiety is a component in all psychological disturbances will get us nowhere. But to say that *inhibition* is a component of all anxiety states will lead us to the excitatory alternatives that are the way out. A theory of anxiety is a theory of neurosis.

"Anxiety is a learned response [I am quoting Mowrer (1)], occurring to 'signals' (conditioned stimuli) that are premonitory of (i.e., have in the past been followed by) situations of injury or pain (unconditioned stimuli). Anxiety is thus basically anticipatory in nature and has great biological utility in that it adaptively motivates living organisms to deal with (prepare for or flee from) traumatic events in advance of their actual occurrence, thereby diminishing their harmful effects. However, experienced anxiety does not always vary in direct proportion to the objective danger in a given situation, with the result that living organisms, and human beings in particular, show tendencies to behave 'irrationally,' i.e., to have anxiety in situations that are not dangerous or to have no anxiety in situations that are dangerous. Such a 'disproportionality of affect' may come about for a variety of reasons, and the analysis of these reasons throws light upon such diverse phenomena as magic, superstition, social exploitation, and the psychoneuroses."

In this excellent passage, we can see that anxiety, as it confronts us in therapy, is first and foremost a learned response. The emotional pattern is innate, but almost all of the stimuli that arouse it are acquired. Watson's studies of how children acquire fear could as well have been studies of how they acquire anxiety and worry. It may be that anxiety feelings originally had something to do with self-preservation—but this is guessing about evolution. Once conditioning sets in, anxiety reflexes remain after any conceivable protective function has disappeared. The anxious individual is afraid of his past experiences.

We need not flog the dead Freudian horses of birth trauma[1] and repressed early sex experiences as the causes of anxiety. In animal experimentation, as Gantt puts it, "The origin of [anxiety symptoms] can be definitely traced back to a known and artificially produced conflict..." (2) In inhibitory humans we can find a sufficient number of inadequate reaction systems (based on past conditionings) that explain later "illogical" anxiety feelings.

Now I should like to comment on the difference between what has been called primary or objective anxiety, and secondary or neurotic anxiety. Anxiety, of course, is warranted when the stimulus precipitating it is a bona fide threat or danger—say, having a revolver suddenly pushed into one's face. Anxiety may be considered unwarranted when it involves, say, an anticipatory fear of being reprimanded. Only the inhibitory will suffer from this anxiety. The excitatory will not feel anxious before, during, or after the reprimand. Once more we are forced to realize that it is not the stimulus that counts. It is the personality of the recipient of the stimulus that determines his reaction to it.

---

[1]   The mother usually suffers more of a birth trauma than the baby.

But Shaffer found that this is not always the case. From a study of 4,504 fliers who had recently returned from combat, he concluded that "the adequate stimulus for fear is a highly motivated situation toward which the individual has no adequate means of adjustment." (3) In other language, the adequate stimulus for fear [or anxiety] is a critical situation about which the individual can do nothing.

Pavlov gave dogs similarly insoluble problems and found that they too broke down. In his own words, "A projection of a luminous circle on to a screen in front of the animal was repeatedly accompanied by feeding. After the [salivary] reflex had become well established" a luminous ellipse was projected onto the screen. This ellipse was not accompanied by food, and "A complete and constant differentiation was obtained comparatively quickly." The dog salivated at the circle and not at the ellipse. Then the ellipse was made more and more circular. Though the dog was able to discriminate to "a considerable degree" between the circle and an almost completely circular ellipse, "After three weeks of work upon this differentiation not only did the discrimination fail to improve, but it became considerably worse, and finally disappeared altogether. At the same time the whole behaviour of the animal underwent an abrupt change. The hitherto quiet dog began to squeal in its stand, kept wriggling about, tore off with its teeth the apparatus for mechanical stimulation of the skin, and bit through the tubes connecting the animal's room with the observer, a behaviour which never happened before. On being taken into the experimental room the dog now barked violently, which was also contrary to its usual custom; in short it presented all the symptoms of a condition of acute neurosis." (4)

It is encouraging to note that Maier (5) remarks that the "conditions which relieve the animal's disturbance" are conditions which give the animal *increased mastery of its environment.* Maier continues,

"1) Masserman found that cats could be cured of their neurotic behavior if they were *trained to manipulate the feeding signal.* 2) Discrimination problems in general, even if the animal cannot learn them, produce no neuroses but in these *the animal determines when it will make a choice.*

3) Maier found that conflict situations in which convulsions occur are *effective if the animal is free to make an abortive or substitute reaction to the conflict situation." [All italics mine.]*

On the human level it is excitation that means environmental mastery and the elimination of fear and anxiety. As for the Freudian talk of the purposiveness of anxiety—that the anxious individual unconsciously wants to regress to a position of dependency on his family—that is nothing but a guilt-breeding way of saying that yesterday's reactions are today's reflexes.

To be rid of his anxiety the individual needs some new excitatory reflexes. His old inhibitory ones do him no good. *The fact that excitatory reflexes cure anxiety tells us that anxiety is the shadow of inhibition.*

Case 35

The following case illustrates the whining low self-sufficiency that often characterizes anxiety states. It is a study in rationalization and in the unimportance of faith for successful therapy. Here is the report as written by the young man, aged 34. The bracketed comments are mine.

About 6 A.M. in early March, while working on the midnight shift at my place of business [a night clerk for the city] I suddenly received a very sharp pain in the left temple. This was accompanied by a short dizzy spell and was the beginning of the symptoms that were to follow in a very short time.

Besides working, I was taking courses in chemical engineering in the manufacture of penicillin. 1 was at the top of my class in these courses, and was just about completing them when I had the symptoms appear and was unable to complete my work. I was driving myself fairly hard, with my regular working hours, lectures, and much outside studying. Just about this time, I had become engaged to be married to a nice young lady of fine family and good education.

Concerning myself, I was an only child of a fairly happy marriage. [He was quite mother-bound and perfectionistic.] I had been a pre-medical student while at college, and due to financial reverses, I never was able to complete medical school. This was very disappointing to me, since all my friends who had been in my class at college managed to get through school. I managed to do some work in chemical research and plant production for a few years. However, having no real connections, I was able to land very poor jobs with little remuneration. [The world owes him a living.] In 19—, I became connected with the municipal civil service because of its financial security, and have remained there since. I never had been happy at this position, and tried to obtain better positions in civil service or scientific work, but with little success.

When the symptoms first appeared, I went to Dr. A., and he believed that it was due to too much overwork and study. He suggested taking a week's rest and then continuing my work and research again. After the week, I started to feel worse and new symptoms showed up, greater pressure on the temples, periods of excitement, dizziness, extreme fatigue, fear, etc.

I was next recommended to Dr. B. He recommended rest, even bed rest for a while, vitamin tablets, and sunray treatments. After about a month under his care I showed no improvement whatsoever, and the symptoms persisted. When going out on the street noises bothered me, dizziness remained, fatigue was very great, pressure on the temples was obstinate.

After this I went to Dr. C., the psychiatrist. He believed it to be nothing at all, merely a childhood attachment to my folks and a fear of leaving them. He recommended immediate marriage and was certain that this would break the symptoms in a very short time. After arrangements for the marriage were made, the symptoms persisted and after about six so-called talks with no improvement, he decided to give me electric shock treatments. I became very annoyed and hated these treatments, but being desperate I went through with the first three that Dr. C. recommended. On the day following the third treatment I was married. How he could have had the nerve to force me into getting married under such conditions I still cannot understand. After the marriage he again recommended my taking three more shock treatments. Having little choice at this time I went through with them. My condition showed very little improvement in all this time. After this he recommended giving me vitamin tablets for a few weeks to help my general fatigue, and then decided to go back to shock treatments again. In all 1 had an even dozen treatments with very little improvement. When I protested to Dr. C. he told me his opinion was that my case was a definite chronic neurosis and there was nothing more he could really do.

By accident, at this time, I heard of you and immediately following my first consultation, I was buoyed up very much in my hopes after having reached a very desperate stage with nothing else to turn to. In your opinion, it was mostly a matter of "emotional constipation" plus home environment through the years. In other words, what was needed was a good "emotional diarrhea," to sort of let go and become a definite extrovert and no more of a gentleman [with an amiable disposition and an asinine smile]. After following this procedure as was definitely planned, there was a concrete upturn after about the sixth consultation. I had never felt as well in all the time that I had been ill as during this short time. After continuing with "giving out with the emotions," plus a conditioning factor that was added [he is referring to some self-suggestion] there has been a definite improvement. It surges "up" and "down," every few days there being a variation, however the "downs" never go down too far. Although it does become a bit discouraging when the "downs' come, I know by now that in a short time there will be a definite "up." It is a matter of gritting my teeth and holding on until the "down" period surges to its lowest stage and then proceeds up again.

Now, at this writing, after eleven consultations [a week apart] things look brighter than they ever did since I have become ill, which is in all about twenty months. The dizzy spells are not as frequent as they used to be. More than this, a "fear" used to accompany these spells. This fear has practically become negligible, and I can get around better both at work and in the social world with greater confidence. The greatest improvement found has been in the extreme fatigue that used to be prevalent at all times. At present, I can do most everything that I used to at home, at work, on vacation, etc., with not the same vigor and vitality I had before I became ill, but I feel my strength unquestionably coming back, and that extreme fatigue becoming a thing of the past. Another symptom that has disappeared has been the "periods of excitement," which were most annoying and came at the most inopportune times.

So in general most of the symptoms are disappearing or have been cut down to a minimum. The pressure on the temples still remains obstinate, plus the occasional dizzy spells. However, you feel very satisfied with the way things have progressed and feel from now on time is the only factor left to bring things back to normal.

Notice that the young man says that it is I who feel "very satisfied with the way things have progressed"—more leaning and doubt. The sequel is not uninteresting. I saw him seven more times, about a month apart. Then I told him that I could help him no further, and we parted quite pleasantly. "Remember," I said. "If you ever have any trouble get in touch with me."

I heard from him eight months later. This once anxious young man, who had been afraid of his own shadow, had given up his safe little job in the civil service. He and his wife had moved to Cuba, where he was representing some American pharmaceutical companies on a commission basis.

Case 36

I have commented on the foregoing case as we have gone along, so without further ado we shall consider the anxiety state of Mr. W. He is 30 years of age, married, and with one child, a new-born girl. He sells law books to lawyers by direct personal solicitation.

He paces back and forth, and assures me that he is going to pieces and will soon be insane. He squints and screws up his face. He has cardiac palpitations and digestive upsets, but physician after physician has assured him that "it's all mental." He scolds himself for being a failure. He doubts himself, he doubts everyone else, and he doubts his own doubts. "I'm afraid of everything, but if you ask me what, I don't know." He buys all of the magazines as they come out—"I practically grab them from the newsstand"—for he hopes that some new method of self-help has been announced. He "almost had a nervous breakdown six years ago," and for the past several years has been seeing a psychoanalyst three times a week. When he was twenty he consulted a psychoanalyst five times a week for a year. All in all, he is a thoroughly apprehensive, bewildered, and excited individual.

In such cases a firm hand is excellent policy. "Sit down," I say sternly, "and stop acting like a hysterical fool." He sits down.

We find the inhibitory roots readily enough, wrapped though they are in the psychoanalytic jargon he has acquired. He has a brother two years younger than himself. His father is "high strung and a strict disciplinarian who believes that children should be seen and not heard." He still remembers how his father once said, "You have no right to think."

His mother is "worrisome and always wanting me to do the right thing." Both parents, of course, are quite perfectionistic. Where and how he picked up his difficulties is no longer a mystery. But what is to be done?

On the Bernreuter, Mr. W. has a high neurotic score, more so than 90 per cent of adult males. Besides, he is low in self-sufficiency—scoring 28.4 per cent. It is my opinion that anxiety states are most difficult to treat in people who have low self-sufficiency—the ones who feel as if they are living in a revolving cement-mixer.

Mr. W. does not know whether he loves his wife and their infant daughter. Perhaps a vacation would help him to get better, but he's not sure. This gives me an idea.

"Yes," I say. "I think you ought to take a vacation."

His face lights up for a moment. "Where do you think we ought to go?"

"There's no 'we,'" I answer. "I don't want you to go with your wife. I want you to go alone."

"And leave my wife and baby behind?"

"That's right."

"I could never do that."

I explain that I want him to get a change of surroundings and that bringing his wife and child with him would be carrying around the same environment. I hammer at this, and he reluctantly agrees to go alone.

The next day his wife telephones me. "By what right," she asks, "do you tell husbands to desert their wives and new-born babies? It's very easy when you have no personal interest in the matter. You're really a home wrecker, and I'm sick of all these psychoanalysts and whatnots my husband has been seeing. My mother-in-law says that people like you ought to be put in jail."

"My dear girl," I tell her. "Don't flatter yourself. Do you call your place a home? It's full of worry, trouble, and fear. It doesn't sound like a very happy place to me... Now, I'm not trying to wreck any homes. I just want your husband to find himself, and then everybody will be much happier. He doesn't have to listen to me, and he can quit seeing me right now."

But her husband actually went on a vacation, and alone. He packed a few bags, and moved into a local hotel—for an hour and a half. Then he checked out and ran back home. He apologized profusely to his wife, and pledged eternal love—which was precisely what I had expected to happen, and which was why I had him go on his solitary vacation. With his low self-sufficiency, there could have been no other outcome. His brain had been full of conflict—did he love his wife, or didn't he? He had to act to find the answer ... and now he felt at peace about his family.

Next I explained to him the origin of his symptoms. "Your feelings of anxiety are feelings of tension stemming from unfinished emotional business. Thanks to your father, you learned the wrong way to react to emotional situations. I call it the wrong way, but you could not have learned otherwise in your childhood environment. Now you are going to learn the right way to react. I'm going to re-educate your emotions."

"But the way I feel is terrible," was his insipid reply, so typical of those with low self-sufficiency.

"I know," I answered firmly. "Your perfectionism dooms you to frustration because it's humanly impossible to be perfect. When you constantly aim for the impossible you're bound to fail. Let's take a look at how a happy cat or dog goes about living," and I proceeded to develop the idea of spontaneity of action.

"But I have such conflicting ideas," he said. "I don't know which to follow."

"Obey your first impulse—whatever it is."

And that is how it worked out. Lying in bed in the morning he told himself that he ought to get up—but then again he might as well remain in bed. His first impulse was to get up, so he forced himself out of bed. But if his first impulse had been to stay in bed, and his second to get up so that he could call on a prospect to try to sell him some law books in order to make a living for his wife and child, my advice would have been, "Without debating, pick the alternative that will be better for you." (Here I was harnessing his perfectionistic desires in order to make him reach decisions quickly.) He then decided that he had better call on his potential customer.

By increasing his excitation and his self-sufficiency he was rid of his anxiety. I found that he had excellent mechanical ability, and at my suggestion he decided to put it to use. He became a manufacturer of small kitchen gadgets, and succeeded beyond his fondest dreams. It is now four years since I first saw him, and he has remained happy and somewhat complacent. Total sessions: 14. I might add parenthetically that his mother who had wanted to send me to jail, and his mother-in-law, have since sent me their other children for treatment, and that I have no stauncher supporters than him and his wife.

In Chapter 12 I explained some "Problems of the Therapist." Here I need only mention that the individual with an anxiety state is sometimes so much of a doubting Thomas that therapy is impossible. Such cases are quite challenging, But unless they do some psychological "homework"—even a little is enough—to continue seeing them will serve no useful purpose. This is unfortunate, especially since the roots of their inhibitory personalities are usually quickly obvious, even to them. But a realization of cause does not effect cure. For that we need good works—excitation.

Case 37

Because I wanted him to practice excitation at home, where it would do him the most good, a man flew back and forth to St. Louis each week between appointments. A prominent psychoanalyst had told him, after two years, that he would never improve unless he moved out of his community, for the complications his personality had caused had thoroughly discredited him there.

Of his childhood,[2] he said, "I always had to be careful to say the right thing... Home had no affection. It was an economic institution. Whenever I came home happy, mother always picked on me. ... Any enjoyment was followed by pain, suffering, punishment, guilt, and self-pity—and that's how I feel about things now. ... I'm always discontented, hurt, and mad. ..." Here, in his masochism and yearning for martyrdom, is the explanation of the anguish he felt in his personal relations.

I told him that his feelings of anxiety were worries about the future; and his feelings of regret were worries about the past. I examined how he was to cope with the real situations that confronted him, and how he was to build his excitation.

"You're right," he said. "I keep my emotions inside. I do this because I find it difficult to bring them out. Nobody ever knows whether I care for them or not." Here was the inhibitory keystone which we have met again and again.

As we approached the end of treatment (fifteen hours in all) he told me that he had successfully applied my ideas to his divorced wife, in an effort to help her recover from a lately completed psychoanalysis.

Sometimes the anxiety state is marked by what Bleuler describes as "the compulsion to examine repeatedly whether a match thrown away no longer burns, whether the doors of closets are locked, whether letters are sealed, or whether no mistake was made in the calculation. ..." (6) A woman had this *folie du doute*, and wondered whether her five secretaries had all done what they were supposed to do. Since she had extensive responsibilities, the ramification and complexities of her doubts and worries were considerable.

Yet by building in excitation, in a half dozen sessions, she was completely cured, not only of her "doubting mania," but also of her other inhibitory quirks.

When the learning attitude is present, the most bewildering symptoms readily respond to excitational therapy. This is true of generalized anxiety as well as of specific phobias. claustrophobia, acrophobia (high places), and agoraphobia (open places). I once treated a woman whose biggest fear in life was to ride in an automobile. In fifteen sessions her neurotic score dropped from 99 percent to 18 percent and she began to relish hazardous mountain driving. She received no specific conditioning in regard to automobiles.

Such persons have more than their particular phobias. They have difficulty in shaking off all distressing stimuli. They suffer from general inhibition.

---

[2] These are verbatim quotations, set down when I saw him.

And so does the insomniac. All day long he pours sand into his emotional machinery, and at nightfall he seeks a few drops of oil for his motor. Then he is distressed when it doesn't run.

He chases slumber further away by trying some pillow-magic that he has encountered in a magazine or best seller. He breathes in and out with great deliberation, he counts sheep, he writes S-L-E-E-P on a mental blackboard, he carefully tucks soft pillows under himself, or tries a hard health board. Then he runs around the room ten times, drinks hot milk, reads mystery stories, puts on a sleep mask, stuffs his ears with cotton—but still he cannot sleep.

Insomniacs make the same error at night that they make in the daytime: The more they try the less they succeed. The more they try to grab sleep by the throat, the more it eludes them. "Easy does it"—but that does not lie within the inhibitory range.

Many people who drink very little, frequently take an alcoholic nightcap in order to sleep. This gives us our clue. Insomnia that is psychological in origin, and it usually is, is a symptom in many inhibitory patterns. It invariably responds to increased excitation, and it is not cured at night. Insomnia is cured in the daytime.

Excitation also cures the excessive desire of those inhibitory personalities who go to sleep readily, and want to sleep all the time. How are we to explain this paradox?

To quote Pavlov, "We have established beyond doubt the fact that sleep is inhibition spreading over all the hemispheres." (7)

In the case of the insomniac we increase excitation to reduce inhibitory intellectuality. This reduces the cortical interference with the sleep-inducing spread of inhibition.

In the case of the excessive sleeper, we increase excitation to reduce the general state of inhibition in the hypothalamus (the sleep center). This prevents sleep from coming so readily.

The same seeming paradox applies to students who cannot concentrate. Though some of them teem with extraneous thoughts as they try to study, and others get sleepy and lie down for a nap, the therapy that teaches them to concentrate is the same excitation.

One such student drove me home, and on the way pointed to a repair in his broken steering wheel. "You see that," he said. "It's your fault."

"What do you mean?" I asked.

"Well," he said, "you told me to express myself, and I disagreed with a friend of mine so strongly that I banged the steering wheel and broke it."

"And that 'self-expression' is the reason they didn't throw you out of college," was my answer.

CHAPTER 17
BODILY CORRELATES OF INHIBITION

We may well agree with Harvey A. Carr that "Consciousness is an abstraction that has no more independent existence than the grin of a Cheshire cat." (1) "Consciousness" and "thought" football of Victorian philosophers are the functioning of physical structures, and accompany material processes in the brain. Thinking is a physiological event, and the laws of mind are laws of matter. They can be nothing else, even if we do not know them.

But we do not have enough physiological knowledge—consequently "the construction of psychophysiological hypotheses becomes necessary."[1] And although we navigate successfully by them, these hypotheses are only tentative. Physiology remains our true north, even if our ignorance often compels a substantial declination from it.

The Freudian metaphysics, which can hardly be considered physiologically oriented, has recently become aware of its deficiency. In an effort to overcome it, they have appropriated the language of physiology, mixed it with a specious transcendentalism about mind and body, and proclaimed the oratorical science of "psychosomatic medicine."

---

[1]   C. C. Pratt. The Logic of Modern Psychology: The Macmillan Company, New York, 1939, page x. Everybody interested in thinking clearly about psychology should read this splendid book.

My comments are fully justified. The Freudian viewpoint can hardly be considered physiologically oriented. What else can be said of a structure with such fundamentals as id, ego, super-ego, libido, and Oedipus complex? Even Heidbreder, who is sympathetic to psychoanalysis, admits that Freud had a "penchant for the vague and the mystical." (2)

Psychosomatic medicine is psychoanalysis wearing a new mask. Witness:

Flanders Dunbar, in her *Psychosomatic Diagnosis,* says, "... up to the present [psychoanalytic technique] is our instrument of greatest precision in diagnosis and control of psychic processes as well as of their somatic manifestations." (3) As for the *Psychosomatic Medicine* of English and Weiss, no one will argue that it is anything but completely psychoanalytic. (4) And in all this the Psychosomatic Freudians have adopted a specious transcendentalism about mind and body. In this connection, I shall quote from a penetrating analysis by Burnham. (5)

"It should be unnecessary here to reiterate the fact that no differences have ever been distinguished which may serve as universal criteria of either body or mind. Consequently, as Pratt states, *If it is impossible to tell the difference between the mental and the physical, then the problem of the relation between them need never arise...* This statement implies that some form of monism only can be given scientific credibility. Further inference reveals that to speak of psychogenic determination of organic disorder *as opposed to* organic determination is sheer nonsense. Both are examples of the same type of determination. There is only one type of determination, or determinism, which is recognized by science and that is of the simple 'if this, then that' variety. Any other apparent difference based on body-mind distinctions is purely at a verbal level. To inquire into the ultimate nature of observable events or relations, from the standpoint of the theoretical scientist, is to be a metaphysical has-been."

Psychosomatic medicine is an oratorical science. And curiously, it is there that it has made its most noteworthy contribution. It has educated many laymen and physicians to an awareness that a nervous system happens to be part of the human body.

Psychosomatic medicine, or more accurately, psychoanalytic medicine, is a transitional stage in the disintegration of psychoanalysis. What it hails with an air of breathless discovery are old saws to those familiar with the classical tradition in psychology—the work of James, Prince, Pavlov, Bechterev, Watson, Thorndike, Hull, Hunter, Lashley, and the physiologists Cannon and Sherrington. These men said it before the devotees of psychoanalytic medicine said it, and they said it better.

Petrova has produced ulcers of the leg and hip, and baldness and eczema in dogs by giving them difficult problems to solve. (6, 7) Gantt remarks that had his dog Nick (in whom an experimental neurosis had been produced) "been a patient he would undoubtedly have been treated for anxiety attacks and been labeled with the terms merergasia [i.e., neurosis] phobias, gastric neurosis, functional tachycardia, asthma, enuresis, [and premature ejaculation]." (8)[2]

These terms are as useless for humans as for dogs. We need only disinhibit the inhibitory, and the entire hierarchy of symptoms, visible and invisible, disappears: the migraine, the obesity, and the circulatory disturbances included—what the analysts call the "somatic manifestations." And when these symptoms go, so do the feelings of anxiety that are always associated with them. The anxiety feelings are just as somatic as high blood pressure, even if their physiology is not now as accessible to observation. This also means that we can do without the psychoanalytic symbolism of conversion, and its presto-chango of mental into physical—what Hollingworth has called the "somatic monument erected in memory of the vanquished complexes." (10)

But there is one important question which we have not yet considered. Why does the inhibitory Mr. A. develop an ulcer, but the inhibitory Mr. B., a pianist, a paralysis of the right forefinger? And the inhibitory Mrs. C. puts on too much weight, but Mr. D., who is also inhibitory, cannot seem to gain any? In other words, how are differences in symptom formation to be explained?

My answer may surprise the reader. I deny that there is any significant difference in the divergent symptoms of the individuals we have just considered. It is true that in a *single obvious* physical sense, they have a different symptom, but in *dozens* of their other inhibitory behaviors, which are equally symptomatic, they are essentially similar. And more than that, as we have seen, for all intents and purposes their backgrounds are also quite similar.

Having established that in these divergent cases there are far reaching similarities in total symptom and background patterns, we have only to explain a minor nuance—the gross physical symptom that so impresses the untutored.

This I would say is probably the conditioned result of the *differences* in their past experiences, and a matter of the routing of nervous energy.

---

[2] See also Watson's eloquent description of a dog conditioned into maladjustment, and of the sterility of the "influence of mind over body" in describing the results. (9)

Sometimes it may only involve simple stimulus substitution: a certain food may make an adult vomit, and only because in childhood he had a distressing experience with it. Rarely is innate predisposition responsible. I grant that we can use more knowledge about this, but at present I must say that the therapy of the inhibitory disorders is much easier, quicker, and thorough when it is based on their manifold and major similarities, than when it is concerned with their minor differences.

Indeed, when it comes to improving our psychotherapeutic technique we have little to gain from the psychosomatic preoccupation with "the bodily organs or systems of organs involved in emotional disturbances...

"The reference of bodily changes to particular organs is a convenient way of organizing the facts. One should remember, however, that it is the organism *as a whole* which responds in emotional situations. Intense emotional excitement includes bodily changes in the glands, smooth muscles, skeletal muscles, nerves, as well as chemical modifications of the blood."[3]

Case 38

Keeping in mind that it is always the organism *as a whole* that responds in emotional situations, we shall turn to the case of Mr. D., age 42. He was born in Italy and came to this country when he was two years old. He was the youngest of five children. His parents were devoted to him, but his father was quite domineering. All through school (he graduated from college) he had excellent marks in spite of his shyness and a slowness in speech. "I was always in an anxious state, fearing I would be called on to recite. I became self-conscious when I was among people. I read a great deal as it seemed to make me feel better. I did not go out with girls much, as I was very shy and was afraid I would stammer when I spoke to them. I blushed very readily."

At the age of 31 he married a girl he had known all of his life. She was two years older than he, and was a dominant school teacher who carried over her classroom behavior into her personal life. When teacher commanded, John and Mary—and her husband— had to jump. She made his life miserable by constantly repeating to him that he was of low social origin, and that his parents were "vulgar peasants."

"I became ill," he said, "having attacks of stomach trouble and palpitations of the heart." He lost weight and was unable to carry on

3   Young, P.T. *Emotion in Man and Animal.* John Wiley & Sons, New York, 1943, pp. 211-212.

his business. His wife told him that only inferior people got sick. She accompanied him to physicians, and when they said that there was nothing wrong with him she would go into tantrums and accuse him of malingering and wanting sympathy. Since she did not want a "sick man" for a husband, she suggested a divorce, which was granted after some religious complications. Right after this his condition became aggravated. His father died of coronary thrombosis, and constant worry about his heart was now added to his stock of symptoms. "Physician after physician never found anything wrong. I was always told to snap out of it. How easily said by someone else who is not suffering! I began to read every book I could get on psychology and medicine."

He remarried three years after his divorce. Fortunately for our therapy this marriage was a complete success. "But I nevertheless remained quite conscious of my bodily functions. I kept on having worries, and I had an apprehensive feeling that something was going to happen. I had dreams that I was dying, or was in an enclosed place where I couldn't breathe. I would wake up in a cold sweat, my heart beating like a hammer. Any situation was an ordeal, producing palpitation, sweating, and a feeling of uneasiness. It was hard for me to make any decisions. I seemed to be at a fork in the road, undecided which way to turn. I was apprehensive over the results of each decision. There was hardly a day that I was symptom free, always having headaches, palpitations, extra systoles, and pseudo-ulcer symptoms. On the off day when I did feel well, I seemed to anticipate an attack because it just didn't feel right for me to feel well. It seemed as if I enjoyed ill health. Each time I had one of these supposed heart attacks I would rush to a physician and he would never find anything wrong physically. Tachycardia and hypertension, yes [he had learned the medical jargon well]—but all caused by some emotional upset. Their reassurances would last a few hours, and then I would again start to think that there was something very seriously wrong with me, but which they wouldn't tell me."

Here is almost every ailment in the psychosomatic lexicon, but as far as we are concerned, all that is wrong with Mr. D. is that he is excessively inhibitory, and, says the Bemreuter, that he has low self-sufficiency, 26.6, to boot. Only this, and nothing more. Disinhibiting him will restore the balance between inhibition and excitation, and all of his symptoms will disappear including the rapid heart rate and hypertension that particularly concern him, and the headaches that accompany his high blood pressure.

I explained to Mr. D. that all of his symptoms were "just warts on the same psychological pickle," and that excitation would make them disappear. His wife, his friends, his employees, his customers—soon everybody became a recipient of his "feeling-talk," and before long, several people remarked, "You know, there's something different about you. I don't know what it is, but you're different."

"Really? he would say. "In what way?"

"I don't know," would be the answer, "but you're different. You have more personality or something."

After fifteen hours of treatment he wrote, "My symptoms seem to be fading away. Days go past without my noticing that my bodily functions are going on. I have few symptoms and I disregard them when I do. I am able to do my own reassuring and make it stick. [I had taught him some techniques of self-suggestion.] An extra systole is now just something physiological [sic], without my worrying that I am having a heart attack.

"I can't say that I am entirely over my condition, but the improvement is so great I can hardly believe it. It is easier for me to work, my business has increased very much, and I am not shy among people. The only thing I am still troubled with is my insomnia and my slowness in speech. It seems the harder I try to woo sleep the more difficult it is to win her. But I don't worry about it any more. When I can't fall asleep I just read a book until I get sleepy."

I took the position that his halting speech was proof that he was not practicing excitation sufficiently. He had to talk more and to think less. The insomnia would take care of itself as he became even freer. Five sessions (and five weeks) later he reported improvement in his sleep and his speech, and I gave him a Bernreuter. Now his neurotic score was 32.2 per cent as compared with the 99 per cent he had scored when I first saw him, and his self-sufficiency score had risen from 26.6 per cent to 47.8 per cent. "Work on your self-sufficiency some more," I advised him. I saw him another ten times at one and, later, two week intervals. By then he was completely symptom free, and to the astonishment of his physician, his systolic blood pressure had dropped from 220 to 140, and remained there. His diastolic blood pressure remained stationary at 90.

I did not hear from him for almost five years. Then I took the initiative and telephoned, for I wanted to know how he was doing. He was still symptom free, he told me, and "life," he said, "is wonderful. You made a terrific change in my psyche."

I have treated several persons whose hypertension was reduced by thyroidectomy, but who found their blood pressure rising back again because their personalities had not been modified. It is indeed possible to help many conditions by sympathectomy (cutting of the sympathetic nerves) and vagotomy (cutting the two branches of the vagus nerve). Often, however, these operations have distressing side reactions. Sympathectomy has been known to render men sterile by making them unable to ejaculate, and in the majority of patients vagotomy seriously reduces their ability to eliminate.

Fishberg's study overcomes many of the limitations of the earlier appraisals of the value of sympathectomy in hypertension. (11) Fishberg points out that his report is "based on patients selected for operation by a single internist and followed by him after operation." He contrasts this with the sympathectomies "reported by surgeons who perform the operation on patients referred by different physicians." Fishberg thus presents "an evaluation of sympathectomy from the point of view of a physician who is at the same time treating other— many more—hypertensive patients without operation and has thus a control in his own experience for assessment of the symptomatic results." He concludes, "One hundred and nineteen patients with severe essential hypertension were selected for sympathectomy and followed by the same observer for an average of thirty-two months... After a weighing of the favorable and untoward effects, it is concluded that sympathectomy is indicated in less than 4 per cent of patients with essential hypertension." Fishberg's findings are surely in keeping with the remark that "Sympathectomy is an operation of desperation or experimentation."

It is of course well known that selected cases can be helped by psychotherapy and without surgery. But at all times we must be sure that old-fashioned lesions and pathology are not behind the cardiovascular (or other) troubles.

Migraine in a sense is as much of a circulatory disturbance as hypertension. In the case of migraine it is the veins and arteries of the head that are particularly involved. They become congested, begin to throb painfully, and are accompanied by a feeling of nausea. An aura of light flashes usually precedes these "sick headaches," and the sufferer tenses in anticipation.

The migraine sufferer is fraudulently excitatory. He is alert, ambitious, and aggressive. He has a pose of casualness, but is really perfectionistic and analytical. He is definitely his own worst enemy, and could just as well have ulcers.

Case 39

I have been fortunate in the treatment of migraine, but the failure which follows is more instructive. It clearly demonstrates the psychological background of migraine.

A woman had been plagued by migraine attacks eleven years. She had consulted dozens of physicians, who had checked her for histamine sensitivity, sinusitis, eye strain, thing else in the book.

"Tell me about your last attack," I said.

She described it in detail.

"When was it?"

"Last Saturday morning."

"And when was the one before that?"

"The Saturday before, come to think of it.

I discovered that most of her attacks for the past two years been on week-ends. She had never quite thought of them that way, but "sure enough, that was about right."

My next objective was to determine the difference between weekends and week-days, from her own personal point of view. Stutterers often speak better on weekends, because the pressure of the world is less, but here was the reverse. Surely, something was happening on week-ends that she didn't like.

She fluttered her eyelashes coyly. She was married and carrying on a love affair, and the week-days were hers with her beloved. But he too was married, and had to spend the weekends in the country with his wife and family. Therefore the migraines. Prior to her involvement with him, her other headaches were fairly well correlated with her personal problems of the time. She was quite beautiful and accustomed to getting whatever she wanted, and when she couldn't, a migraine would be part of her distress.

In later sessions, she constantly begged me to convince her lover to divorce his wife and to marry her—for I was also treating both him and his wife. (Everybody concerned knew that I was seeing everybody else.) But the ending was old-fashioned. She went back to her husband, and her lover remained with his wife. As events later proved, this was the only correct solution to the problem. And I did not help her migraine one iota.

I am always suspicious of people who have stomach trouble, because pathology aside, it is usually the internal badge of inhibition. Ulcers, spastic colitis, or nervous indigestion—they are all the same for our purposes.

Contrary to the assertions of the psychologically naive, ulcers are not the result of mental processes. Ulcers are a single component in an inhibitory pattern which involves the entire organism.

Because they are more inhibitory, men with ulcers outnumber women by four to one. If they were not married they would be perfect old maids. The typical sufferer is intense and perfectionistic, and in a great rush. Every minute he saves probably costs him an hour of life. He often seems superficially confident and self-possessed, but the Bernreuter will unmask him every time. Though he is not foaming at the mouth, he is foaming at the gut.

Worry about his poor health may have affected his personality, but we will always find that his pre-ulcer behavior was also inhibitory. High-pressure executives have ulcers not because of the stress under which they operate. They have ulcers because of their pre-stress personalities, and because these personalities not only do not know how to cope with stress, but are constantly manufacturing it. Hormones, and milk and mush diets may have their place in the treatment of gastrointestinal disturbances, but substituting honest excitation for inhibition frequently remains the more fundamental therapy.

The plain unvarnished truth is that the woman who is too fat eats too much. Too many calories get into her stomach by way of her mouth. Although it is more comfortable to blame the glands, modern endocrinology finds them "Not Guilty."

Lewis H. Newburgh, a distinguished endocrinologist, expresses the consensus of the great majority of his colleagues:

"... many painstaking investigations ... have failed to disclose any abnormal process that accounts for the accumulation of fat."(12) Endocrine imbalance can no longer be blamed for obesity. Many people believe the contrary, but it simply isn't so.

Massage, exercise, and steam cabinets on the one hand, and thyroid and benzedrine on the other, are all symptomatic treatments, and as we saw earlier, it may well be that women who smoke in order to keep on a diet do more than kill their appetites. They kill themselves. To quote another endocrinologist, S. Charles Freed, the fundamental therapy is something else again. "The psychologic factors in obesity are paramount. . . . Treatment of the patient should be based on understanding of the psychologic reasons for his overeating." (13)

This is fundamental, even though sometimes obesity may have no particular personality involvements, and is solely a matter of habit or custom in the quantity and types of food that are eaten. These persons aside, the obese—or overly plump—bemoan their lack of will power and for once they are right. They lack will power, and they have big appetites, because they are inhibitory. It is the excitatory who possesses true self-control. And now we are on familiar territory again.

Case 40

Besides a diet list and a thorough physical examination, the overweight person must have a sincere desire for cure. The following case illustrates what happens when this crucial desire is absent:

Miss T. is 22 years of age, and 30 pounds overweight. She has a sweet and attractive face enveloped though it is in fat. She wants to lose weight in order to take a screen test. "Fond dream," I think. Nevertheless, I learn that she has an extensive dramatic education (her parents have always pushed her in this direction) and that a bona fide offer of a screen test had been made to her four months ago. This occurred at the end of her summer vacation, and when she had no excess weight.

"Oh," I said. "So you *can* lose weight sometimes."

She remained expressionless. "Yes, but I can't seem to get enough will power now. Things seem to have changed.

"Tell me. Why did you lose weight this summer? Was there a man in the picture?"

"Yes."

"And you lost weight because you wanted to appeal to him."

"Yes."

"And what happened?" I asked, although I could guess.

"We broke up."

"And you put on weight again."

"That's right."

Here I decided it was time to break through her impassiveness. A brutal attack with a bludgeon is sometimes better therapy than gentle and considerate guidance. "I'll tell you why you can't lose weight. I'll tell you exactly why. . . . You lost weight this summer. That's fine. Then you broke up with this young man. Clear enough. Then you went into a blue funk and put on weight. Now, although you can lose weight—as we see by the record—you nevertheless don't want to now. Why? It's very simple. You don't really want to take the screen test. You know that hardly anyone ever gets a job from a screen test—and if you fail—all of the efforts of you and your family will come to naught. You don't want the screen test or any other test. You're afraid you haven't got what it takes."

She bit her lip, and then began to sob bitterly. I felt a little guilty for having acted cruelly, even though it was correct therapeutic strategy... After she quieted down, she told me that she had always been "shy and sensitive," and had not been happy about the dramatic aspirations that her parents had always cherished for her. I am not familiar with the outcome of this case, for after a tearful session she left, and I never saw her again.

Case 41

The following case is important because it shows us the basis for the correct treatment of obesity. A young woman of 23 was definitely inhibitory and discontented. She had crying spells and acute feelings of inferiority, and had been taking one grain of thyroid daily for the past four years. "Throw away your thyroid pills," I said, "and learn to be honest..." I saw her ten times in all. As she became more excitatory she became happier, and was able to lose the weight she wanted to. A little over a year later she came to see me again. She had been married three months earlier, and had quickly become overweight all over again.

The obvious possibility struck me—her marriage was a failure, but after I discussed it with her I saw that I was wrong. She was quite happily married. What then?

"I shall be stubborn," I said to her. "When people relapse it is because they are neglecting the fundamental principles of excitation. Remember, the more you get off your chest, the more you get off your rear. Are you expressing your honest feelings sufficiently?"

"Yes," she said, "though I haven't much occasion to."

"What do you mean?"

"My husband and I lead a quiet life. We have a few nice friends and we take it easy."

"There's nothing wrong with taking it easy," I said, "but it may be that you are living—shall we say—a sort of happy bovine existence. It's not that you need more physical exercise. You need more verbal and mental exercise. You're neglecting our old friend feeling-talk."

"I think you're right," she said. "Perhaps I've become too much of an old married woman... ." She paused for a moment. "The more I think of it, the more I know you're right. Before I was married, that is just after I'd seen you, I was much more outgoing than I am now, and lately, since I feel happily settled, I must have been taking it easy on the things you told me to do."

For the next week she worked hard at her excitation, and thereafter remained excitatory without any effort. Soon enough she lost her excess weight. It is now four years since I saw her last, and she has remained slender and happy.

The bodily correlates of inhibition are extensive, and what I have said in this chapter applies as well to the treatment (for example) of hypochondria and certain of the asthmas; but I have selected these cases because they are typical and because they illustrate the fallacy of emphasizing the obvious symptom. In the words of Cohen and Nagel, "Theories are... frequently regarded as 'convenient fictions' or as 'unreal.' However, such criticisms overlook the fact that it is just certain selected invariant relations of things in which science is interested, so that many familiar properties of things are necessarily neglected by the sciences." (14)

Inhibitory behavior is the selected invariant relation in all the so-called psychosomatic manifestations. When we treat inhibition, we are getting at its bodily correlates.

CHAPTER 18
MASOCHISM AND SEX

Lorenz, the great orthopedic surgeon, tells of a patient whose spine was shattered by a bullet. (1) The pain was excruciating until he was put into a plaster cast, and after that he eventually made a complete recovery. But then he found himself with a new problem. Because he had become accustomed to sleeping in stone pajamas, as it were, he was no longer able to sleep on a soft bed. Whereupon he slept in his plaster cast, took it with him when he traveled, and was able to sleep soundly thereafter.

This neat little story illustrates the genesis of masochism. We see an association of pleasantness (sleep) with unpleasantness (plaster cast). And we also note that this association has nothing to do with sex. The story is so simple that at first thought masochism seems much too strong a word for it. But let us consider the following.

Pavlov found that if a hungry dog were given an electric shock, and at the same time food was put into his mouth, after enough training sessions, "the electric current, be it ever so strong, becomes the signal, the representative, of food, and a conditioned stimulus for ... a food reaction: the animal turns toward the experimenter, makes licking motions, etc., as before eating. The same is observed if the electric current is supplemented by burning and wounding of the skin." (2)

Erofeeva says of this electric current that if it were applied to a man, it "would make him feel such intense pain that he would instantly withdraw his hand. The dog at first had a defensive reaction, and tried to remove the electrodes with his teeth or by shaking the affected part. He howled with pain. [After sufficient practice] ... the dog went willingly to the laboratory, and allowed himself to be immobilized. ... Before the conditioned reflex was formed, application of the current would stop both pulse and respiration, and then they would become fast and irregular. After the reflex, *there was no change.* " (3) (Italics mine.) Severe pain had become the dog's normal way of life, and his body had become adjusted to it.

Slutskaya performed a similar experiment with young children. (4) She pricked them repeatedly with a needle, until they acquired a conditioned fear of the very sight of it. After that, she pricked them with it and fed them immediately thereafter. In five of the eight children, "the avoiding nocuous conditioned reflexes first weakened, then disappeared, and finally" just the sight of the needle would make the children open their mouths and swallow. They had become conditioned to pain, just as had Pavlov's dog in the experiment with electric shock.

This adjustment to pain is typical of the masochist and is rationalized in different ways:

Mrs. A. says, "You must be tough with me. It helps me more than any other way."

Mr. B. says, "I always feel that something is going to happen to spoil my good feeling."

Mr. C. says, "I am convinced that everything worthwhile comes as a result of hard work."

Mr. D. says, "I don't know. I always like to act like Pagliacci."

Miss E. says, "I often feel that I have to enforce a penalty on myself."

Every inhibitory person is a masochist, because early in life failure and frustration become his habitual lot. He is not comfortable when things are going well, because they are going against the grain. He is always looking for trouble, and if he can't find it he manufactures it. He makes the worst of everything, and his biography is the story of a man's struggle to be a failure. With his behavior determined by his conditioned responses, as we watch him we may well describe his activity as "pain-seeking" or masochistic. Yet it is vulgar oversimplification to say that the masochist "enjoys" pain. His reaction systems simply don't feel complete without it.

Masochism is a useful concept, even though its definition is symptomatic and it is only an aspect of inhibition. As we look at symptoms we find that:

1 Patterns exist which may conveniently be termed "masochistic."
2 These symptom patterns have important implications for our therapeutic technique.

Unfortunately, in current practice masochism is usually dragged in by the heels to apologize for the failures of inefficient and concept-ridden therapies. "They just don't *want* to get well." Marked masochists, as I shall demonstrate, can be cured, and are genuinely delighted when they are cured. Their old habits were equivalent to "not wanting to get well," but those very same habits can be manipulated until they have been annihilated.

Masochistic reactions are a comment on the past. They may seem ridiculous at times, but they are perfectly valid neural connections.

Man is "against himself" and has a "drive to self-destruction" and "an unconscious desire to retain his neurosis" only when he has inadequate reaction patterns. He attracts trouble and constantly repeats his errors because he has acquired no other methods of coping with his environment. When he says, "I don't want to let go of my troubles," what he really means is, "my troubles [habits, that is] won't let go of me—because they are habitual."

It is a fact worth repeating, and a truism of epic proportions, that *habits have a tendency to remain habitual.*

Case 42

The following case illustrates the degree to which masochistic habits can become rationalized. For that matter, all other habit patterns are rationalized just as thoroughly.

A man asked me to hypnotize his mistress, who was waiting outside, and to find out whether she had ever been unfaithful to him. He handed me a small memorandum which he had prepared to facilitate my questioning. It read as follows:

The names of some of her men acquaintances in the business world are: A—, B—, C—, D—, E—, and F—. In an exposure which occurred probably from about the 22nd of March through April 6th or 7th, a pregnancy developed. It was appropriately controlled, but I would like to find out who she believes was responsible, and with whom of the individuals she is intimate. How about G—?

Has she seen H— since she came to Chicago? Has she been intimate with him since her arrival here?

The same for I—. What of J— on her visits to Louisville?

Did K— of—, Inc. put her to bed?

What happened on the afternoon and early evening of March 23rd? (She had a theater appointment with me and she arrived 'high.')

What happened on March 31? She had a date for a birthday party at my home and arrived tight and said during the course of the evening, 'Don't marry me ever. I'm no good.'

What is her relationship with L—? . . . with M—?

Are there any other individuals in whom she is interested and with whom she has been intimate? How about N—?

Has she seen O— since her arrival in Chicago? Been anywhere with him?

It will be noted that he was suspicious about her relations with no less than fifteen men! I needed no diagrams to realize that he was quite masochistic, even if he was intelligent and well-spoken.

I smiled. "I'm sorry. I won't hypnotize her, but I'll be glad to talk to her and form a general impression. I also intend to tell her that I'm seeing her in order to form that impression."

He was insistent that I hypnotize her, but I was adamant. He finally gave in, saying, "Very well. She's defiant, and though she lies constantly about little things, she says that she always told me the truth about the big ones." Which not only made him a masochist, but probably indicated that she was a full-fledged psychopath. He stepped out and she walked in.

She was attractive in a dark, sultry way, and a bit confused. "What's this all about?" she asked me quite correctly.

I told her that I didn't know much more than she did. "But," I said, "Tom seems to want to know if you've remained faithful to him since you've been having your affair."

"Absolutely," she said, eyes blazing. "I'd like you to tell me why is he always so suspicious, anyway?"

Not a bad question, I thought. We had a chat, in which she was completely uncooperative and defensive about what she had been doing lately and about everything else. What she wanted to know was what was wrong with him that he kept hounding her so.

I then had her leave the room, and he came back in again. "Don't you think it possible that you need some treatment yourself?" I said. "Obviously you must be quite masochistic, whether or not she's been unfaithful to you with any or all of these characters." I waved the memorandum at him.

"Oh," he said casually, "I know I'm masochistic. I've been thoroughly psychoanalyzed, and I know all about it."

"Then what good would the truth be?" I said. "Chances are that you'd feel much happier if she'd been unfaithful with all of these men."

"I see what you mean," he said brightly, "but nevertheless I'd just like to know whether or not she *had* intercourse with any of these men." He then recited several instances of her so-called purposeless lying, and of her great ability to fascinate everyone she met.

"She sounds like one of these charming psychopaths to me," I said. "The kind whose word means nothing."

He nodded. He was familiar with the concept of psychopathy. A month before, he amplified, he had had detectives follow her, and they had reported that she had engaged in homosexual relations with a Negro prostitute.

That was enough. "Listen," I said. "Let me set up the questions and let me answer them.

"Question one, has she been unfaithful to you? Answer, I don't know, but if we're to take your estimate of her seriously, and if we can make any deductions from character, the answer is almost certainly 'yes.' " I did not ask him whether he thought homosexual relations with a prostitute to be indicative of infidelity.

"Question two, what's wrong with you?" He made a motion with his hand as if to demur. I continued, "I know you didn't come to see me about yourself, but you might find my observations of interest. You're a bright, masochistic person and you could use some therapy yourself."

"This is all very interesting," he said, "but you still haven't answered the question that brought me to see you. What I want to know is whether or not she's been unfaithful to me . . . etc., etc.

Soon the conversation became somewhat repetitious, and I said, "Look, there isn't much more I can tell you beyond what I have said, so if you're not happy, I'm sorry."

Two weeks later he wrote me a letter expressing his opinion of his session with me. He concluded:

"I appreciate that this note is purposeless, yet I also felt that a candid expression of my lack of satisfaction was in order."

Everybody constantly seeks objective support for emotional reactions. Nevertheless, sometimes they want to change them, and even when masochistic patterns predominate, successful treatment is still possible.

In the treatment of masochism the therapist must take a friendly but authoritarian approach, much as in the treatment of low self-sufficiency. He must be friendly, but fundamentally stern. He must build up the difficulties of treatment. "Maybe I can help you but I'm not sure. This is going to be difficult. You'll have to work hard—very hard." If you assure him that treatment will be easy and rapid, he will crack the whip at you. "I won't let you relax for a moment. Do you understand? …I'm going to lay down the law, and you're going to obey—whether you want to or not." Praise the therapist from whom all punishment flows! Under no circumstances should we ever tell a masochist." These rationalizations feeds his masochism and block his efforts at self-realization.

A case of mine told me how she treated her masochistic husband. 'I tell him that I'm angry at him, and then after a while, I tell him that I'm 'glad' at him. He loves it."

In general, polite sadism is the correct strategy. Just as masochistic dogs respond only when they are burnt and given severe electric shocks, so do masochistic humans respond only to the harsh treatment that they have known before.

Masochism and the low self-sufficiency with which it is usually associated have important political implications. A startling percentage of persons respond more readily to an iron fist than to a velvet glove. And that is the basis of our therapy, except that we take advantage of the masochist's tendency to be a follower in order to browbeat him into being a leader. These techniques will be effective even with the masochists who read this and who know the purpose of every therapeutic move. If a conditioned dog read a biography of Pavlov, he would still salivate when we rang the bell.

We must be sadistic to those who have known no other way of life. We must slap them because they bite the hand that feeds them. It is impossible to insult them, no matter how harsh we may be, and how vociferously they may complain.

They have a conditioned association of goal with barrier. Unless there is a barrier, there is no goal. They keep on coming just because we put them off. You can't fool them! Nothing in life comes on a silver platter. Life is earnest, life is real. If everything in life were easy everybody could do it. It's the sweat and the problems that we get paid for... All very plausible, but nevertheless rationalizations for masochism.

A man of great culture and breeding once came to consult me. The newspapers had made me familiar with his masochistic history and with his elaborate procession of wives who were much inferior to him. We got along quite well, and as he was about to leave, in order to spare him some inconvenience, I presented him with a book I had written. His attitude toward me changed instantly. He turned on me, and became flippant and almost obnoxious. I had patted him on the head, and that had been an error. I know better now.

Here the psychoanalysts possess a great advantage. By keeping their patients at arm's length at all times, and being distant an aloof—perhaps because they have nothing to say—they keep them coming back for more. Familiarity with a stimulus reduces fear, and fear is a technique of control with masochists.

I sometimes wonder if this also explains why the inhibitory are so attracted to psychoanalytic literature. Its boring and tedious analyticism probably keeps them at a distance, and certain that here indeed is a barrier worth overcoming. Besides, the inhibitory find it difficult to feel, and therefore place a great premium on intellectual hair-splitting. They are veritable Medusas, with wriggling cortical angle-worms.

In the treatment of masochism our first concern is disinhibition, regardless of the individual's prior conditionings. Disinhibition reconditions him because he learns new and more rewarding response patterns, and therefore does not repeat the inhibitory response patterns of masochism.

As one of my cases put it, "You have to uncover yourself. Be naked. Give the neighbors a treat. You usually want to do the wrong thing so it's a good idea to spite yourself. I have a complete catalogue covering forty years of what I have done, so I know just what not to do." Notice the perversity inherent in this, but for a masochist it is quite normal and is an excellent therapeutic tactic.

Case 43

Above all, the masochist must be inculcated with a thorough going sadism. That's what he understands best of all. A sadist is a doer. A masochist is done to. For masochists the slogan is, "Sadism now. Down with pity!"

"Right you are," said one of my cases. "There's no point in talking to me about these normal things. I have to step on others just the way they've stepped on me."

He kept some notes of our sessions, and repellent as his observations may seem, we must remember that he was trying to goad himself into normality after a lifetime of kowtowing to everybody, an having no mind of his own.

You're a masochist, and your desire for cure is not sincere until you become more sadistic. You have to be pitiless, aggressive, a selfish—intentionally, and this to everybody. Make sincere feeling the basis of life. Memories dissolve by positive means, that is by applying these rules instantly. Don't try to suppress or forge. Ventilate your feelings through joy in sadism. Beware of pity—of yourself or others. Don't give a damn for anybody particularly your friends! To all men be fully their emotional equals and intellectual superiors. Don't be witty except to satisfy your own feelings. Anything else is only to please people. Emphasize malevolence, to hell with the world! It's a mass of poor conditionings that interferes with your feeling liberation...

Sadism should be vented in grinding down others, and in malevolence, and pitilessness. It yields power, respect, and self-control.

Bad memories, regrets, nursing grudges, imagining persecution, are masochism—deliberately inflicting punishment on yourself to derive pleasure. The antidote to this, of course, is sadism inflicting punishment on others to derive pleasure. At all costs, ventilate your feelings because a vigorous offensive is the best defense against masochism. If you want to be pitiless and sadistic to someone, why worry about the impression you make? Spit on the world and achieve independence! Get down to fundamentals! The world is only a veneer. Get basic. You have seen several examples of how true it is that "malevolence is a lift and tonic to a masochist." Capacity for feeling is man's greatest gift. Your only mission is to build an emotional habit pattern. Use an emotional horsewhip on everyone. You are heading for trouble when you are afraid or reluctant to hurt people.

In forming emotional habits, introspection is not enough. You have got to use physical practice. Neuroticism is internal seething. Whenever you get into trouble, it's because you're ignoring the triumvirate:

1 Selfishness
2 Malignance
3 Sadism
   Permit no exceptions.

Brutal as these precepts may sound, a moment's reflection reminds us that selfishness is more innate in the human beast than self-abnegation; and sadism, rather than masochism, is usually the healthier adaptation to adverse circumstances. The objective of therapy, though, is not the manufacture of sadistic Mr. Hydes. The objective is the disinhibition of frozen, sanctimonious Dr. Jekylls by infusing into them some of the hot blood of the Neanderthal-like Mr. Hydes. A burning alkali neutralizes a burning acid.

Case 44

Mr. Y. is 24 years of age. He is unmarried and is interested only in girls who have a deformity or defect of some sort. A limp, a face disfigured by a birthmark, or excessive fatness is enough to attract him. At side-shows he is much intrigued by women freaks, and particularly by midgets.

"I don't think I'm as normal as the next fellow," he said. "My mother always kept an eye on me. I couldn't go more than five blocks from home. … I was never permitted to develop naturally, and when we moved I couldn't measure up to the other children in the neighborhood. They would play ball, but I couldn't. Mother used to dress me in velvet pants and fancy shirts, and everybody always made fun of me."

There was, however, a lame little girl with whom no one cared to play. Since she was the only child who looked at him favorably, though he did not especially like her, they often played together. He assured me that they had never engaged in any childish sex play. They were playmates from the time he was six until he was nine, when his family moved away again. "I know how it feels to be hurt," he said. "That's probably why I'm always too considerate of people."

That he is an inhibitory personality in need of disinhibition there can be no doubt, but this case presents us with a more important problem. If the young man had had some infantile sex experiences with the lame little girl, but was now unable to recall them, or was simply denying them to me—that is, if his interest in defective women came from a simple bit of early sexual conditioning—would disinhibition help to overcome his masochism? The answer is that even without sexual experiences with the little girl, the young man's masochistic attitude toward women, surely in part, had been associationally created by her. And further, both in childhood and adulthood, his social relations with everybody else were equally masochistic and inhibitory.

Reassociation and disinhibition go hand in hand. To disinhibit is to reassociate, and to facilitate this reassociation we build new linkages into the individual. Various purely associational techniques may be necessary, and I shall describe them, but disinhibiting the total personality is our primary task. We treat sexual problems as primarily difficulties of social, and not sexual, relations; and by and large, the solution to all sexual stimulus substitution problems is to learn to approach the environment for direct and uncomplicated stimuli.

There are those who say that masochism is primarily a sexual phenomenon. By definition it is possible to delimit it accordingly, but as I have shown earlier in this chapter, whenever masochism and sexual disturbances appear together, it is in all probability a special case. Nevertheless, I agree with Gantt that there is a "close biological association of the emotions of pain and sexual excitation." (5) Kinsey presents a list of 43 "apparently non-sexual stimuli which bring erection in younger boys. Included are such situations as "being scared," "anger," and "looking over [the] edge of [a] building... The record suggests that the physiologic mechanism of any emotional response (anger, fright, pain, etc.) may be the basic mechanism of sexual response." (6) Of course, sexual response patterns, at first quite generalized, become thoroughly conditioned.

Among adults, I have never encountered or heard of a case of sexual masochism in which the individual was not also masochistic in his social relations. Some typical statements:

Everybody treats me like dirt.
I have developed wonderful muscles for crosses.
The purifying value of suffering is highly exaggerated. I know.
I put all my troubles together and I call them "duty."
I can always understand and get along with a girl who has troubles.

To return to the young man who played with the lame little girl. "You don't get around enough," I said. "You have to loosen up more," and I explained the idea of disinhibition and how he was to become more expressive with his co-workers, and with his friends and acquaintances. "I want you to practice this with girls too," I said. "All kinds. Good-looking and bad-looking, and crippled and not. Do what I say and we'll see what happens."

I saw him three weeks later, and reviewed his behavior with him. "I'm starting to see what you mean," he said. I developed the principles of excitation in more detail, and I arranged to see him in another month. Then he reported further progress, but I made his next appointment relatively soon in order to keep at him while he was in a malleable mood. I saw him in two weeks, at which time his progress had leveled off. We agreed that he was doing well, and I vaguely told him to get in touch with me in a few months. We had our fifth and last session three months later. He felt more at ease with everybody now, and had lost his interest in girls who were deformed—with one exception. Girls who wore glasses still appealed to him simply because they wore glasses, though he was considerably less fascinated by them than before.

I decided to let it go at that. "If a girl's deformed," I said, "and you like her for her other traits, that's fine. But if your love for her is based upon her deformity, that's another story."

Case 45

In the following case, unlike the previous one, the sufferer is older, the sexual masochism is more intense, and the origin of the behavior deviation is unknown. Nevertheless, disinhibition is still the treatment of choice.

Mr. N. is 50 years of age and looks like a handsome, gray-haired matinee idol. Actually, he is a mechanical engineer who works as an efficiency expert in a large factory. He has always disliked his work, and for the past year has been worrying and fretting constantly and has developed an increased inability to keep his mind on his work. He was divorced 30 years ago, and has never remarried.

He considers himself "the lowest person on earth." He spends his evenings hunting for streetwalkers, and on finding one takes her to his apartment. There he serves coffee, and engages her in conversation in an effort to elicit curious and humiliating details of her sexual encounters. One guest described how she had intercourse with a man in a phone booth, and another told him how she had once accommodated a patron on a vacant lot near a busy thoroughfare. Reports of sexual perversions in which his guests had participated also interested him, yet at no time did he find any of this sexually exciting. He was aware that the streetwalkers, like Scheherazade, realizing what sort of customer he was, may often have invented and embroidered their narratives. Nevertheless, he didn't care, and after listening to their recitals would pay them and see them to the door. He would then go to bed for a night of insomnia and self-recrimination. He would lie awake visualizing what his guests had told him and asking himself over and over again, "What sort of a low, horrible, no-good person am I, anyway? I must be lower than low."

When he came to see me he was in a state of great anxiety. "What shall I do?" he asked. "I can't stop thinking these degrading thoughts.

I can't work, I can't sleep, I can't do anything. I think I'm going crazy."

Many questions come to mind. Is he a sadist because he enjoys stories in which women are humiliated? I think there is something in this, yet I find that he has never pursued women, but that women have always aggressively pursued him. Besides, he has never had any feelings of cruelty toward them. On the contrary, he has always treated them with gentlemanly consideration. "I keep women on a pedestal."

This makes me believe that he feels sexually attracted only to women of inferior social status, but he tells me that neither the streetwalkers nor their stories arouse him sexually. He also disclaims any fear of disease. "It's something else," he says. "I just don't know what."

Does he seek, quite unwittingly, in the stories of his guests, a sexual pattern that through some obscure conditioning has the power to excite him? Perhaps, but not one of the stories he has heard has ever excited him the least bit. Is he really a homosexual at heart? Not at all. In his fifty years of life, he says, he has had no homosexual hankerings or activity. Is he lonely, and just likes company? He smiles for the first time. "No. I have friends who, if I may say so, are very fine people... I can't understand why I do things like this."

"Tell me about your divorce," I said. "Who divorced whom?"

"She divorced me. She didn't like women chasing me all the time, and she saw I was just bored with her. I didn't care one way or the other."

Before coming to see me he had had half a dozen sessions with a psychoanalyst. "He asked me to tell him my dreams," he said, "but I told him I dreamt only when I ate something that disagreed with me."

I took a firm approach. "Your problem has nothing to do with sex. You're not a pervert, if that's what you mean. You have a great deal wrong with you, but it's not sexual at all. It's just that you're a Milquetoast. People walk all over you. You've been sailing under false colors. Your good looks get you by, but they're just a front. You're really very shy, and are always worried about the other fellow. Isn't that true?"

"Yes," he said, "that's me, all right, but why do I act the way I do?"

"You feel inferior to men and to women," I said, "to the whole human race. And when you don't have the guts to sleep with any of the women you pick up, the more they tear themselves down, the more you enjoy it. In fact, you go out in the street looking for them, don't you? You pursue them—even though you know women who'd be glad to go to bed with you. What you're doing is a twisted method of punishing yourself."

He nodded.

I worked with him as if his problem were solely the well-bred neurosis. When he criticized people he supervised, which he had to do very often, I told him to quit wrapping each bit of criticism in an elaborate coat of candy. "Serve it straight," I said. "Talk man to man, and forget the inhibitory sugar coating. When you have some honest praise, give it. Don't walk around the factory giving praise to people the way a mechanic squirts grease from a grease gun. People know the difference, and the efficiency expert winning-friends-and-influencing-people approach is quite nauseating. As for women—build up your aggression. Become a living, vital, male animal, not a good-looking fraud who can turn on the charm. You're the perfect bachelor. A smile, a kind word, and no involvement."

At our eighth and last session, in talking about his sexual masochism, he said, "You know, when I think of it now, it shocks me." It is four years since I have seen him. At the present writing, he is interested only in healthy and uncomplicated sex. He still dislikes his work, but somewhat less so. Life has become easier. "I'm fine," he said. "Thank you. Fine. Don't worry about me. You can write me down as cured."

Many well-bred masochists are tremendously attracted sexually to women of inferior social or intellectual status. At times it is because their early sexual experiences were on this level, but often it is because they are inhibitory with women of equal status, even when these women are as attractive and even more readily sexually available. And after the scion marries the waitress, and his sexual ardor fades, it is with a sense of horror that he asks himself, "What did I ever see in her, anyway?" Love at first sight is often followed by incompatibility at second sight.

Fetishism, i.e., the erotic attachment to a handkerchief, a glove, or some other object, is also a result of association. Through conditioning, the fetish becomes an objective in itself.

L. W. Max, in treating a case of homosexuality, found that "the homosexual behavior usually [followed a] fetishistic stimulus." (7) Under laboratory conditions, the stimulus (its precise nature is not mentioned in the published report) was presented in conjunction with extremely severe electric shocks. "Though the subject reported some backsliding, the 'desensitizing' effect over a three months period was cumulative. Four months after cessation of the experiment he wrote, 'That terrible neurosis has lost its battle, not completely but 95% of the way.' " Max is aware of the limitations of this technique, but it surely merits further experimentation.

Guthrie sums it up. "In terms of a systematic associationalism," he writes, "the requisite for detaching a stimulus from an undesirable response is only that the stimulus be presented and, by one means or another, the response be prevented." (8) This, I must say, with its ramifications, is the cardinal technique of psychotherapy.

I treated a peeping Tom, and readily enough found that as a boy he had helped his widowed mother operate a boarding house and that his first knowledge of sex came from looking through keyholes and transoms.

And in cases of gerontophilia (love for much older persons) we will always find childhood associativities with fathers, mothers, and uncles that explain the pattern. But our findings will avail us little. Disinhibition, and its attendant environmental expansion, will set the stage for the reconditioning that heals.

Case 46

This applies even to cases as complicated as that of Mr. H., who sits dejectedly before me, and tells me that the only thing that interests him about women is drinking their urine. "I often brood about this," he says. "Am I a pervert, am I going crazy, or what? . . ."

He is a stocky young man of thirty with a psychiatric discharge from the Army, and a long record of psychiatric treatment. I ask him whether he gets an orgasm from drinking urine. "Almost," he says, "but not quite." He further explains that sexual intercourse without it is not completely satisfying.

An associativity of some sort is certainly involved, perhaps several steps removed. Sexual stimulus A may have been associated with stimulus B, and B in turn with C, and C finally with urine. In Pavlovian terms, this is a higher-order, or "secondary conditioned reflex." (9)

Experimentally, this may be illustrated as follows. The hungry dog naturally salivates to food. This salivation was associated by Frolov with the ticking of a metronome, until the metronome alone elicited salivation. Then the metronome was linked to the "appearance of a black square in the dog's line of vision." (10) After a while, the black square, though it had never been presented with food, acquired the ability to elicit salivation. We may restate the principle of higher-order conditioning by saying that under appropriate circumstances things associated with the same things become associated with each other.

After analyzing this and other related experiments, Hull (11) says, "In normal human organisms it would appear . . . that there is practically no limit to the degree to which higher-order conditioning may be carried under suitable conditions." This, I suggest, explains the degeneration and transformation that habits undergo in time, and the extraordinary patterns often encountered in therapy.

But back to the young man who drank urine. "I think of the other person constantly," he says. "I always feel I must say something interesting. ... I'm the only boy among four sisters. Much as my mother tries to keep me tied to her apron strings, I really don't feel that I have any degree of blood relationship with the family..."

"What was the first time you recall drinking urine?" I asked. He told me that when he had been eight years old a girl cousin, aged ten, had presented him with a glassful and said, "Come on, drink it!"

I stopped him. "And at that moment you felt very inferior to her, and thought you simply had to obey, otherwise she'd be angry. She was the boss and you had to behave. Isn't that the way you felt?"

"Yes," he said, with surprise. "How could you tell? That was just the way I felt. She was the boss and I had to obey."

Perhaps he was simply being agreeable to me, I thought. I spoke casually, taking a logical chance, "Would you rather have intercourse with your mother or with one of your sisters?"

He was horrified. "That's a disgusting thing to ask. Why do you say that?"

"I guessed right," I thought to myself. "You're only human," I said aloud, "and if you have certain early emotional experiences, they leave certain marks on you."

"I had emotional experiences, all right," he said, "but they didn't leave those marks."

On the next day, at his second session, he told me that he had stayed up most of the night and written a long report for me. I had not asked him to do so, but his extensive psychiatric experience had guided him. His report included such significant material as:

I will see an ad in the paper saying "Eat where the stars eat", and I don't go because I'm afraid I will be embarrassed if I do.

Followed a girl in the railroad station for about 45 minutes because she had such nice looking legs. [I had him develop this thought, and I soon found he had a clear case of leg fetishism.]

I was eating in a restaurant and there was an exquisite girl sitting near me. She said something to another girl about not talking to strangers. Under normal circumstances I might have engaged her in conversation, but at the sound of the word "strangers" fear crept up in me. I do not know just what I was afraid of unless I was afraid I would blurt out confidences that I had been talking to you about.

Yes. I think I would like to have intercourse with my youngest sister, at least more so than my mother or other sisters. You were right. I don't know how you guessed it. [I had simply assumed that a boy with four sisters might well have been sexually conditioned by them.]

Yes. I liked the taste of that Panamanian whore's urine. I remember the taste distinctly. It was tangy and sexually stimulating, but at the same time the idea of it was revolting to my sense of morals.

At age ten he had masturbated a dog and himself simultaneously. At age twelve he had kissed the hired girl in the pantry. "I'm going to tell your mother," she said, but she never did. She left his family shortly thereafter. Three years later she had a baby. He went around sick for several weeks believing that he had fathered the child.

His report continued:

I feel that my subconscious wells up to meet my conscious shows in my face. For instance, if I am sitting in a theatre lobby thinking of going someplace to eat, the feeling comes to me that when I go to the restaurant and ask for food the pent-up emotions will show in the tone of my voice, or in my face, or the words I use, or the actions I go through after I get the food. In other words, I am afraid of getting feeling of my soul being on parade.

He has dreams of his father:

Vague dreams about gangsters shooting desperately. I can't identify any of the actors, but it seems as if gangsters fool the police and decoyed me away from the job of protection in order for them to carry out some crime. When I returned under my own power I said, "This father of mine called me crooked and that's the man I want."

Here we see that he wants to murder his father, and earlier we saw that he wanted to sleep with his mother—a perfect Oedipus complex to any psychoanalyst and even to me. Shall we say that every boy with a cruel father and an over-protective mother develops an Oedipus complex? Yes, if we feel mythological. Shall we say, with the psychoanalysts, that *every boy and girl without a single exception,* goes through an Oedipus stage? Yes—if we reject truth and stretch out words like molasses taffy.

I treated him as a problem in shyness, and in two months and fifteen sessions the young man was able to look people in the eye and to feel at case with them. His approach to women became more direct, and his sexual masochism disappeared completely. "I still stare at women," he said, "but the interest is academic and not personal."

I saw him two months after our last session. He was confident and buoyant, and successful at gainful employment. He told me, with a smile, that all of his friends had commented on the change in him. "I just told them that I had decided to get a grip on myself."

I have not heard from him for some years. Shall we chalk him up as a cure? From my point of view he was just a thoroughly inhibitory young man who had picked up some logical and disturbing sexual conditionings. When he was disinhibited, and his environment and his sexual outlets were broadened, and when he felt happier and was more productive, and began to love the father he had hated—when all this was accomplished, I assumed that the therapy had been worthwhile.

Though male erectility is an innate response, the entire question of potency soon becomes complicated by conditioned restrictions. A man spent his wedding night at an Egyptian hotel. He had married his wife for her money, and was sexually uninterested in her. He suggested that she prepare for bed first, and she went to the bathroom down the hall. After she came back, he sallied forth, not to the bathroom—but to his Eurasian mistress, for whom he had reserved a room on the same floor. With her, he told me, he "had the virility of a lion." After a few minutes with his mistress he was thoroughly aroused, whereupon he quickly ran back to his wife, who was much flattered by his ardor.

When an important part of the desired sexual stimulus pattern is, say, plumpness in a woman, or buck teeth—a man may find it easily enough. But what if satisfactory potency depends on a half-witted sister who is now committed in an institution? Or what if it necessitates a different woman every few months—a luxury he cannot afford? Or what if early conditioning surrounds sex with such shame that the entire hierarchy of sexual responses is thoroughly confused and inhibited?

The result is usually impotence. It ranges from lack of erectility, to partial erectility, or premature ejaculation. It means unhappiness for the man and frustration for the woman.

In these cases I am opposed to simple suggestive therapy, because even though it is sometimes helpful, it does nothing to get at the roots. In conjunction with disinhibition, though, hypnosis is something else again.

It is disinhibition that is the fundamental therapy for impotence. It broadens the man's sexual environment, and frees his potency from the limits of its old conditioned requirements. At times, these old conditioned requirements remain, but the individual finds that he is also potent under a multitude of other circumstances that were once fatal to sexual fulfillment.

To put it in rough laboratory terms, the dog now salivates to a bell, and to a green light, and to the sound of bubbling water—besides to the red light (the half-witted sister) to which he was once limited. A little inhibitory conditioning of the man against sexual responsiveness to his sister, and our task is complete.

At times, when we broaden the sexual response patterns, we will find that the old limited conditionings disappear simultaneously. If they remain, they are eliminated by teaching the subject how to direct his mental imagery. More specifically, he is taught how to blend inhibitory images with recollections of actual (or even imaginary) sex experiences. When sexual behavior is otherwise satisfactory, such sexual inhibition is distinctly beneficial.

Some men use imagery to excite themselves into potency. They may have to imagine their sex partners as somebody else, they may first have to read the adventures of Frank Harris and Fanny Hill, or they may have to go through such play-acting as making believe that they are drunken sailors and their sex partners are dissolute whores. All these techniques are comments on the conditioned sexuality of the individual, and respond to general disinhibition and specific reconditioning.

Disturbed sexual activity always involves excessive inhibition in personal relations, such causes as fatigue, locomotor ataxia, and multiple sclerosis excluded. To become introspective about most bodily acts, whether it be swallowing food at table, or sustaining an erection in bed, is to spoil them. Primitive personalities who live only for the moment do not suffer from these difficulties.

Here are some extracts from a report written by a man whom I successfully treated for impotence.

I have really been conditioned! Damn! To worship women–hands off–bow down at a distance—Women can't do wrong—remember your mother—you know the slop I mean:
  (a) Always treat any woman as you would your own sister or your mother. Put her up on a shrine and burn incense.
  (b) Sex is unclean and is forgiven only if indulged in to procreate a blessed, blessed event.
  (c) Masturbation makes little boys go crazy and makes the brain turn to water. The penis was made to urinate through exclusively-unless you want a disease.

(d) Don't pay any attention to girls till you are all ready to marry. (Then grab the first bitch you see?) In the meantime desire them from a distance with burning lust in your eye till everybody thinks you're queer. Then masturbate regularly because you enjoy it even if you do lose sleep wondering what the first signs of that certain insanity will be. Get so sex conscious you're silly in the presence of females..

(e) When everybody makes fun of you don't fight. You know, the meek inherit the earth. Be a Mr. Milquetoast in anything rather than stick up for your rights.

(f) "I'll tell you, son, you will have to work and suffer to become a worthy Christian."

(g) When you are tempted by any earthly, worldly, fleshly desires— just lecture at the top of your lungs against such evils and you will come out all right. The world will admire you for it.

The misguided and the well-meaning have tried to talk people out of their bodies for centuries. It can't be done.

Sometimes impotence seems to involve only simple association. Meignant (12) presents the case of Mr. R., aged 35, who had become impotent six months earlier. All medical assistance had been in vain, but significantly he remained potent with his wife in hotel rooms and whenever they traveled. Six months earlier they had moved to a new apartment. Mr. R. thought there was something familiar about the bedroom, but he couldn't decide what. Meignant, however, found that prior to his marriage Mr. R. had been caught in bed with a woman by a third person who suddenly walked in and found them *in flagrante delicto*. It seems that the pattern of the wallpaper in the bedroom of the new apartment was almost identical with that of the bedroom in which he had been discovered. Mr. R. had the bedroom of the new apartment redecorated, and his potency became normal.

It is my impression, from the published study, that although the similarity in wallpapers was the immediate cause of Mr. R.'s impotence, Meignant did much to help his patient work off his guilt feelings. If this be the case, it would make repapering the bedroom only part of the therapy. In general, the cases of impotence with a good prognosis are those who allow us to approach their problem as one of social relations. At all times, and in all problems, the balky ones who try (however obliquely) to guide the therapy will have a poor prognosis.

The female equivalent of impotence is frigidity. It includes everything from an inability to achieve an orgasm to a complete absence of genital excitement. It is inhibition of all or part of the response patterns attendant to sexual stimulation. The woman's sexual conditioning has considerably greater effect on her orgasm capacity than the man's sexual technique, but once we establish that the male's technique and the woman's anatomy are not at fault, frigidity is best treated like its brother, impotence, by disinhibition and associational reconditioning.

Pavlov's differentiation between internal and external inhibition is helpful in considering the causes of all psychological disturbances. Here I shall confine myself to their application in the treatment of frigidity.

By *external inhibition* Pavlov meant that a conditioned response was diminished by some outside stimulus acting as a distraction. This is illustrated by the dog in whom conditioned salivation diminished when "some quick change in illumination would occur, the sun suddenly going behind a cloud [and darkening the experimental room]." (13)

On the human plane, we may speak of *external inhibition* in referring to the woman who became frigid because her attempts at sexual intercourse were repeatedly interrupted by such distractions as "a knock at the door, the arrival of a third person, [or] the ringing of a telephone." (14)

Much more important therapeutically is *internal inhibition*.[1] *This* refers to situations in which, in Pavlov's words, "the positive conditioned stimulus itself becomes, under definite conditions, negative or inhibitory. . . . Conditions favouring the development of conditioned reflexes of the negative or inhibitory type are of frequent occurrence ..."(15)

One form that internal inhibition can take is experimental extinction. In experiments with dogs meat is associated with the ticking of a metronome until the metronome alone elicits salivation. Then the metronome is presented repeatedly without meat. The salivation diminishes progressively and then ceases completely. In Pavlov's words, "the positive conditioned stimulus is temporarily transformed into a negative or inhibitory one by the simple method of repeating it several times in succession without reinforcement." (16)

We may consider experimental extinction to be exemplified by the woman who becomes frigid because her husband has difficulties with potency. Repeatedly, she is sexually excited, and repeatedly she is frustrated. Extinction of sexual response—frigidity—is the result.

---

[1] Pavlov finally considered external inhibition as being the same in nature as internal inhibition.

The term inhibition of delay is almost self-explanatory. When there is too much of a delay between sexual stimulation and satisfaction, sexual responses become inhibited. The rate at which men and women become sexually aroused is quite different. Men are quickly excited and quickly satisfied. Women are slowly excited and slowly satisfied.

Perhaps the most important type of internal inhibition is conditioned inhibition. Our usage of the term is much looser and broader than Pavlov's, who says that, "this form of inhibition might more appropriately have been termed 'differential inhibition.' "(17)

When Mrs. X. receives sexual stimulation from Mr. X., her responses are inhibited. When Mr. Y. (who unlike Mr. X. does not include stimuli reminiscent of her father) arouses her, Mrs. X. has intense orgasms. This illustrates conditioned inhibition. Mrs. X. has sexual reaction patterns that function perfectly as long as certain conditioned inhibitory stimuli are absent.

Strictly speaking, we would call it *differential inhibition* if Mrs. X. through constant masturbation (i.e., reinforcement) conditioned herself to prefer digital manipulation to sexual intercourse. Then sexual intercourse acts as an inhibitor of orgasms. Through satisfying repetition [reinforcement] one stimulus elicits conditioned responses. Through non-reinforcement another stimulus inhibits them. It is differential inhibition, stemming from personal experiences, that underlies the elaborate Freudian congeries of fixations, complexes, and fetishes.

"Inhibitory conditioned reflexes," says Pavlov, "can, however, also be obtained by a totally different procedure. If an inhibitory stimulus is applied simultaneously and repeatedly for short periods of time together with some neutral stimulus the latter also develops an inhibitory function of its own." (18)

It is this *higher-order conditioning,* and the juxtaposition of unfortunate circumstances, that account for symptoms encountered in psychotherapy.

Many women deceive their husbands into believing that they have orgasms. This practice is more prevalent than might be believed, for some studies have reported that from 33 (19, 20) to 40 (21) per cent of women never attain an orgasm.

It has been contended that once a woman learns to achieve an orgasm, all of her psychological problems are automatically solved. It is actually the converse that is true—when a woman is appropriately reconditioned, then is able to achieve an orgasm—but put this way it is no longer an attractive hypothesis to the sexually bewildered. As for the psychoanalysts, who say that frigidity is caused by a woman's desire to take revenge on men for the woman's lack of a penis—to mention it is to dispose of it...

I would say, especially if the woman has ever had orgasms in the past, that with patience and cooperation from her sexual partner, frigidity can usually be cured. Frequently, however, cooperation is one-sided because one sexual partner really doesn't care for the other. And when they both happen to care for each other, they don't feel that changes in their sexual relations are a result of "mental treatment." A little therapeutic skill, though, can take us over this obstacle easily enough.

Case 47

Mrs. J. is in her late twenties and looks like an attractive kewpie doll. She had an active sex life before she was married, and after marriage had no difficulties in attaining an orgasm. But after four years of marriage her husband ran into business difficulties and his potency became distinctly irregular. Soon she had no orgasms, even when his potency was satisfactory, a perfect example of Pavlovian experimental extinction.

Somewhat prior to this, while her husband's potency was still satisfactory, he began to get on her nerves, though, as she said, "I never let him know it." She started to contrast him with other men, and decided that beneath his pose of strength he was simply an innocuous, ineffective, well-meaning, good man, like millions of others—no better and no worse—but not good enough for her.

She became involved with another man, for the first time after her marriage, and with him she had orgasms repeatedly. Soon, though the man remained sexually attractive, her orgasms began to diminish in frequency and intensity. This disturbed her, so she went to a psychoanalyst. After a half year of analysis she protested that she was still not having any orgasms. The analyst advised her to find another lover and to see what would happen. It was her previous experience all over again. She started off with orgasms, and they soon disappeared. She gave up her analyst, continued seeing her new lover, and came to see me.

My first objective was her social relations. She was much too politely well-bred and tense. I explained the techniques of disinhibition, and how she was to express more of her resentments and less of her hypocritical compliments. As far as I was concerned, hers was simply the well-bred neurosis. "You know," I said, "you have been brought up to be so disgustingly well-poised that I'm surprised that you don't take a lorgnette with you when you go to bed." This struck her fancy.

In addition, by the methods I have explained earlier, I taught her how to relax by self-suggestion.

"Now," I said to her after a few sessions, "you can relax much more, and your emotional responses have become much freer. The time has come for you to imagine former orgasms with your friend when you next have intercourse with him. In other words, mix actual sex with your friend with daydreams of past sex with him."

On her first attempt with her lover she failed to achieve an orgasm. On her second try, at another time, she had a full orgasm, and what is more, it was more intense and satisfactory than any she had ever experienced before in her entire sexual history. This meant that the therapy had thoroughly freed her entire orgasmic capacity, which happens when anything happens at all.

After several weeks went by, and her orgasms with her lover remained stable at this intense and thoroughly satisfactory level, I spoke to her as follows,

"Your husband's potency is quite satisfactory, even though you don't respond to it. Isn't that right?"

"Right," she said. "Sex with my husband is the same thing as dishwashing on the maid's night out, or any other job."

"Now we have to take one more step," I said. "This time I want you to blend actual sex with your husband with imagined intense orgasms with your friend. It's the same technique you used before, only applied to your husband."

On her first attempt with her husband she had only a slight orgasm, but thereafter they were full and intense. This convinced her that she was now in "good mental and physical condition" and not "one of those awful neurotics," so she divorced her husband and with the substantial alimony she receives and an occasional sexual affair, she assures me she is quite happy.

Blending past sexual experiences with present ones is a delicate technique, and its use in therapy must be carefully timed and managed if it is not to become a form of mental masturbation. I have even been able with this method, in conjunction with disinhibition, to recondition a woman who could only achieve an orgasm when she imagined herself being raped at an orgy.

Antithetical as they may seem, nymphomania and frigidity almost always go together, and are treated similarly. Even the few exceptions who have healthy orgasms are best treated as problems in social disinhibition and sexual reconditioning. Such cases as I have encountered have all been affection starved, and sex to them has become a conditioned method of controlling their environment. "I remember... how surprised I was to find that with sex I could get a man to do anything I wanted." Excitatory methods of social manipulation and some sexual reconditioning are all that is needed to cure nymphomania. Strong masochistic trends are always present an must be treated accordingly.

The connection of sadism with masochism has been frequently noted in the literature. Although I agree that they are often found together, I am singularly unimpressed with the diffuse explanations that are usually given. I shall venture an explanation of the relationship that I hope will be simple and accurate...

The masochistic individual has learned to thrive on pain. He is an inhibitory personality with inadequate reaction systems for coping with his environment. As we know, some of the inhibitory, when they have been goaded and prodded sufficiently, turn on their environments like foxes snapping at the dog pack that has cornered them. On the human level this takes the form of sadism, and it is sometimes mistaken for excitation. The excitatory personality is at peace with the world, and the sado-masochist is in a state of chronic irritation at all and sundry. He thinks to himself, "If you want it, you'll have to work hard for it, my friend." The excitatory personality has an attitude of give and take.

When it comes to therapy, the best approach is to treat the sadist as a masochist. That permits us to beat him into malleability. For that matter, we might as well treat him for anxiety, because we will always find him to be anxious and confused.

Many of these sado-masochists are profoundly certain that they have been entrusted with a staggeringly important revelation for the world. As a famous one put it, "Most people consider me a messianic mess." To help such an individual, we forget he is a messiah, and treat him as a masochistic mess. The messianic component originates much like the desire for acting. We start out with an inhibitory individual who is thoroughly wrapped up in himself. He wants to communicate thoughts which he considers important, but he cannot communicate them enough to give him release. He runs around like a chicken with an egg stuck in its cloaca. He has a message for the world, but it pays him no heed. He loathes people in particular, but professes a great love for humanity in general.

Greatest of all is his love for himself, which makes him, according to the Freudians, a narcissist and unamenable to psychoanalysis. By definition narcism is self-love, and self-love is a very obvious affliction of the inhibitory whose world is centered in themselves. When they are made more excitatory and their environment is broadened their narcism fades. The Freudians who bemoan their failure with the "narcissistic neuroses" are really bemoaning the inadequacy of their therapeutic techniques.

We might wonder what happens when a thoroughgoing narcissist marries a fervent admirer or when a masochist marries a sadist. Do they live happily together ever after?

They do not. The narcissist and the excessively humble, the sadist and the masochist-all are thoroughly unhappy individuals who are unable to get along with each other for any extended period of time.

Most women have what may best be termed normal feminine masochism. They like their men to dominate them—not necessarily with a bull-whip, but in a pleasanter and more subdued sort of way. Whether this feminine masochism originates in cultural conditioning, or from brute differences between the sexes, does not concern us here. My guess is that historically speaking, brute differences were primary, and cultural patterns and differences in individual experiences sanctified them. In any event, normal feminine masochism must be reckoned with as a therapeutic reality.

I am not referring to the masochism of the woman who said to me, "You know, I have a fondness for coarse men," or the one who told me that her sexual excitement increased tremendously when her husband said, during sexual intercourse, "I don't love you, but you're handier than [masturbating]." I mean the warning against masochism in the proverb, "Faint heart never won fair lady." The inhibitory male never won anything else either, and often loves his wife in a way she doesn't want to be loved.

Every woman knows that men are emotional fools, but few men realize that every woman knows this. I think it is more difficult to be a good wife than a good husband, because men expect everything from their wives, and women expect little from their husbands.

In marriage, people who have never been able to get along with others before they were married, find that they have to get along with each other. And when these persons who know nothing of social relations get involved in sexual behavior involving mutually obscure conditionings, we can only expect great difficulties in adjustment.

And to reverse the picture, if they are sexually well-adjusted, in time they may suffer from spasmodic negative adaptation. The constant repetition of the sexually stimulating situation reduces its effectiveness. They become "adapted" to it. This need be no cause for alarm. A vacation from each other and some variations in their sexual technique will restore the responses to their original level.

Modern sex education is to be preferred to ignorance, but familiarity with sexual stimuli, however acquired, reduces the sexually exciting power of the bona fide stimuli and can contribute to an elaborate series of unsatisfying sexual relationships. Good sexual conditioning requires a delicate balance between knowledge and mystery.

CHAPTER 19
THE PSYCHOPATHIC PERSONALITY

Come, listen, my men, while I tell you again
The five unmistakable marks
By which you may know, wheresoever you go,
The warranted genuine Snarks.

Lewis Carroll

The distinguishing characteristics of snarks include a meager and hollow taste, a habit of getting up late, and slowness in taking a jest. Not much more enlightening are the earmarks of the psychopathic personality. Usually, by a psychopathic personality, we mean a cold, callous, completely egocentric person, who would as soon cut your throat as say "good morning." Beneath his facade, the psychopath is: emotionally hard, completely egocentric, sensitive (in the sense of bruising easily), insincere, emotionally shallow, conscienceless, thankless, fickle, unreliable, disloyal, treacherous, antisocial, cynical, hostile, infantile, daydreaming, self-deceiving, pity-seeking, and pitiless.

This is not a pretty picture, and sure enough, in social relations the psychopath will usually mask his egocentricity with fraudulent solicitude, and his thanklessness with protestations of gratitude. Nevertheless, a study of his biography will invariably show all of the traits I have enumerated above, scattered though they may be among data that are only tangential to the diagnosis.

The term "psychopath" is often an ambiguous and misleading sort of label, and consequently, it would seem not commensurate with the simplest scientific principles. Yet in practice, those of us who come in contact with it in the courts, in psychotherapy, or in marriage, know that though its definition may be vague and symptomatic, it is a tangible and maddening reality when we have to cope with it. We may find it where it does not exist, we may overlook it where it is carefully hidden, and we may be perplexed by a borderline case—but it is a perfectly valid clinical entity nevertheless. The term "psychopath" is a psychological necessity. If it did not exist we would have had to invent it. In the cases which follow, I have italicized the particularly psychopathic features for emphasis.

Case 48

Johnny S. has just been expelled from university. At a meeting in chapel, foregathered to unveil the portrait of a banker who left the college ten million dollars, after much ceremony and oratory the flags covering the painting are pulled aside. *There, in the frame, is the picture of a beautiful movie actress with a well-inflated bosom.*

Johnny smiles proudly as he tells me the story, and I too find it amusing. "Why did you do it?" I asked.

"Oh, they were a bunch of stuffed shirts, and I thought I'd teach them a lesson."

Johnny had once almost been expelled from another college. It was something about having women sleep over in his rooms, but his uncle was a member of the board of trustees and Johnny was permitted to resign because of poor health.

Johnny is 20 years of age. Next year he gets the first million of the five million his grandfather left in trust to him. He is a handsome and clean cut young man, dressed like a fashion plate and with a neatly knotted silk tie. At college, when he felt in the mood, he earned excellent grades. He plays a fine game of polo, and was "practically born in the stirrups." He goes to the race track whenever he can, and bets with a lavish hand. There he is usually accompanied by the girl he is currently wooing. He has two heiresses on his string at present. Johnny gives a slow ingratiating smile. *"The six million dollar one is more fun than the twenty million dollar one. I don't suppose there's really much difference between six million and twenty million.*" I believe him when he says that either of the girls would marry him if he proposed. Says Johnny of his relationships with people, "Once I have the upper hand, they're goners."

Johnny is the oldest of three children. He has two younger sisters. His parents are divorced and both have since remarried. *Last year Johnny sent his stepmother and stepfather several anonymous letters telling them of highly plausible, and completely fictitious, sexual escapades of their respective mates— that is, of his parents.* At camp one summer, when Johnny was fifteen, he found out that one of the saddle horses had been a trained steeplechaser. Each evening in the early twilight, Johnny would sneak the horse from the stable and go *jumping. His obstacle course was a neighboring cemetery, and the tombstones were the hurdles. One tombstone, Johnny told me, was really difficult, and his horse would sometimes balk at it.*

In all this, *Johnny does not manifest the slightest feeling of guilt, remorse, or embarrassment.* Life is so very interesting, and people are such fools. It's a pity not to exploit them.

Kahn would call Johnny a psychopath of the "active autist and egocentric variety." (1) Henderson would diagnose him as a psychopath of the 'predominantly aggressive" type, (2) and Cleckley would call him a "partial-psychopath." (3) I would call him just a "psychopath."

Case 49

Mr. A. In prison because of a $450,000 swindle. Married a prostitute with whom all his friends, acquaintances, and business associates had had relations. A man of considerable charm and glibness. Remains optimistic after three years in prison with seventeen more to go. It is not a question of good adjustment. He simply does not understand the predicament he's in.

Case 50

Mr. B. Has cheated two consecutive business partners out of their fortunes. Quite intelligent and untutored. After he impregnated a secretary he had hired two weeks earlier, *her mother came to complain but remained to succumb, and he had sexual relations with both mother and daughter for six months.* Constantly chattering away with a cynical, weird humor. "Just watch me," he says. "Why go to a nuthouse?" His wife once said of him, apropos of the great distress his satire had caused her brother, *"He likes to destroy everyone he meets."*

Case 51

Mr. C. An actor, married and divorced four times. *He once simultaneously had three women pregnant by him.* He laughs. *"A fourth one had the decency to fall down some stairs and miscarry."* Once, after weeks of maneuvers, he was about to go to bed with a movie star, but a waitress with whom he had had sexual relations some months earlier telephoned him at the star's bedside. *On talking to her he immediately left the star to rejoin the waitress.* Comes of good family, and considers it important to have as many children as possible so that his valuable germ plasm will not die out.

Case 52

Miss D. Bright, attractive. Has ruined three men. One committed suicide. Another, who was a lawyer, has become a salesman and drifts from job to job. The third was fired from his position as head of a college department and became an alcoholic. Is quite promiscuous, but really nonsexual. When her fourth husband was about to marry her, her third ex-husband hobbled up to him in a railroad station and said, "Believe me, I have nothing to gain by this, but don't marry her! She'll ruin you." But this only convinced number four that his predecessor was jealous and wanted to remarry her himself. He found out better.

Her father adores her. Each time he visits the city in which she lives, he has dinner with her at his hotel apartment. She always leaves at about eleven o'clock, telling him that she is going home. *Instead, she goes upstairs to another part of the hotel to the room of her present paramour. This arrangement, she feels, is convenient, because her father comes to town rather often.*

Case 53

Mr. E. When he was a professor at a women's college, he seduced many of his students, often under incredible circumstances. Says he, "I really hate dirty minds, but somehow I think I have one myself." Has many unpaid loans, all of which he could repay if he wanted to. *He talks his way into the highest scientific and academic circles, and then does something completely stupid and is thrown out of his job.* But soon enough, because of his great ability, he gets another one. Says he, "I believe that I have never known love. I am ashamed of my situation and of many things I have done in my life, and yet I believe I will do them again."

Add to these cases Rasputin, Kreuger, Hitler, and Aaron Burr. And Ponzi and Dr. Cook. And in literature, Becky Sharp, Mephistopheles,

Scarlett O'Hara, and Matt Saxon. And on another level, the man who murders someone for two dollars and then goes home to sleep, the fascinating scoundrels, the confidence men, the weird black sheep, and many (not all) prostitutes—in general, the persons who in the 1800s were called "moral imbeciles." These are the psychopathic personalities, the ones with the weird egocentricity and the stones in their hearts. It is of no relevance to our diagnosis whether the person in question is aimless and given to purposeless folly, or practical and enterprising, or exhibitionistic, boastful, polite, flattering, affable, intelligent, verbally facile, shrewd, acquisitive, dishonest, criminal, sarcastic, alcoholic, suicidal, narcissistic, masochistic, or sadistic. These terms may or may not apply. They are different lacquers on the hard-cored callous egocentricity that underlies the diagnosis of psychopathy.

To call someone a psychopath usually implies that he is completely unamenable to therapy, when actually, with a little effort, he can often be helped. To which Cleckley has replied in essence: if he's amenable to treatment, he's not a psychopath. My definition refers to a carefully delimited group of intelligent, emotionally shallow, self-defeating personalities. In our present stage of knowledge it, would be best to keep them confined in mental institutions.

Without doubt, this is the best course to take with a great number of psychopaths.

Karpman also believes in "indefinite confinement" for this group. (4) He calls them the primary psychopaths... no matter how hard and how deep one studies [such a] case it is quite impossible to find any specific psychogenesis for his behaiour. He is what he is and he does what he does by reason of what he always was and always did. The reaction is so deeply ingrained in him that it seems [my italics] "*as if it had been with him from birth.*" Consequently, this behavior "is in all probability not the result of any deep-seated conditionings and conflicts." (Preu neatly points out the two-edged character of the "evidence or hereditary predisposition to psychopathic development."(5) every argument in favor of it serves just as well as an argument against it.)

In connection with his theory of primary (or non-environmentally caused) psychopathy, Karman has published two illustrative case histories. It seems to me that both of these cases negate his thesis. It may be that his choice of cases was unfortunate, but they are the only ones available for use in evaluating his ideas.

Karman presents the case of a 45 year-old white male. (6) "What we know of the patient's early life," he says, "is exceedingly meager though numerous efforts have been made to secure such information." This handicap usually conceals highly significant diagnostic data, but Karman declares that if numerous efforts to get information have failed, the information is probably nonexistent.

This 45 year-old patient was the sixth of seven children. One brother, deceased, had been an epileptic. The patient's mother had died when he was four. The father, who was "moderately alcoholic," kept all the children at home, and remarried four years later. This marriage gave the patient two half-brothers and one half-sister. "From the first, the patient rebelled against the stepmother, and for the next several years he spent most of his time at the home of an older sister. It is stated that the stepmother showed a decided preference for the patient's younger brother and it is suggested that this may have been the basis for the patient's dislike.

"From the age of six until he was eight, patient attended a boarding school ..."

Here indeed is a psychological jumble, even if we do not have enough information to work out its precise convolutions. Surely, Karpman is not justified in saying that, "We find hardly one psychogenic fact" in all this. And it seems somewhat evasive to say that "The death of the patient's mother when he was only four years old could hardly have had much *conscious* [my italics] effect upon him."

Karpman's second illustration, published six years later, is even less convincing. (7, 8) This, however, is reported in great detail, an is well worth reading. Freudian psychogenesis falls down here, as happened before and will happen again. If ever a case illustrate conditioned inhibition—or conditioned neglect and parasitism this is it.

Walter Manson can barely remember his father, who died when the boy was only five years old. He was of a roving disposition an alcoholic. Walter's mother has said that he had spells when she would have to leave home because she was afraid of him. [His influence on Walter could hardly have been favorable.] The mother...[possessed] more sentiment than sense. [For which read she protected her son completely."]

[As a child he was sickly and] he was badly pampered and when he was subsequently denied anything, he would have tantrums into fits of rage. His next reaction was to take the things he wanted when his parents were not looking.

The father's death [when the boy was five] reduced the family to poverty, and it was necessary for the mother to place the three children in an orphan asylum. [Over-protection + deprivation = Parasitism.] There the patient had diphtheria and scarlet fever, and he continued his fits of rage when he was required to take medicine and was not given candy afterwards ...

Four years later his mother opened a boarding house and took the children to live with her, but apparently she could not make a go of it, and while an aunt took the girl, the two boys were placed in a manual training school where they remained for two years more.

From our point of view, these details provide enough in his background for two people. Walter grew up to be a full-fledged parasitic psychopath, and included robbery and manslaughter among activities.

Karpman proves the conditioned character of his patient's psychopathy when he concludes, *"Against all expectation* [my italics], the therapeutic efforts seemed not to have been entirely fruitless as the man appears to have been able to maintain himself after leaving the hospital without getting into trouble for eight years, by many times the longest period in his life."

Kavka, much influenced by Karpman, presents the case of a twenty-six-year-old Marine whose history seemed to indicate bona fide non-environmentally caused psychopathy. (9) Further study, however, necessitated reclassifying him as a case of "symptomatic psychopathy," in which "emotional maladjustment... [was] outlined against a backdrop of serious family disharmony and disrupted parent-child relationships."

Without doubt, the psychopathic personality is a result of early conditioning, usually, in the words of Heaver, of "the type of early environmental conditioning provided by a mother who overwhelms her son with her indulgence and solicitude, and by a father who is highly successful, driving, critical and distant." (10) Greenacre (11) has also found this to be true, but I should like to side with Levy (12) who adds to the "indulged" psychopath a so-called "deprived" psychopath—what Bender refers to when she says, " [Psychopathic behavior in children] is caused by early emotional and social deprivation, due either to early institutional or other neglectful care, or to critical breaks in the continuity of their relationships to mother and mother substitutes." (13) See also Lowrey (14) and Goldfarb. (15) As we saw earlier, a multiplicity of different backgrounds can produce an inhibitory personality, and that is precisely what the psychopath invariably is.

Johnny S., the young man at the start of this chapter who rode steeplechase in a cemetery, had a Bernreuter neurotic score (B 1-N) of 90.2 per cent. This is close to the average B1 -N score of 89.5 per cent that Schmidt and Billingslea found for fifty-seven "constitutional psychopaths" in the U.S. Army Air Force. (16) Caldwell, in an important study of thirty psychopathic personalities, reported that "All cases showed neuropathic family histories, neurotic personalities or clinical neuroses, indicating a basic neurosis underlying the psychopathic type of behavior." (17)

The psychopath is a product of inhibitory conditioning, and those who say that the psychopath is not a "neurotic" because he has no "conflicts" have a rather restricted view of maladjustment. I agree, in essence, with Caldwell that "... egocentrism combined with neurosis and antisocial behavior equals the psychopathic personality..." (18)

There is not one feature of psychopathy that does not occur in the other inhibitory patterns. The difference is that the psychopath has more of these features, and they are all more deeply dyed. Egocentricity and callousness, and all of their ramifications, are classical inhibitory characteristics, and the emotional shallowness that we always find in the psychopath often occurs in low self-sufficiencied persons who by no stretch of the imagination can be termed psychopathic.

Nor may we call a man a psychopath because he is a civilized Mundugumor. Margaret Mead has described the Mundugumor, a primitive tribe in New Guinea. (19) "The Mundugumor man-child is born into a hostile world, a world in which most of the members of his own sex will be his enemies, in which his major equipment for success must be a capacity for violence, for seeing and avenging insult, for holding his own safety very lightly and the lives of others even more lightly."

Contemporary culture, with its rapacity, its pitiless exploitation of personality, and its conscienceless drive to "get ahead" fosters Mundugumor behavior. Yet fatal as it may be to those who get in its way and to those who initiate it, by no means is it per se proof of psychopathy. The businessman brought up in Mundugumor style is not a psychopath if he is a sincerely loving husband, father, son, and friend. But if he has no real love for anybody, and carries his Mundugumor-like activity into his personal relations, he may unhesitatingly be classified as a psychopath. The basic cause of the psychopathy of every big-business psychopath I have ever studied has been his early familial conditioning. Contemporary culture simply put a premium on his maladjustment.

The treatment of the psychopath is based on the fact that he is inhibitory and particularly inaccessible. His quiet groaning about his past errors is not regret, and his solemn head shaking is not agreement. His earnestness is as fraudulent with the therapist as it is with everyone else.

The weird real situations he will get into, the extraordinarily subtle rationalizations he will present, and the many false hopes of progress that he will arouse, will tax the therapist. Yet all of these features are symptoms, and the therapist should no more resent them than a physician resents a high fever. The well-adjusted therapist will not mind the psychopath's monkeyshines, but one less integrated will take them personally, and will exasperate himself and antagonize the individual under treatment.

"There are none so deaf as those that will not hear." In this adage we have the whole problem of psychopathy. The psychopath's early kennel training precludes our getting near him, and until we do, our best efforts will be wasted. For successful therapy we must fight through to rapport.

In this necessity for rapport, the treatment of psychopathy differs from most of the other inhibitory patterns. The run-of-the-mill inhibitory personality has a great multitude of honest feelings, and these feelings are the metal that we hammer into shape. But the psychopath feels nothing when he gets what he wants, and only shallow anger when he doesn't. No matter how we hammer such material, it can never be shaped into an emotionally wholesome personality. We have to find some new metal to work with, and we do this by giving the psychopath new emotional experiences in his relations with the therapist. It would do just as well if he could get those emotional experiences outside of the office, as do the non-psychopathic inhibitory when under treatment. But with the psychopath we need to control the stimuli a great deal in order to insure their appropriate impingement on his nervous system.

In general, if we give him lavishly of our skill and patience, and act the way his parents should have acted, we can change him. A simulated interest cannot be carried off for long, and the psychopath, being an emotional fraud himself, is well equipped to scent any psychological sham in the wind. Sometimes, indeed, it is difficult to summon up any enthusiasm for changing a prurient barfly into a peaceful clubman, so unless the therapist is really interested, it is only fair to refuse the case.

In the background of even the most hardened psychopath may be found a human relationship of sincere involvement. It may have concerned a grade school teacher, a girl in the neighborhood, or an uncle whom he rarely saw, but if we can find such a conditioned pattern, it will be of great therapeutic value. For by sympathetically discussing its ramifications we will find that we can produce an astonishing softening of the psychopath. It is a matter of looking for helpful bells, and hitting them hard when we find them.

Once we have established rapport (and this calls for imagination and flexibility), if we tread warily a little while longer, victory will be ours. For the core of the psychopath's difficulty is an inability to enter into emotional involvements, and once he has done so with the therapist, he is no longer a psychopath—though I shall continue to call him one for convenience. Now he will listen, and now he will obey, and he will practice the principles of excitation that will make him into a human being.

The psychopath must try to practice excitation every time he opens his mouth. *The psychopath has feelings, even if they are superficial and about relatively unimportant matters.* With a little introspection on his part, and guidance from the therapist, he will learn to recognize an ephemeral and spontaneous feeling when it flutters across his brain. And as soon as it does, he must utter it, without decoration and without hypocrisy, for the psychopath is a master at forging emotions. At no time must he lie about facts or feelings. To make believe he is sincere will not be enough. He must be genuinely so, and he himself must be his severest critic. It is not enough to simulate feelings. He must utter feelings *that he really feels,* and as he does so he will develop deeper and more serious emotions. No more will he be dead to deep love and hate, but both shall be reborn in him.

Every psychopath is a shyster Mephistopheles. He emphasizes minor issues, and when he is defeated he switches so quickly and leaves such a thick smoke screen of "objectivity" that you doubt your own logic. But when you shut him off with "Just a moment," and recapitulate what he has said, you will see that he is more interested in obfuscation than in truth, and in psychotherapy it is truth that brings victory.

The psychopath even argues with himself, but it is not a true conflict. Though he goes through the motions of being open-minded, he knows precisely what he wants. And as one of them put it, "Whenever I decide to be noble, I'm always contradicting myself by my actions."

A psychopath can charm the birds out of the trees. He is a master at telling you what you want to hear, and is often known as a "smooth" or a "fast talker." With moving sincerity he can defend the most arrant nonsense, or even a perfectly worthy cause. He pushes the magnetism at you as soon as he sees you, but only, as one of them said, "because I always feel that I'm proving something to somebody else, but never anybody I know."

I told a psychopathic young woman that she was exploiting everyone she met. She answered, "I don't try to be foxy, but it comes out that way." Not only must the therapist try to protect others from the psychopath's depredations, but he must also take care not to be exploited himself. Personally, I believe it is much better to be victimized a bit, than to keep the psychopath at arm's length. This will have a hollow sound to those who have almost been destroyed by psychopaths, but I have found that with care even the most cunning of them can be outmaneuvered and hoist by their own petard. Friendly firmness should be the attitude of the therapist, and when he is in doubt, he should be friendly rather than firm.

A conscience is a set of conditioned emotional patterns. Since the psychopath lacks those patterns, to talk of conscience to him is to try to hit nonexistent bells. The objective of therapy is to build those missing emotional patterns into him, and once we do so, our task will be complete. The moralistically inclined will then say that he has a conscience. The more scientifically-minded will say that he has become excitatory.

To be excitatory is to be sincere and to respect other people's rights. To be excitatory is to be able to become involved and to love. In brief, to be excitatory is not to be a psychopath.

The successful treatment of psychopathy is not easy, but it is definitely possible if we pick our cases carefully and remain skeptical of our results until we are absolutely certain. Johnny S., who rode steeplechase in a cemetery, is no longer a psychopath and neither is a young man who spent a year in a reformatory and then teamed up with crooked gamblers all over the country—and neither is a brilliant businessman to whom I owe some excellent insights into the mechanisms of psychopathy. But we will have our failures too, who will kick over the milk pail when it is more than half full. I like to believe, and I think it is true, that the lessons of my therapeutic defeats are often the reasons for my therapeutic victories. Sometimes, and I am not talking of psychopathy alone, therapeutic success seems possible only if we could use a gun freely on some of the friends and relatives of the individual under treatment. Fortunately, or unfortunately, this is not yet a therapeutic prerogative.

CHAPTER 20

ONLY SCIENCE, ABSOLUTE SCIENCE

This is the last chapter of the book. I have tried throughout not to repeat myself, but since psychotherapy is an elaborate study in synonyms, some redundancy has been inescapable. That at least is my explanation. In this chapter I shall first make some general observations on psychotherapy, and then I shall turn to its connection, world peace, for without world peace there will be no human with anything to gain from psychotherapy.

The history of the individual is stored in his protoplasm, his actions, his history repeats itself. Through psychotherapy we manufacture new history, which repeats itself in his new actions.

Man is the prime symbol-seeker of the animal kingdom, cultural anthropologist can show how man's personality is formed in the matrix of society, and the reflex psychologist can show how phenomena of society can be interpreted in psychological terms. But to the individual who absorbs certain patterns, it does not matter whether they are societally conditioned or individually conditioned. They are neural patterns and they determine his behavior.

Psychological events are physiological events, and conditioning is the modification of tissue by experience. But since our knowledge of these changes is incomplete, we manufacture psychological hypotheses. The closer these hypotheses parallel physiology, the more accurate our conceptions will be, and consequently the more helpful. We do not want psychology to be a science of sterile abstractions, we are therapists, mechanics if you please, and the theory we want is the theory that leads us to what to do to change the material we work with. Perhaps someday we may be able to do this chemically, but at present we do not know enough about the biochemistry of the tissue modifications involved in the learning process. Surely, to tell someone that he has anxiety feelings because his cholinesterase activity is up, or because his acetylcholine production is down, will not be very helpful.

Associationalism is important in understanding the origin of behavior problems, and Pavlov's differentiation between inhibition and excitation is important in understanding their treatment. Our goal is to disinhibit the inhibitory, and this we attain by what may be termed *verbal chemistry*. Words, spoken by the therapist, travel along appropriate nerve tracts in the person under treatment, and produce chemical modifications in his nervous system. These changes are associated with behavior changes, which in turn precipitate more bio-chemical modifications and more behavior changes.

Maladjustment is a learning process, and so is psychotherapy. Maladjustment is malconditioning, and psychotherapy is reconditioning. The individual's problems are a result of his social experiences, and by changing his techniques of social relations, we change his personality. Experience is not only the best teacher, it is the only teacher. We are not especially concerned with giving the individual stratified knowledge of his past—called "probing." What concerns us is giving him reflex knowledge for his future—called "habits."

When the individual's emotions are disinhibited, the extensive ramifications of his changed behavior prove the fundamental quality of our therapy. Consequently, to call the reflex approach superficial "character analysis" as opposed to "depth analysis" is to be both inacurate and scientifically naive. The reflexes are the man, and the experimental studies of induced neurosis in animals point in the same direction. We can agree with Maier. "The animal work appears to encourage the notion that much of disturbed behavior is without a motive. For the frustrated individual the behavior is more an end in itself than a means to an end." (1) The means become the ends.

Although in psychotherapy we persistently emphasize excitation, certain social situations call for inhibition. Says Pavlov, ". . . a continual and proper balancing of these two processes lays the basis of a normal life for both man and animal. These two opposite processes, it is necessary to add, are coexistent and equally important in the nervous activity." (2) Gantt (3) remarks that the literal translation of Pavlov's term for disinhibition is "unbraking"—and that is precisely what restores the dynamic equilibrium between inhibition and excitation. In a single precept: *The solution of all problems of the self comes from unbraking the individual's behavior with other people.*

With the conceptions of conditioning, inhibition, disinhibition, and excitation, it is possible to make a science of reflex therapy—systematic in structure and scientific in application. But unfortunately, history is not always ready for the construction of a science. Sears points out, "If Freud had learned his academic prejudices a quarter century later than he did, if Pavlov, Bekhterev, McDougall, and Watson could have influenced him, psychoanalytic theory might have had a very different systematic texture. But by the time the stirrings of behavioral science had led to reexamination of subjectivism, Freud had long since conceptualized his psychiatric observations in terms of conscious and unconscious processes." (4)

Yet it is true that in psychotherapy *post hoc* is not necessarily *propter hoc*. And it is in this spirit that I have written this book. Although I have advocated a body of therapeutic theory, and presented a series of case histories consistent with it, I have tried to make abundantly clear the intrinsic limitations of absolute proof in psychology.

But undeveloped as psychology is as a science, it has established some important conclusions which may have much to do with whether nuclear fission will render this a dead planet.

We know that there is no inborn desire to wage war.

We know that the inhibitory are more prone than the excitatory to be filled with hatreds. We know that though the characters of people may vary under different societies, disinhibition is the same thing organically and chemically in any culture, and individuals in a state of excitatory-inhibitory balance will get along quite well with each other.

We know that the Commandment to "Love thy neighbor" is based upon human experience, and that the person conditioned to the contrary cannot love his neighbor or anybody else.

And we know that it is one thing to have knowledge, and it is another thing to distribute that knowledge over the face of the earth and to see that it is *applied* in complicated human relationships. For as long as the findings of psychology, and of social science in general, remain in academic seclusion, the layman regards them with amused tolerance. But the instant they are put into practice they inflict pain on his conditioned protoplasm, and cause him to rationalize and to counterattack vigorously. The scientist tries to draw his conclusions from organized and carefully checked data. The layman deduces his conclusions from his rubbish heap of accidental experiences and historical deadwood.

De-adrenalized speeches, heavy laden with intellectualities about peace and good will, do nothing to implement the lessons of psychology for world peace, nor are books that demonstrate the fallacies of prejudice, hatred, and greed any more helpful. The training must be on an emotional level, and this is best done in day to day experiences in childhood.

Implicit in the psychological approach to world peace is the assumption that since human nature underlies human institutions, the science of human nature can solve all human problems. In Pavlov's words, "Only science, exact science about human nature itself, and the most sincere approach to it by the aid of the omnipotent scientific method, will deliver man from his present gloom, and will purge him from his contemporary shame in the sphere of interhuman relations." (5)

Although I believe that world peace is individual happiness multiplied, and that governments of excitatory people will not be interested in working their citizens into a lather for war, I cannot join the hosts of psychologists who believe, as Montaigne said, that "the same reasons that make us quarrel with a neighbor cause war" between nations.

Science is a declaration of causes as preceding certain effects. The choice of the sequences of causes and effects depends upon the subject matter of the science. But there are other sciences besides psychology. Sociology, cultural anthropology, and history (a veritable quicksand) deal with sequences of causes and effects. Consequently, though social organizations are composed of individuals, there are broad hierarchies of social causes and effects that may be studied with only passing reference to the personal psychology of the individuals involved in them.

Because there are different sequences of cause and effect besides the psychological, action in other spheres than the psychological is required if we wish to interrupt these sequences. Nationalism has certain cause and effect relationships to war. The conflicts of economic systems have cause and effect relationships to war. And even a cursory glance at history shows that organized religion has sometimes ideal-conditioned people into bloody slaughter. History, I think, even shows that ideal-conditioned societies have been fully as war-like as thing-conditioned societies.

When the sewage of society gives persons emotional typhoid, they need psychotherapy. Preventive public health tries to keep the sewage out of the drinking water, but persons still contract typhoid, and need treatment—which means that we must favor both prevention and cure.

Some biologists and physicists, perplexed by the problems of contemporary life, have been rationalizing the emotional training of their childhoods into books and articles invoking the assistance of a "higher moral force." Simultaneously with this they have been boasting of how little science knows of the "ultimate nature of things" (whatever that may mean) and asserting that "scientific materialism with its false values and standards" threatens our civilization.

It is possible to agree that happiness is not a matter of automobiles, refrigerators, and bathroom fixtures without taking refuge in the vacuum of dogmatic theism.

We do not need less science. We need more science. It is science, and only science, that has made it possible for us to live like people, and not like brutes. It is science and only science that has made it possible for us to live longer and more fully. And it is through science and only through science that the world can have enough to eat, for only the man whose feelings and whose gut are well fed can afford to love his neighbor.

The development of physical science has produced weapons of inordinate deadliness, yet only the application of more science can save us. Now it is the pudgy infant hands of the social sciences that hold the key to the future. If we help them to grow, and we apply their knowledge to the solution of concrete problems, we can face the future with the certainty that there will be peace, plenty—and even happiness—for all.

AFTERWORD

William J. Salter, Ph.D.

Why Reprint *Conditioned Reflex Therapy?*

As noted in the Foreword, Andrew Salter was my father. But I am also a Ph.D. psychologist, as is my wife. Only when we began graduate school at Yale in the late 1970s did we realize that my father's claims to be "the father of behavior therapy" were true: that his work had introduced ideas on which hundreds of academic careers were built and that his contributions helped perhaps millions of people to be happier and to live more successful lives. One reason for this new edition of *CRT* is to help to secure my father's rightful place in the history of what has become a dominant psychotherapeutic approach. It is also, candidly, an homage to him. But these are not compelling reasons for most people to read it.

The best reason to read *CRT* is that it can still help people. Although ostensibly not intended as a self-help book, it is one, and has been since its publication. I believe it still stands out in the now crowded field of self-help.

CRT possesses a vigor and clarity of expression that belie its age. My father took justifiable pride in his prose and treasured the praise it received from Aldous Huxley, Thomas Mann, Vladimir Nabokov, and H. G. Wells.[1] This vigor, and a host of striking metaphors and

---

[1] Wells's career stretched from Queen Victoria's reign through Hitler's and Stalin's. *The Time Machine* appeared in 1895, and he was still publishing almost up to his death in 1946. He died before *CRT* appeared but read *What Is Hypnosis*—the copy sneaked to him in wartime England aboard an air force transport plane—with "admiration and approval," a quote that appeared on all editions. Wells went on to say, overoptimistically, that with this book, "The destruction of psychoanalysis is conclusive." I saw this text quoted on a bookstore's web listing

memorable one-liners, communicate the excitement of his novel ideas even now, when they are no longer new.

On a recent rereading I was struck by its lack of jargon. Although many of its ideas have become pervasive, much of its terminology has not, which gives the seventy-year-old text, paradoxically, a certain freshness. For example, scores of books have been written about "assertion," an idea introduced and elaborated in *CRT* though the word does not appear there. My father talked about "excitation" or "excitatory behavior," using terms from the Pavlovian lexicon; the novelty of the language, for most current readers, underscores the novelty of the ideas.

Brief Personal and Intellectual History

Andrew Salter was born in Waterbury, Connecticut, on May 9, 1914, to Russian immigrants who had fled anti-Semitism and forced conscription in the czar's army. He died in New York on October 6, 1996, a few months after seeing his last patient. His father was a watchmaker who worked in Waterbury's factories and then, when his union organizing got him blacklisted, opened a small watch repair shop. Andrew was recognized as something special in elementary school; researchers from the Gesell Institute at Yale interviewed and tested him repeatedly as a child, and his parents fostered his lively intellectual interests. The family moved to New York City when Andrew was fourteen, first living in two rooms behind his father's store, then moving to an apartment.

As a boy he was fascinated by magic tricks and cryptography, and spent many hours at a dingy magic shop in Manhattan where Howard Thurston hung out, listening to older magicians and learning tricks. He wrote a (paid) weekly column on codes and cryptography for the *New York World* in his early teens. His interest in conditioning arose in part from youthful observation of the way magicians manipulated attention and suggestion to achieve some of their effects.

An avid socialist, he developed a small street following for his wit in soapbox debates with communists. That same quick wit was deployed to great effect in televised debates with psychoanalysts during the 1950s following the publication of *The Case Against Psychoanalysis* in 1952.

He entered the uptown campus of NYU in 1931, majoring in physics. His freshman grades were only fair, and he realized that although he wasn't sure what he wanted to study, he knew it wasn't physics. Then, at

---

for a used copy in 2000—quite a distance from the world in which H. G. Wells and my father lived, but both would certainly have approved.

the height (or depth) of the Depression, this only son of a hardworking immigrant family dropped out of college for two years and spent most of his time at the New York Public Library. He read deeply in hypnosis and psychology, much preferring Pavlov and the Russians to Freud and his ilk. He read widely as well about yogis and mystics, about popular ideas on hypnosis through the years, and about the manipulation of attention and mastery of suggestibility practiced by the stage and parlor magicians he had encountered as an adolescent. I am convinced that this breadth of interests, which he maintained all his life, helped lay the groundwork for his innovative ideas. Upon returning to NYU, he switched his major to psychology and did well, graduating in 1937 with a B.S. and ending his formal involvement with an academic institution.

My father was repelled by Freudians' dogmatism, arrogance, and obsession with sex, and attracted by the simplicity of Pavlov's and Bechterev's ideas. He was determined to do something important in psychology building on learning theory and behaviorist psychology, but "had no desire to spend the rest of my life studying the reactions of rats lost in labyrinths" (Wickware, 1941, p. 86).

He had been interested in hypnosis for years. My father's younger sister and a friend from those early days swore that my father was experimenting with hypnosis in college, inducing standard phenomena like glove anesthesia and inability to rise from a chair, and investigating ways to hypnotize people more quickly and even to rid them of bad habits. Indeed, in her late seventies, that old friend still fondly credited her elegant fingernails to my father's having cured her of nail-biting when she was in high school.

He was convinced that hypnosis was deeply linked with the phenomena of conditioning being investigated in laboratory animals by the behaviorists of that era and began to use hypnosis with stutterers, nail-biters, and some phobics. Within a few years, he had developed his ideas sufficiently to write the article *Three Techniques of Autohypnosis* (Salter, 1941), eventually accepted by Clark Hull for the *Journal of General Psychology* after my father had "Americanized" his name from Saltzman. This article clarified the concept of self-hypnosis, introduced the idea of using it in therapy, and presented three practical methods for self-hypnosis.

Essentially, my father taught "subjects" (as he called them) how to rapidly induce a hypnotic trance in themselves, using procedures quite similar to those he used when hypnotizing them. They were to invoke these brief self-induced hypnotic states to reinforce in their everyday lives the learning and changes made in my father's office via hypnosis. This has three major benefits: first, subjects can maintain the desirable effects of hypnosis (such as eliminating nail-biting, overeating, procrastination, and so on), overcoming the common problem of hypnotic therapy that its effects quickly fade. As my father put it, "Autohypnosis completely surmounts this diminution of hypnotic suggestion" (Salter, 1941, p. 435, as are the other quotes in this paragraph). Second, through this ability to *voluntarily* reinforce the effects of hypnosis, the subject learns to feel—and actually to *be*—in control. This increases feelings of self-efficacy (not that my father used the term) and rapidly "weakens the feeling of dependency upon the psychologist held by most cases under treatment." The third advantage is the practical consequence of the second: "It means a good deal to a subject not to have to revisit persistently the psychologist for frequent hypnotic aid, whether it be for the problem under treatment or in another connection."

Amazingly, this brief article in a professional journal by an obscure twenty-seven-year-old was discussed approvingly in the *New York Times* (Kaempffert, 1941, p. D5), *Time* magazine, and in an extensive article in *Life* magazine (Wickware, 1941). The *Time* article was titled "Everyman His Own Svengali," complete with a photograph of an intense, already balding Andrew Salter (*Time*, June 2, 1941, p. 40). My father must have used a publicist.

He opened an office in the Waldorf Astoria while still living with his parents in the Bronx, an act of amazing chutzpah, given his economic circumstances. Within two years he moved his practice to 1000 Park Avenue, where he stayed for close to forty years.

About a year later, he was "discovered" by the widely syndicated newspaper columnist Elsa Maxwell. From a poor family, with little education (though very intelligent), she was wonderfully lively—excitatory, one might say—as a collector of interesting people and as a hostess to whose parties those people flocked. Her column of December 4, 1942, is devoted to him. It begins: "I lunched several days ago with one of the most remarkable men of our time. His name is Salter, Andrew Salter. A brilliant fellow, only five years out of college." She concludes that she would "like to see certain of our Senators and Congressmen visit Mr. Salter." Her column of August 6, 1943, discusses (imperfectly) his use of hypnosis, illustrated with the example of "a certain golf champion I know." (He is case 30 in *CRT*, pp. 125–127.)[2] And on April 27, 1944,

---

[2]   My father was perhaps not an ideal golf coach, however. He recommends that "Tournament golfers on a new course should practice as little as possible before teeing off." He also advocates

she describes her "small dinner in honor of Lewis B. Mayer of MGM." My father was apparently the after-dinner speaker; Maxwell includes responses to his talk from Dorothy Thompson (the most famous woman journalist of the time) and Margaret Mead.

I can find no evidence that Maxwell was ever a patient. Although there must be some backstory—maybe that golf pro?—I suspect that she simply found my father "remarkable," as she said, and a suitable addition to her menagerie. Her interest demonstrates the head-spinning course of my father's career. Still in his twenties and years before *CRT*, he had become a minor intellectual celebrity in Manhattan—a long way from the back of his father's watch repair shop and his ardent debates with communists a decade earlier.[3]

This early work can be seen as a major step toward cognitive behavior therapy, since it fundamentally involves patients telling themselves things to change how they feel.

An important source of my father's ideas (mentioned in Salter, 1941) was his interest in the trances of yogis, who were able to self-induce a variety of states seemingly identical to deep hypnosis (such as catalepsy, anesthesia, and changes in various autonomic processes). He remained fascinated by such phenomena for decades, convinced that they bore striking similarities to "standard" hypnotic phenomena yet exhibited crucial differences from them. Extensive work beginning in the 1960s with Charles Tart's edited collection *Altered States of Consciousness* (1969) and continuing with Herbert Benson's work at Harvard Medical School on "mind body medicine" showed the merits of this idea. *The Relaxation Response* (Benson, 1975) was a best-selling treatment of this and associated concepts. My father also raised the question "What connection, if any, is there between autohypnosis and progressive relaxation?" (Salter, 1941, p. 436) as a direction for further research. Progressive relaxation, in innumerable variants, has since become a mainstay of behavior therapy.

His work by this time had attracted the attention of a few writers and editors in New York—his closest friends, then and throughout his life, were generally writers, actors, playwrights, advertising executives, and other creative people—who were skeptical of psychoanalysis and impressed by my father's ideas, results, and personality. This led to an extensive profile in *Life* magazine—then immensely popular—complete with a photograph of his eyes through the horn-rimmed glasses he wore

---

a brisk approach to putting, observing that a golfer should visualize the line between the ball and the hole "and hit the ball down the line without even thinking" (both quotes p. 126).

[3] I imagine he would have been an adept user of social media.

his entire adult life—stressing that "the majority of his patients…rarely see him" after "five or six interviews" (Wickware, 1941, p. 91). From that day on, he had a waiting list. At age twenty-seven his career was fully launched, despite his lack of an advanced degree or university affiliation.

By 1944 he had expanded his ideas on hypnosis into a small volume titled *What Is Hypnosis*, which also vigorously attacked the dominant Freudian thinking of the day as unscientific and at best generally useless to patients. This little book (less than 100 pages) caused quite a fuss, with reviews pro and con in specialist and general interest publications. It remained in print for thirty years and was eventually used in many college psychology courses.

Although my father retained his interest and involvement in hypnosis to the end of his life,[4] as his clinical experience accumulated, his techniques expanded beyond hypnosis to conditioning more broadly, specifically conditioning focused on making people more "excitatory" and less "inhibitory," ideas explicitly credited to Pavlov. *CRT* presented many of the ideas and techniques he had developed in less than ten years of clinical practice, ideas and techniques that pervade behavior therapy today. A fascinating article in *Victory* magazine presents the best pre-*CRT* discussion of this I have been able to find (*Victory*, 1945, vol. 3, number 1, pp. 42–44).[5] My father's view of hypnosis is described as "the production of reactions in the human organism through the use of verbal or other associative reflexes" (p. 42), an extremely broad characterization. This led to his use of auto-hypnosis, the subject of Salter (1941). The article then discusses my father's debriefings of successfully hypnotized subjects in which he elicited their specific reactions to having been hypnotized. He employed these responses to teach them auto-hypnosis: "the subject's individual conditionings were found and 'fed back' to him" (p. 42). That is, he used the subject's "private, personally conditioned language" (*CRT*, p. 75), a major innovation in therapeutic practice.

---

[4] A few months before his death, when his practice was quite limited, my father spoke eagerly about a new hypnotic induction technique he was developing that combined brevity with effectiveness.

[5] *Victory* was a very successful publication of the Office of War Information, the government's propaganda arm. Similar in format to *Life*, it ran from 1942 through 1945 and was published in multiple languages. Issues were undated and all articles were unsigned. Kenneth W. Purdy, who originated the idea and served as editor, became my father's closest friend. I suspect that Purdy wrote this article. Author of *Kings of the Road* (1952) and many other books and articles, he was for two decades the country's leading automotive writer—a nice contrast with my father, who never drove a car. His wife was my mother's closest friend, and one of my daughters' favorite people. For more on Purdy, see Kimes (1993) and W. J. Salter (1994).

But, since only a minority of patients are good hypnotic subjects, my father "in recent years… has broadened his concepts to such an extent that it is possible for him to eliminate hypnosis" (p. 44); that is, by the early 1940s, before the publication of *What Is Hypnosis* (Salter, 1944), my father was already moving beyond hypnosis. His therapeutic approach is characterized as "discover[ing] inhibitory symptoms in his cases—symptoms of which the cases themselves are usually unaware—and suggest[ing] specific re-conditioning procedures to eliminate them. Each person presents a different problem but [Salter's] purpose with all of them is identical—to provide a free, outward-flowing personality in which true emotions are expressed in speech and action" (p. 44). The concern with individual symptoms may appear inconsistent with my father's stance that the origins of an individual's problems are irrelevant to treatment; it certainly seems so to me. But the sharp focus on the identical purpose of therapy, despite the "different problem[s]," perfectly captures my father's approach to treatment for the following half century.

He treated hundreds of patients, honing his methods for effective brief therapy, developing his insights, and constructing an overarching intellectual framework. And it is those ideas, and associated methods, that are documented so vigorously in *CRT*. (My father would have said that the ideas led to the methods, but I am convinced that he would have been mistaken.)

CRT was quite successful and broadly reviewed in both local newspapers and professional publications. It was also widely translated (including into Pavlov's Russian, although that never yielded a ruble of royalties). My father's clinical practice boomed, and he began to be sought out as an articulate anti-Freudian. In 1952 he published *The Case Against Psychoanalysis*, a vehement (one unsympathetic reviewer called it "bombastic," and I can see what he meant) attack on psychoanalysis. It combined methodological critiques, a review of therapy outcome studies, and what might be called commonsense argument. This led to interviews and television appearances, mostly debates with Freudians. My father always did very well in such debates, due at least as much to his quick wit and excitatory personality as to the rigor of his arguments.

Gradually, my father's ideas about behavior therapy began to spread. Joseph Wolpe first came to America from South Africa in 1956, on a fellowship at Stanford; he had contacted my father earlier, encouraged by Leo Reyna (then also in South Africa). My father and a few other therapists began to exchange ideas; the academics among them wrote papers. Arnold

Lazarus, a student of Wolpe's, arrived from South Africa in 1966 and began his influential American career and life-long friendship with my father.

On the pop culture front, in the mid-fifties my father became friends with the novelist Richard Condon. They had many conversations about conditioning and hypnosis and their potential applicability in brainwashing. Condon transmuted those ideas into *The Manchurian Candidate* (1959).[6] My father's work is discussed at length in the book, and he is mentioned in the movie by the chief North Korean, Dr. Yen Lo. In the copy of the book he inscribed to my father, Condon says that all those pages about Yen Lo "could not have been written" without him. Some friends and patients even saw aspects of my father's personality in Yen Lo's cheerful extroversion and conversational breadth.

In 1962 the first conference on behavior therapy ("the Charlottesville Conference") was convened, followed two years later by the volume of edited conference papers, *The Conditioning Therapies* (Wolpe, Salter, & Reyna, 1964). My father conceived of this conference, helped to invite speakers and attendees, and funded it with money from a foundation he had established a few years earlier to support various research projects. In 1966 he was one of the founders of the American Association for Behavior Therapy (AABT, which originally met in my parents' living room and is now the Association for Behavioral and Cognitive Therapies, or ABCT), along with Reyna, Wolpe, and a small group of psychologists, psychiatrists, and neurologists—Joseph Cautela, Edward Dengrove, Herbert Fensterheim, Cyril Franks, Leonard Krasner, Arnold Lazarus, Robert Leiberman, John E. Peters, and Dorothy Susskind. Behavior therapy was on its way to becoming legitimized as a central component of clinical psychology.

My father was quite involved in the AABT during its early years, serving on the board and in various official and unofficial capacities, and always attending meetings. Gradually, as behavior therapy became more mainstream, his involvement diminished. Professors trained graduate students (as they should); my father had none. Inevitably, and due to its success, most of the work in behavior therapy became incremental "normal science" (Kuhn, 1970), which my father frankly found boring.

As the name change from AABT to ABCT suggests, cognitive behavior therapy has become a dominant approach in behavior therapy; indeed, few contemporary behavior therapists fail to include cognitive aspects in their

---

[6] Condon's apartment was in the same building as my father's office, and they may have been introduced by a doorman. Condon often took ideas from the ambient intellectual climate and pushed them beyond their limits in his fiction.

work, regardless of how they describe themselves. The key distinction is that CBT explicitly includes identifying and altering "faulty or unhelpful ways of thinking," in addition to "learned patterns of unhelpful behavior." In both, the driving idea is that "people can learn better ways of coping with [those "unhelpful ways of thinking" and "patterns of unhelpful behavior"], thereby relieving their symptoms and becoming more effective in their lives."[7] My father certainly tried to find and change "unhelpful ways of thinking" in his patients, as well as to help them to change their behavior.

In the discussion below, the term "behavior therapy" is sometimes used where "cognitive behavior therapy" might be more technically correct. I'm sorry if some readers find that confusing or if some professional therapists are offended. Some of the specific methods now used in *cognitive behavior therapy* (CBT) are also present in *CRT*.

His clinical practice flourished; he pursued a number of other interests unconnected to psychology; behavior therapy continued to grow and prosper; academics elbowed each other for credit as the second generation of behavior therapists emerged. My father began to be cited less frequently, in part because his ideas had been incorporated into the zeitgeist, in part because he had no academic affiliation and essentially stopped publishing in 1964, and in part, it seems likely, because he first made a splash in general interest publications rather than in professional journals.

As Gerald Davison put it in his obituary, "Ironically, being an innovator often makes a given contribution less visible. Just as references to psychoanalysis seldom cite Freud, one often encounters 'assertion training' and the origins of behavior therapy with no citation to Salter" (Davison, 1996, p. 31). Davison, a friend, surely knew my father would have gotten a perverse kick out of the comparison with Freud.

A brief description of what my father was like: He was, as one would expect, excitatory; he established instant rapport with cab drivers and doormen, with my friends and my brothers', with patients of diverse backgrounds. He was not, again as one would expect, excessively modest, but his unabashed self-confidence had an unusual inclusiveness, incorporating his listeners into his own self-esteem and boosting theirs. A number of people—close friends, patients, even casual acquaintances— have reported this interesting quality.

Verbally quick, he loved puns, vivid expressions, clever turns of phrase. And he was a font of jokes. Many of his patients were writers or in advertising, and his office became an informal joke exchange, with patients

---

[7] www.apa.org/ptsd-guideline/patients-and-families/cognitive-behavioral

striving to bring a new joke to each session, confident that they would be rewarded by new ones to take away. Several times he mentioned that a patient had told a joke at a party and was then approached by a stranger who asked if he or she was seeing Andrew Salter. When I said this at his funeral service, several heads in the audience nodded. One of his favorite lines was "always leave 'em laughing," and this he often did.

Approach to Therapy

When *CRT* was published, psychoanalysis was by far the dominant approach to psychotherapy, usually conducted by physicians who had themselves been psychoanalyzed, and generally requiring years of treatment consisting of three or four sessions a week.[8] Behaviorists, on the other hand, worked in laboratories, conducting carefully controlled experiments with rats and dogs, and few people saw connections between that work and therapy. My father's approach sought to apply ideas derived from learning theory to practical problems of human happiness.

I do not attempt to review the vast literature here; my goal is to show that my father's general approach and many of his specific ideas form the basis of behavior therapy. I also include a few examples of his ideas in areas where he did not make important contributions to show the breadth of his interests and the depth of some of his insights.

In the third paragraph of *CRT* my father says that by "building our therapeutic methods on the bedrock of Pavlov, we can keep out of the Freudian metaphysical quicksands" (p. 9).[9] This may be overstated; a fairer characterization of the interplay of Pavlovian theories and my father's methods is that his techniques were "inspired by theory," if you will, rather than derived from it. They were guided by his strong ideas about the importance of conditioning and actions in the world, his belief in the value of excitatory behavior, and his exceptional clinical insights. We had many lively discussions about this in the two decades preceding his death. He vigorously disagreed with me, but I am convinced that his greatest and most lasting contributions to behavior therapy—and thereby to increasing human happiness—can best be evaluated by focusing on the enduring value of his methods and his

---

[8] If a psychoanalyst's patients come four times per week that means about 180 hours per year, so ten patients will generate 1800 billable hours per year. If a typical patient of my father needed ten sessions, then 180 patients are required to fill 1800 hours. Brief therapy is much better for patients, of course, but creates challenges for therapists trying to make a living.

[9] The metaphorical contrast of Pavlovian "bedrock" and Freudian "quicksands" is typical of my father's linguistic playfulness, which characterized his conversation as well as his writing.

insights, not on the relationship of his methods to a rigorous theoretical framework. When therapeutic insights and theory conflicted in his practice, therapeutic efficacy virtually always won. Moreover, theoretical frameworks change over time; today's are very different from those of seventy years ago.

The opening remarks at the Charlottesville conference in 1962, the first meeting of therapists interested in behavioral methods, were made by Ian Stevenson, M.D., chair of the Psychiatry Department of the University of Virginia Medical School (the host institution), an old-school but open-minded psychiatrist and trained psychoanalyst. "I regard these new therapies," he said, "as far more important than their concomitant theories, which I think have nothing whatever to do with the question of whether or not these new therapies are better than the old ones" (Stevenson, 1964, p. 4).

Although that was not my father's position[10] (or, almost certainly, that of the other conference attendees), it is a critical observation. In those days—the early 1960's—behavioral therapies were new, terminology was often imprecise, and theories were often underspecified.[11] Stevenson's point was that if a therapy works, it should be used, and is worthy of further study and elaboration, regardless of theoretical motivation or the rigor of theoretical analysis.

My father's therapy was driven by one essential goal: enabling people to be happier. They came to him because they were unhappy or unsatisfied, sometimes with an identified problem, sometimes with more general malaise. He believed that the path to greater happiness, whatever the problem, required action rather than focusing on insight. "The history of the individual is stored in his protoplasm, and in his actions his history

---

[10] Indeed, my father wrote: "Although we solemnly swear that the theories we work with are experimentally supported and internally consistent, and that our therapeutic practices are derived solely from these theories, the fact remains that our therapeutic practices and our results can be evaluated quite apart from these theoretical bases" (Salter, 1964, p. 30).

[11] Behavior therapy now has the opposite problem: a proliferation of theories and associated terminologies and therapeutic methods, making ever finer distinctions. Over the past decade or so, David H. Barlow and colleagues have been developing theories and applying techniques based on the idea that "splitting disorders into…fine [Diagnostic and Statistical Manual of Mental Disorders] categories may be highlighting relatively trivial differences" (Barlow et al., 2014, p. 344). They conclude that neuroticism, an old idea in psychopathology and personality theory, explains a variety of anxiety and emotional disorders, and, crucially, that neuroticism can be changed and is therefore a high-value target for therapy. My father had a similar idea. From the beginning of his practice, he used personality tests, first the Bernreuter, then the MMPI, typically before therapy began and again at its end. Dozens of case studies in CRT mention improvements in patients' neuroticism scores as evidence of effective therapy.

repeats itself. Through psychotherapy we manufacture new history, which repeats itself in his new actions" (p. 234). His recommended action was of a particular kind: being more excitatory ("assertive" in today's language) in their daily lives. "Inhibition becomes excitation only through action" (p. 144). This would provide positive feedback and in turn help to form new, healthy habits. It is hard now to believe that these ideas were revolutionary, but in 1949 they were. Although he was interested in theory, his focus was always on clinical work. His emphasis on excitatory behavior pervades *CRT*.

If patients already knew how to behave in order to feel better, they wouldn't need to see him; if they would not change, they were wasting their time and his. He was highly directive: in several case reports he explicitly discusses urging patients to a divorce. "These women [who come seeking to change how they feel about difficult husbands] need divorce and not psychotherapy".[12] He would often say that the easy part was knowing what patients should do; the challenge lay in getting them to do it.

Although his therapeutic strategy was the same for virtually all his patients, his tactics were eclectic; he would do whatever it took. This exemplifies his strongest motivation and his greatest gift. In conversation, he referred to this idea as "getting the hooks in," meaning finding ways to motivate the patient to listen. In addition, he would leverage their feelings for him, and in *CRT* he discusses "the constructive use of past conditionings" in therapy (chapter 7, pp. 50–59). He provides a number of examples of how he used elements from his subjects' prior lives and relationships and exploited their relationships with him to encourage excitatory behavior. Once they became excitatory in their lives outside the office, they would get positive reinforcement from their actions and interactions.

"People are faithful to the grooves in their emotional phonograph records," he posited, "and rather than bemoaning this, it means that with a masochist we must be stern, with a club man type we must be amusing, and with a scholarly person we must be as analytical as possible" (p. 50).[13]

---

[12] In 1970 he sued Gary Grant for nonpayment of fees for treating him and Dyan Cannon, his then wife. Grant claimed that he didn't have to pay because "Salter failed in treating and counseling my wife so that the condition of estrangement was not corrected or ameliorated but was in fact aggravated" (Albelli, 1970, p. 68). That is, my father would be paid only if Cannon did not divorce Grant. Albelli's article in *The New York Daily News* – the city's most popular tabloid – was titled "Cary Sued by Psychologist." A friend of mine who wrote for *The New York Post* – the other major tabloid – said that the headline should have read "Salter Sues Actor." I suspect that this was, deep down, how my father thought of it. A settlement was reached with which he was quite pleased.

[13] Cyril Franks, the first president of the AABT and the first editor of its flagship journal, quotes

The quote concludes: "As I have stressed, there is no communication except in terms of the person being treated." Or, as he says in the prior paragraph, "We must talk to people in their private, personally conditioned language. Anything else is gibberish."

A more traditional way to say this is that building rapport was a critical element of his approach. Of course, this was not unique to him or to behavior therapy in general, but he was unusually explicit about it. Despite my father's contempt for the Freudian idea of "transference," he uses what psychoanalysts would certainly call transference in some of his clinical examples. Transference is an endlessly complicated topic in psychotherapy, and I have neither the interest nor the competence to discuss it in any detail. It essentially means "transferring" (and perhaps transforming) feelings for others onto the therapist. My father cared about his patients' feelings for him but used them to motivate—even manipulate—the patient to do what he thought they should, rather than to gain insight into the sources of their problems. His goal was *action*, not *insight*. Anticipating my father's approval for an action or seeking it when reporting it to him facilitated therapy; he didn't care, and didn't think patients should care, about *why* they valued his approval, although he employed a number of techniques to wean them from needing it. Indeed, he says "Despite my belief in directional therapy, my objective is to get the individual to do the correct thing by himself" (p. 120).

He did, however, accept a central idea behind transference: that aspects of behavior and emotional life could indeed be reflected in interactions with the therapist. In speaking of patients who do not establish rapport due to attitudes of "satire and cynicism," he observed that "those who act this way toward the therapist do so in all of their other personal relations" (p. 112). But he did not use this to help them understand those "personal relations"; rather, he would try (not always successfully) to break through and get them to take his advice. So he used a Freudian notion with a nod to behaviorist ideas ("private, personally conditioned language") toward an explicit behavioral goal.

this, with some ambivalence, in discussing how the therapist can develop reinforcing stimuli suited to the particular patient, after saying: "Unfortunately, generalized verbal reinforcers cannot be standardized for universal application. The therapist needs to adapt his behavior to the history of the patient" (Franks, 1969, p. 455). Systematic desensitization, popularized by Wolpe (1958), provides a useful contrast: it is indeed systematic, and describes the steps the *therapist* should take (rather than focusing on the patient). That has the advantages of making it easier to teach and enabling less gifted therapists to deliver therapy, but it is applicable only to a fairly narrow range of problems: phobias and some anxiety disorders.

Most of the case studies in *CRT* demonstrate his flexibility. As a later example, he treated a successful Broadway composer soon after *CRT* was published, who eventually became a friend. (Such friendships were acceptable in those innocent days, and occurred frequently in my father's clinical practice.) Coincidentally, more than forty years later, the director of a successful revival of one of this composer's shows was also a patient. My father told me that he was having trouble "getting his hooks in," so in the second or third session he reached into his desk and handed the patient a small sketch the (long dead) composer had made of him. My father pointed at the patient and said, "He was sitting right there." He told me that this made all the difference in the patient's commitment to therapy, and it illustrates his ability to improvise when necessary. That sketch hangs above my desk as I type this.

At my father's memorial service I told a story my mother had related a few weeks earlier to illustrate the idea that he would do whatever it took for his patients. Just months before he died, a young woman arrived for her appointment looking tired and a little disheveled. When she came out an hour later, she looked much better, "Like your father had brushed out her hair," my mother told me. This got a laugh, as people visualized my frail father standing behind the patient chair—where many of them had sat—wielding a brush and, of course, talking. After the service, an elegant young woman approached me and revealed that the story was about her. "No, he didn't brush my hair," she said, "but he sure made me feel better."

Despite his intentions, my father's methods were not always tightly coupled to his theoretical positions. Cyril Franks, in the first detailed review of behavior therapy, was fairly dismissive of *CRT* owing to the disconnect between techniques and theory: "The publication of Salter's *Conditioned Reflex Therapy* (1949) aroused some popular interest in the idea of applying conditioning methods to abnormal behavior but the book had little impact among psychologists because the main clinical method described had no apparent relationship to experimentally established principles" (Franks, 1969, p. x).

Goldfried and Davison (1976) echo this critique but note that "While many would disagree with [Salter's characterization] of the relationship between his theory and his practice, he nonetheless occupies a central role in the development of behavior therapy" (p. 5). Kazdin (1978) agrees that the linkages between theory and practice in *CRT* were unconvincing but affirms the importance of its contributions: "Although the specific Pavlovian notions of inhibition and excitation that were posed as the theoretical base of conditioned reflex therapy have been refuted, fuller versions of techniques initiated by Salter are still being employed" (p. 174). This remains true today.

A Man Ahead of His Time

Although my father's appeals to theory were not compelling, his therapeutic insights and methods have stood the test of time, and many of the techniques he presented in *CRT* are pervasive in behavior therapy now, seventy years after publication. Efforts by scholars to tie them to contemporary theories would be welcome.

CRT was the first book about behavior therapy. It also introduced many techniques in use today. Lay readers may well not care about these claims; as long as *CRT* is interesting and useful, it shouldn't matter whether my father was first. Some professional readers might be skeptical, not having encountered my father's work in their training. Such readers should consider reading *CRT*. If they are immersed in the field, they will recognize its primacy; if not, their opinions are of little importance.

In this section I cite a range of secondary sources to document my father's professional contributions. There are also a few examples of his prescience about other topics to illustrate the breadth of his interests and insights despite the fact that he did not make substantive contributions to them.

Several standard histories of behavior therapy from the late 1960s to the late '70s acknowledged my father's contributions. I cite some of them below. However, as noted above, beginning in the 1980s and continuing to the present day, his work has been cited less frequently.

In 1997, the AABT (now ABCT) celebrated its thirtieth anniversary and commemorated it with two special issues of *Behavior Therapy*, its primary scientific journal (Summer and Autumn 1997; volume 28, numbers 3 and 4), discussing the history and future of behavior therapy. None of the 43 articles cites my father. Twenty-two cite Joseph Wolpe, 13 of them referencing *Psychotherapy by Reciprocal Inhibition* (Wolpe, 1958). I note, however, that four past presidents of AABT have provided blurbs for *CRT*, as have two former presidents of the American Psychological Association. The AABT's Lifetime Achievement Award was posthumously awarded to Andrew Salter in 1996.

According to Kazdin, "The importance of Salter's work to behavior modification lies in its roots in conditioning and learning theory and its emphatic focus on therapy... The innovative feature of Salter's approach was not simply to use conditioning principles to explain existing therapy techniques, as Dollard and Miller (1950) had done, but to devise specific treatments and apply them clinically" (1978, p. 173). His detailed discussion of *CRT* on pages 171–174 is quite sympathetic and useful. Kazdin also cites *CRT* as the earliest of four "landmarks" in the history of behavior therapy (pp. 202–203). Twenty-five years later, in his review of the 2002 edition of *CRT*, he writes: "Salter applied conditioning much more broadly to therapy and therapeutic problems than had been the case previously. His leap from learning theory and research to treatments for clinical practice was novel and groundbreaking" (2003, p. 408).

Davison's obituary of my father (1996) reaffirmed this: "Salter used learning principles as a guide to devising new therapeutic methods. Salter thus courageously and successfully challenged the establishment and articulated a vision and a set of techniques that have become so widely accepted and applied that he is often not formally cited" (p. 175).

Below is a brief discussion of some of the techniques first introduced in *CRT*.

My father's goal of enabling patients be more excitatory in their lives outside the office is the now ubiquitous idea of *assertion*, stressed in dozens—perhaps hundreds—of self-help books. "Early recognition of the problem of unassertive behavior was provided by Salter," according to Goldfried and Davison (1976, p. 153). The "patient was given training in assertive behavior (Salter 1949, Wolpe 1958) in order to substitute a more adaptive behavior for the 'escape' and 'denial' afforded by 'hysterical symptoms'" (Franks, 1969, p. 262). Similarly, Kazdin (1978) says that: "The use of assertive responses had been advocated by Andrew Salter (1949), whose therapy technique was based upon Pavlovian concepts. Salter claimed successful treatment of several disorders by having individuals behave assertively in everyday interpersonal situations. Wolpe was impressed with Salter's results although he rejected the theoretical basis of the technique. Wolpe used assertive responses for inhibiting anxiety in interpersonal situations but interpreted the technique according to the principle of reciprocal inhibition" (p. 156). "Pavlov's theory inspired a number of applied behavior therapists, most notably Andrew Salter (1949, 1964) who developed his conditioned-reflex therapy. For Salter, the neurotic individual is suffering basically from an excess of inhibition, thus blocking his or her normal output of excitation. Therapy is therefore designed to encourage the patient to express feeling directly. Wolpe's (1958) 'assertive' response approach represents a very similar technique and conceptualization" (Levis, 1982, p. 42).

As part of his excitatory training, my father encouraged patients to use the word *I* intentionally; indeed, his discussion of General Eisenhower's healthy emotions in *CRT* (pp. 20–22) makes much of his use of that word. One of his "six techniques for increasing excitation" is "the *deliberate* use of the word *I* as much as possible" (p. 70). Fritz Perls's emphasis on "I-Talk" (Perls, 1969) illustrates the importance of this insight.[14]

The early women's movement embraced the idea of assertion. Although that application was certainly not part of my father's original concept, he took great pride in it and cherished the letters and inscribed books he was sent by first-wave feminists thanking him as the women's movement advanced.

As early as 1941, my father was committed to the idea of *brief therapy*. He was convinced that successful therapy—"successful" defined as the patient's being happier—could often be accomplished much more rapidly, building on the work of the behaviorists and applying his approach to hypnosis. In the article in *Life*, the author reports that "The majority of Salter's cases learn the [autohypnosis] routine after five or six interviews, and rarely see him afterwards" (Wickware, 1941, p. 91). That is less than two weeks as opposed to the hundreds of sessions commonly required by psychoanalysis. On the first page of *CRT* my father stakes out a typically strong position: "I say flatly that psychotherapy can be quite rapid and extremely efficacious. I know so because I have done so. And if the reader will bear with me, I will show him how…we can…help ten persons in the time that the Freudians are getting ready to 'help' one" (p. 9). The idea of brief therapy, and specific approaches to it, originated in my father's work years before managed care and the strictures of insurance coverage (which, like virtually all individual health care providers, he loathed).

CRT introduced the idea of using *relaxation* via *imagery linked to positive affect* for reducing phobias and anxieties and for changing behavior such as nail-biting, insomnia, smoking, stuttering, and more complex social problems. *CRT* also introduced a number of specific techniques for inducing relaxation and employing imagery. The method of *systematic desensitization*, later named and elaborated by Joseph Wolpe, who had just finished training as a psychiatrist in South Africa when *CRT* appeared, is a detailed—and indeed systematic—application of this approach to phobias and related disorders. My father used relaxation and imagery much more broadly, beyond phobias and beyond the therapist's office.

---

[14] This is not to say that my father believed in a simple linear relationship between saying *I* or *me* and mental health. For example, he would almost certainly have characterized Donald Trump's frequent use of the first person as a sign of pathological narcissism.

Kazdin observed, "Salter (1949) may have been the first to employ imagery in behavior modification. He manipulated imagery to alter the client's mood and feelings in the therapy sessions as well as in his everyday experience to overcome maladaptive reactions such as anxiety. In therapy, Salter's use of imagery paralleled desensitization very closely" (1978, p. 222).

Wolpe's method of *systematic desensitization by reciprocal inhibition* (1958) is commonly viewed as a founding document of behavior therapy, cited more than 7,500 times as of late 2018, compared with slightly over 700 citations for *CRT*. Although it is the first rigorous articulation of a behavioral approach to therapy, its essential ideas were based on *CRT*.

"Systematic desensitization by reciprocal inhibition" is based on two simple ideas. "Systematic desensitization" involves constructing an ordered list (called a "hierarchy" in the literature) of fear- or anxiety-inducing stimuli and then systematically reducing anxiety beginning with the item lowest in the list. For example, a person with a snake phobia might have a list beginning with a photograph of a worm, then a photograph of a snake, then a video of a snake, and so forth. "Reciprocal inhibition" is the method by which anxiety is reduced for each item: the patient simultaneously is given a positive stimulus with the anxiety-provoking one, so responses to the two stimuli "reciprocally" inhibit each other. For example, the patient might be taught to imagine a soothing image and to relax when shown a picture of a worm. Once the worm picture no longer evokes anxiety, the therapist moves on to the next item in the list. Although the particular hierarchy and counteracting stimuli must be developed individually for each patient, the process of doing so is well-defined.

The core of the method is the association of a positive response, typically relaxation, with aversive stimuli. This concept pervades the case studies in *CRT*. Various academic psychologists support my father's primacy. Two quotations above from Kazdin (1978, pp. 156 and 222) and one from Franks (1969, p. 262) say this explicitly, as do Hazlett-Stevens and Craske (2008): "One of the most influential exposure techniques is the procedure of systematic desensitization developed by Salter (1949) and by Wolpe (1958)" (p. 223). His obituary in *The New York Times* also noted his contribution to systematic desensitization: "The therapy Mr. Salter employed encouraged patients to express their emotions and used visual imagery to reduce anxiety. It also moved people past their fears by gradually getting them accustomed to being around the things they feared" (Freeman, 1996).

My father also emphasized ways for patients to be excitatory in their *real life outside the office*, with spouses, colleagues, friends, and strangers. These interactions would provide positive feedback, thereby producing healthy new habits. This emphasis on *homework, rehearsal,* or *in vivo exposure* has become another central feature of behavior therapy (Hazlett-Stevens & Craske, 2008).

Franks (1969) calls it "instigation therapy," and defines it as "the systematic use of specific suggestions and assigned tasks in the patient's daily environment... The patient is taught to modify his extratheraputic environment and to apply learning techniques to his own behavior. The approach is best characterized as one in which the patient learns to become his own therapist" (p. 552).[15] He reports that "Salter has applied instigation techniques to a host of neurotic problems" (p. 457). Hallam (2015, p. 63) puts it well: "Salter's aim was to arrange for new emotional experiences through what the person did. What was new about this at the time was his emphasis on action... His objective was to get the person to do the correct thing by himself."

Some methods now used in *cognitive behavior therapy* (CBT) are also present in *CRT*. Indeed, Albert Ellis, widely considered the founder of CBT, thought so: "I was not the first therapist to use what became known as cognitive behavior therapy (CBT), since a few practitioners—such as Herzberg (1945) and Salter (1949)—had employed aspects of it previously" (Ellis, 2003, p. 91).

As noted in the Foreword, my father held the virtually universal belief that homosexuality was a problem that should be fixed. Due to the stigma of homosexuality at the time, my father's homosexual patients were ashamed of it—"emotionally inhibited"—in his vocabulary. They came wanting to be "cured". Gay pride did not exist; Stonewall was 20 years in the future. Homosexuals wanted to feel better, and they were convinced that the way to do so was to "stop" being homosexual.

Despite the outdated premise in the early editions of CRT, my father takes startlingly modern positions on the origins and morality of homosexuality. "As for society's reactions to homosexuality, that serves to intensify the [homosexual's] inhibitory patterns" (Salter, 1961, p. 285). Talking about experiences that precipitate active homosexual behavior, he says that "Incidents may pull the trigger but the gun was loaded before" (p. 287). And he argues that "The legal penalties against homosexuality

---

[15] This emphasis on "self-therapy" was central to my father's earliest work on autohypnosis (1941), which discussed how patients could apply it in real time, in real-world situations.

are as stupid as those against drug addiction" (p. 300; his position on drug addiction is still not fully accepted).

There are also occasional mentions of homosexuality in the current text, particularly in the case studies, that reflect the prevalent attitude, primarily addressing the issue that homosexual behavior or desire can cause problems in heterosexual relationships.

While my father almost always failed to "cure" homosexuals, many of those "failures" went on to become happier people, albeit homosexual still. He eventually came to believe, in the decades after CRT, that he was right about homosexuals' need for emotional excitation, but wrong about the focus of that excitation: it should be used to enable them to be comfortable with their sexual orientation, not to "cure" them of it. And this he did for many of them.

In Salter (1964, pp. 25–27), my father discusses the importance of the *orienting reflex* in his approach to therapy. The orienting reflex is, simply put, the response of an organism to novelty. It is thus, in a sense, the opposite of a conditioned reflex and has clear adaptive advantages. He thought that inhibition of the orienting reflex was unhealthy and found that eliminating that inhibition had "a very strong impact on the patient" (p. 26). Indeed, he had come to believe that "freeing the orienting reflex" was a foundation of healthy "feeling talk." Note that simple real-world exercises can be used to (re)develop an appropriate orienting reflex: for example, on entering a room (restaurant, cocktail party, business meeting, conference, and so on), a patient should look around and notice who is there. This does not require any interaction, and so will be easier for the inhibited patient than, say, starting or joining a conversation. However, it serves as a useful step toward pursuing interactions, which, of course, my father encouraged. In addition, it helps patients to respond *contingently*— that is, authentically—to their environment. This disinhibition of the orienting reflex can be seen as a form of "*social mindfulness*."[16]

In *CRT*, my father was explicit about the *risks of smoking*, decades before they were widely acknowledged. "By now everybody knows that the more you smoke the quicker you die—that is, everybody knows except the advertising agencies, the cigarette manufacturers, and certain paid

---

[16] I want to thank Mark Davis, of the The UK College of Hypnosis and Hypnotherapy, a psychotherapist psychotherapist and trainer of therapists, for drawing my attention to the importance of this idea, which Davis uses effectively in therapy and therapist training. He was also responsible for initiating this new edition, by calling me and encouraging it, and, crucially, by introducing me to the publisher.

researchers" (p. 170). He told me that in the mid 1940s he used to ask his secretary for an occasional cigarette until one day he picked a pack up from her desk before he had formulated the thought that he wanted a cigarette. He realized that smoking had become a habit no longer under his conscious control; he put it down and never smoked again.

My father was ahead of his time in his interest in the *interplay of evolution and the environment*. He was convinced that many important aspects of personality and human endowment in general are inborn, but also that much was malleable. He touches on this issue frequently in *CRT*. The first words of Chapter 2 are reasonable and useful even after the explosion of genetic knowledge in the seven decades since its publication: "Everybody talks about heredity but nobody does anything about it. It is immutable one second after conception. Consequently, let us concern ourselves with environment, because it is the only thing we can change after we're born. Physical traits, and this includes intelligence [a contentious position he never abandoned], are inherited, but happiness is not based upon them. Happiness or misery is determined after the child is born" (p. 14). The therapist (and the patient) had to work with what they could change: "If heredity is everything, then therapy can only be nothing" (p. 109).[17]

He had a strong view of the fundamentally animal nature of human beings: "Man's physical and emotional equipment is the same as it was ages into obscurity. Yet modern man finds himself enmeshed in a web of constraining social forms with which he has more and more been required to conform, belying his essential nature, and denying that the human is now, as then, an animal—predatory, sadistic, craving, and emotional" (p. 18). The burgeoning field of evolutionary psychology is driven by a more sophisticated version of this idea. The tension between it and the preceding—that only environmental factors can be changed— runs through the current political and social debates about evolutionary psychology and will probably continue to do so regardless of which scientific details are eventually accepted.[18] This is not to suggest that my father contributed to our understanding of the ways in which nature

---

[17] My father's statement about the origins of homosexuality above: "Incidents may pull the trigger but the gun was loaded before" (*CRT*, second edition (1961), p. 287). Can be viewed as a primitive, intuitive version of epigenetics: the idea that environmental influences affect the expression of genetically encoded traits or processes. See Weinhold (2006) for a detailed discussion of epigenesis, which has since become a major research focus.

[18] My father's commitment to the power of conditioning-based methods for increasing human happiness, despite his belief in the fundamentally animal nature of humans, may have come from the same impulses that made him such an advocate of socialist ideas as a teenager.

and nurture interact, but it shows his keen intuitive sense of what was interesting and important in ambient intellectual life.

Also intriguing to him was what has come to be termed *cognitive neuroscience*: the ways in which neurology and studies of brain chemistry can enhance our understanding of phenomena commonly thought of as mental (emotional and cognitive both). Of course, Pavlov was a physiologist, but his interest in neurology went beyond Pavlov and lasted his entire life. In typically vigorous phrasing, he wrote: "Psychological events are physiological events, and conditioning is the modification of tissue by experience" (p. 234). His basic theoretical framework, that learning consists of strengthening cortical pathways and that such pathways can be either reinforced or inhibited, has become a commonplace in contemporary neuroscience. His involvement in neurology was so great that he and a colleague developed a digital electroencephalograph that was awarded U.S. patent number 3,841,309 for "a method of analyzing bioelectric outputs of living things by sensing, amplifying and comparing such outputs with selected predetermined values and providing indications of each occurrence of the departure of a discrete value of such outputs from such predetermined values." (1974). And he anticipated, in general terms, that progress in electronics might revolutionize investigation of mental processes: "[B]y the end of the century…[p]rogress in electronic miniaturization will allow us to check, in our offices, how the patient 'really' felt when he visited his mother last Sunday, or got up before an audience, or had an argument with his wife" (Salter, 1964, p. 23). It took longer than he thought it would, but sensors and associated applications on smartphones have come frighteningly close to realizing this vision.

In cases 10 and 11 (pp. 66–69) my father uses *paradoxical interventions*—encouraging patients to induce the very symptoms they seek to eliminate—as a mechanism to give them control over their habits in order to inhibit the undesired behavior. He did not originate this idea; indeed, he quotes *Women in Love* (Lawrence, 1921) as the source.[19] In case 10, he uses the metaphor of logical and emotional "batteries" that can power behavior and explains that it is the emotional battery (which he defines as the autonomic

---

[19] My father's quotation from Lawrence: "A very great doctor taught me…that to cure oneself of a bad habit, one should *force* oneself to do it, when one would not do it—make oneself do it—and then the habit would disappear…. If you bite your nails, for example. Then, when you don't want to bite your nails, bite them, make yourself bite them. And you would find the habit was broken."

nervous system) that makes the patient blush involuntarily. When the patient blushes, the logical system will tell him—futilely at first—that he should not blush. But learning to blush intentionally "will put logic in charge of blushing. It will neutralize the involuntary emotional impulses and condition, or train, a deliberate control over blushing. When you control it, that will be the end of it" (p. 77).

This example also anticipates the "*two systems*" that are the foci of *Thinking, Fast and Slow* by Nobel Laureate Daniel Kahneman: "System 1 operates automatically and quickly with little or no effort and no sense of voluntary control. System 2 allocates attention to the effortful mental activities that demand it" (Kahneman, 2011, pp. 20–21). Kahneman's overarching goal was enabling people to make decisions using System 2 (my father's "logical battery") to overcome the emotional, involuntary impulses that too often drive them. This is similar to my father's objective in case 10—eliminating the effects of System 1 on undesired behaviors and reactions. However, his fundamental goal in therapy was essentially the opposite of Kahneman's: to make people *more* excitatory, assertive, spontaneous, in touch with their feelings, thereby enabling them to live healthier emotional lives, their behaviors less driven by what he saw as the repressive System 2. He says this in various ways throughout *CRT*, perhaps occasionally too strongly. For example, he tells a patient to "[L]et your emotions run your mind as nature intended" (p. 132). Of course, he did not advocate making consequential life decisions without careful analysis, but his focus was on emotional health, not optimal decision making.

In his discussion of treating addictions (Chapter 15, pp. 147–173), he approvingly cites a 1931 paper in which the therapist provides a conditioned stimulus of massaging the arm of a morphine addict while giving him the unconditioned stimulus of a morphine injection. Over time he decreases the amount of morphine in the injection until it is only sterile water, and found that there were no withdrawal symptoms. My father then speculates that "Perhaps it would even prove as effective if the patient were told the truth when he was receiving the sterile water, especially if he had been given a simple explanation of conditioning for its suggestive effect" (p. 169). This precisely anticipates the counterintuitive idea of "*open-label placebos*" that has emerged as an active research area over the past decade. Such interventions, with such explanations, have shown effectiveness for lower back pain, irritable bowel syndrome, even major depressive disorder. (See, respectively, Carvalho et al., 2016; Kaptchuk et al., 2010; and Kelley et al., 2012.) Although my father had no influence on placebo research, this is another example of his intuitions about psychological phenomena. For many years when he suspected underlying organic issues, he referred patients to Arthur K. Shapiro, a psychiatrist and friend. Shapiro was an author of a widely cited book on the placebo effect (Shapiro & Shapiro, 1980).

As an example of his wide-ranging interests, he became interested in skin chemistry in the late 1950s, specifically in the effects of cold creams and the like. He spent hours experimenting with various oils and additives and testing with litmus paper to measure pH. His idea was that skin had an inherent—that is, "natural"—acidity, and that most skin creams altered it, to detrimental effect. This research resulted in a product, test marketed by a major company, called Placid, that was intended to preserve the "natural acid mantle" that protects the skin.[20] Placid was not a commercial success, but the idea of marketing a product as "natural" and "restoring nature's own protective mantle" seems shockingly modern. Although he did not contribute to advances in skin care or product marketing, he clearly had a clever idea.

A Final Personal Note

Preparing this new edition of *CRT* has been, among other things, a labor of love, for my father, of course, but for my mother as well. She was a crucial contributor to his clinical practice, not only as a loving and supportive spouse, but also in the office, where she worked with him for almost thirty years. Patients would often come early for their appointments in order to talk to her, and a number of former patients reached out to her after his death, seeking her wise counsel. In his review of the 2002 edition of *CRT*, Alan Kazdin (2003, p. 410), after describing my father as "perhaps the most unforgettable character I ever knew, ... a wonderful mix of childish mischief and wisdom," went on to say that "[I]f there were another unforgettable character to compete with this title [his wife, Rhoda] would be the other person." He warmly concluded that, "If one were on a debating team, an infinitely long voyage, or in need of comfort from a horrible personal loss, Andy and Rhoda would be the choice partners."

My mother was also responsible for the organization of my father's extensive files, from patient intake cards from 1941 through

[20] I have a one-by-two-inch brochure included in boxes of Placid explaining that it "is a delicate blend of seven protective acids [that] keeps the skin smooth, soft, and glowing." These "seven natural essential acids...restore and maintain nature's own protective mantle." And "With Placid you always look your prettiest!"

correspondence with hundreds of patients, former patients, and strangers—some famous, but most of them ordinary people—to his notes on innumerable topics, many far from psychology. There were many treasures in those files.[21] She kept our household functioning and the office as well. She was also a wonderful mother in the traditional senses.

This edition has new blurbs from three eminent psychologists: David H. Barlow, Steven C. Hayes, and the late Francine Shapiro; only Barlow knew my father, from conversations at AABT meetings in the 1970s. I was touched that all three of these busy people thanked me for reaching out to them, said how much they enjoyed rereading *CRT,* and affirmed that it remains a valuable resource now, not merely a historical artifact.

Preparing this edition gave me increased understanding of my father. He made contributions that have endured for decades and will endure for many more. Also—something I didn't appreciate until I dug into his files—from his mid 20s through his late 30s, he was astonishingly

---

[21] Here are some of them.

There is a lengthy transcript of an all-day meeting in mid-1944 of my father, Paul de Kruif, and Charles F. Kettering (Kettering, de Kruif, & Solter [*sic*], 1944). Kettering was a friend of de Kruif, head of research at General Motors—perhaps the world's leading industrial research center—for almost thirty years and responsible for many of GM's inventions (including the electric starter), as well as a founder and the organizer of the Sloan-Kettering Cancer Center. I like to imagine my father, a slight thirty-year-old Jew from New York, with these two tough, accomplished WASP outdoorsmen, de Kruif in his midfifties, Kettering almost seventy. Several times de Kruif affectionately refers to him as "this boy," a term Kettering frequently used for the young engineers who worked for him. They agreed that the lot of the innovator is difficult because people refuse to accept ideas that differ from what they have been taught. Kettering predicted that in getting his ideas accepted, my father would "have the same troubles as Darwin…had when you to try to go from [Pavlov's] dogs to humans" (Kettering et al., 1944, p. 3). They discussed free will. They lamented anti-vaccination laws and Kettering remarked that "It depends altogether on whether the preachers are for it or not, not on whether the doctors are for it." De Kruif's most famous book, *Microbe Hunters* (1926), dealt extensively with the history of vaccination, for which he was an important public advocate. Kettering was a major medical philanthropist. (This was a decade before the polio epidemic and the Salk vaccine.) Kettering urged de Kruif to listen to my father's advice about facilitating his writing. De Kruif remained one of my father's closest friends until his death in 1970

A copy of an answering service message from a 1970s giant of Wall Street thanks my father for "last night's very successful election," which surely referred to activities in the bedroom rather than the boardroom. There are dozens of birth announcements, over four decades, for children named Andrew or Andrea. There are thick files of correspondence with my father's four former secretaries, including postcards from their honeymoons, baby pictures, and marriage announcements for those now grown babies. An advertisement from the late 1940s seeks a new secretary with a college degree "in any field except psychology." And there is a legal document in which Cary Grant affirms that he will never sue my father.

productive in his professional life. Three books, one of them a landmark in the history of psychotherapy; building and maintaining a thriving clinical practice; those frequent mentions in national publications; the day with Kettering, one of the most revered public figures in America's 20th century industrial progress – these were products of, among other things, his capacity for diligent hard work.

I hope this republication of *CRT* can help even more people to benefit from that hard work and the brilliant insights that went into it.

BIBLIOGRAPHY

FOR THE AFTERWORD

Albelli, A. (1970, March 6). Cary Sues Psychologist Over Bills. *New York Daily News*, p. 68.

Barlow, D. H., Ellard, K. K., Fairholme, C., Farchione, T. J., Boisseau, C., Allen, L., & Ehrenreich-May, J. (2011). *Unified protocol for the transdiagnostic treatment of emotional disorders*. New York, NY: Oxford University Press.

Barlow, D. H., Sauer-Zavala, S., Carl, J. R., Bullis, J. R., & Ellard, K. K. (2014). The nature, diagnosis, and treatment of neuroticism: Back to the future. *Clinical Psychological Science*, 2: 344–365.

Benson, H. (1975). *The Relaxation Response*. New York, NY: Morrow.

Carvalho, C., Caetano, J. M., Cunha, L., Rebouta, P., Kaptchuk, T. J., & Kirsch, I. (2016). Open-label placebo treatment in chronic low back pain: a randomized controlled trial. *Pain*, *157*(12), 2766–2772.

Condon, R. (1959). *The Manchurian Candidate*. New York, NY: McGraw-Hill.

De Kruif, P. (1926). *Microbe Hunters*. New York, NY: Harcourt, Brace and Company.

Davison, G. (1996). Andrew Salter (1914-1996): Founding Behavior Therapist. *APS Observer*, *9*(6), 30-31.

Ellis, A. (2003). Cognitive Restructuring of The Disputing of Irrational Beliefs. In W. O'Donohue, J. Fisher, & S. Hayes (Eds.); *Cognitive Behavior Therapy: Applying Empirically Supported Techniques in Your Practice* (pp. 79-83). Hoboken, NJ: John Wiley & Sons.

Freeman, K. (1996, October 9). Andrew Salter, Behavior Therapist, Dies. *New York Times*. https://www.nytimes.com/1996/10/09/nyregion/

andrew-salter-behavior
-therapist-82-dies.html.

Franks, C. (1969). *Behavior Therapy: Appraisal and Status*. New York, NY: McGraw-Hill.

Goldfried, M. R., & Davison, G. C. (1976). Clinical Behavior Therapy. New York, NY: Holt, Rinehart and Winston.

Hallam, R. (2015). *The Therapy Relationship: A Special Kind of Friendship*. London: Karnac Books.

Hazlett-Stevens, H., & Craske, M. C. (2008). Live (In Vivo) Exposure. In W. O'Donohue, J. Fisher, & S. Hayes (Eds.); *Cognitive Behavior Therapy: Applying Empirically Supported Techniques in Your Practice* (pp. 223–228). Hoboken, NJ: John Wiley & Sons.

Kaempffert, W. (1941, June 8). Hypnotizing Yourself. *New York Times*, D5.

Kahneman, D. (2011). *Thinking, Fast and Slow*. New York, NY: Farrar, Straus and Giroux.

Kaptchuk T.J., Friedlander, E., Kelley, J. M., Sanchez, M. N., Kokkotou, E., Singer, J. P., et al. (2010). Placebos without Deception: A Randomized Controlled Trial in Irritable Bowel Syndrome. PLoS ONE 5(12).

Kazdin, A. (1978). *History of Behavior Modification: Experimental Foundations of Contemporary Research*. Baltimore, MD: University Park Press.

Kazdin, A. (2003). Book Review: Conditioned Reflex Therapy. *The Behavior Therapist*, *26*, 408–410.

Kelley, J. M., Kaptchuk, T. J., Cusin, C., Lipkin, S., & Fava, M. (2012). Open-label placebo for major depressive disorder: a pilot randomized controlled trial. *Psychotherapy and Psychosomatics*, *81*(5), 312–314.

Kettering, C. F., de Kruif, P., & Solter [*sic*], A. (1944, May 27). *Stenographic Transcript of a Meeting*. Detroit, MI: General Motors Research.

Kimes, B. R. (1993). Ken Purdy: King of the Road. *Automobile Quarterly*, *32*(2), 34–49.

Kuhn, T. *The Structure of Scientific Revolutions* (1962/2012). Chicago, IL: University of Chicago Press.

Lawrence, D. H. (1921), frequently reprinted). *Women in Love*. London: Martin Secker.

Levis, D. J. (1982). Experimental and Theoretical Foundations of Behavior Modification. In A. S. Belleck, M. Hersen, & A. E. Kazdin (Eds.); *International Handbook of Behavior Modification and Therapy* (pp. 27–51). New York, NY: Springer Publishing.

Maxwell, E. (1942, December 4). Elsa Maxwell's party line: Svengali in Modern Dress. *New York Post*, p. 12.

Maxwell, E. (1943, August 6). Elsa Maxwell's party line: Andrew Salter and "Auto-Hypnotism." *New York Post*, p. 12.

Maxwell, E. (1944, April 27). Elsa Maxwell's party line. Midweek roundup, II. *New York Post*, p. 12.

Perls, F. (1969) *Gestalt Therapy Verbatim*. Lafayette, CA: Real People Press.

Salter, A. (1941). Three techniques of autohypnosis. *Journal of General Psychology*, 24(2), 423–438.

Salter, A. (1944). What Is Hypnosis: Studies in Auto and Hetero Conditioning. New York, NY: Richard R. Smith.

Salter, A. (1952). The Case Against Psychoanalysis. New York, NY: Henry Holt.

Salter, A. (1961). *Conditioned Reflex Therapy, 2nd Edition*. New York, NY: Capricorn Books.

Salter, A. (1964). The Theory and Practice of Conditioned Reflex Therapy. In J. Wolpe, A. Salter, & L. Reyna. The Conditioning Therapies: The Challenge in Psychotherapy (pp. 21–37). New York, NY: Holt, Rinehart & Winston.

Salter, W. J. (1994). A Profile of Ken Purdy. *Car Collector and Car Classics*, 17(1), 52–57.

Shapiro, A. K., & Shapiro, E. (2000). *The powerful placebo: From ancient priest to modern physician*. Baltimore, MD: Johns Hopkins University Press.

Stevenson, I. (1964). Opening Remarks. In J. Wolpe, A. Salter, & L. Reyna. The Conditioning Therapies: The Challenge in Psychotherapy (pp. 3–4). New York, NY: Holt, Rinehart & Winston.

Tart, C. (Ed.). (1969) *Altered States of Consciousness*. New York, NY: John Wiley and Sons.

Time, (1941, June 2). Everyman His Own Svengali, p. 40.

Weinhold, B. (2016). Epigenetics: The Science of Change. *Environmental Health Perspectives*, 114(3): A160–A167.

Wickware, F. S. Andrew Salter and Autohypnosis (1941). *Life Magazine*, 11(19), 83–92.

Wolpe, J. (1958). Psychotherapy by Reciprocal Inhibition. Palo Alto, CA: Stanford University Press.

Wolpe, J., Salter, A., & Reyna, L. (Eds.) (1964). The Conditioning Therapies: The Challenge in Psychotherapy. New York, NY: Holt, Rinehart & Winston.

REFERENCES

CHAPTER I: FUNDAMENTALS: HYPNOSIS AND WORD AND EMOTIONAL CONDITIONING

1. PAVLOV, I. P. *Conditioned Reflexes.* Oxford University Press, 1927.
   ———. *Lectures on Conditioned Reflexes.* Volume 1. International Publishers, New York, 1928.
   ———. *Conditioned Reflexes and Psychiatry.* International Publishers, New York, 1941, p. 83.
2. HUDGINS, C. V "Conditioning and the Voluntary Control of the Pupillary Light Reflex." *Journal of General Psychology,* 1933, 8: 3-51.
3. DIVEN, K. "Certain Determinants in the Conditioning of Anxiety Reactions." *Journal of Psychology,* 1937, 3: 291-308.
4. HERRICK, C. J. *Brains of Rats and Men.* University of Chicago Press, 1926, p. 5.
5. WOLFLE, D. "Factor Analysis in the Study of Personality." *Journal of Abnormal and Social Psychology,* 1942,37: 393-397.

CHAPTER 2: INHIBITION AND EXCITATION

1. FROLOV, Y. P. *Pavlov and His School.* Oxford University Press, New York, 1937, p. 134.
2. PAVLOV, I, P. *Lectures on Conditioned Reflexes.* Vol. 1. International Publishers, New York, 1928, p. 126.

CHAPTER 3: THE EXCITATORY PERSONALITY

1. New York *Herald Tribune,* June 19, 1945: p. 5, Associated Press Dispatch.

CHAPTER 4: THE INHIBITORY PERSONALITY

1. BERNREUTER, R. G. "The Measurement of Self-Sufficiency." *Journal of Abnormal and Social Psychology,* 1933-34, 28: 291.
2. SHELDON, W. H. *The Varieties of Temperament.* Harper & Bros., New York, 1944, pp. 38,41.
3. *WATSON, J. B. Psychological Care of Infant and Child.* W. W. Norton & Co., Inc., New York, 1928, pp. 81-82.

CHAPTER 5: THE RATIONALIZATION OF CONDITIONING

1. CANTRIL, H. *The Invasion From Mars.* Princeton University Press, Princeton, 1940, p. 93.
   KORZYBSKI, A. *Science and Sanity.* Science Pa., Lancaster, Pa., 2nd edition, 1941, p. 466.
   MORGAN, C. T. *Physiological Psychology.* McGraw-Hill, Inc., New York, 1943, p. 373.

CHAPTER 6: RECONDITIONING AND DISINHIBITION IN THERAPY

1. RIVERS, W.H.R. *Instinct and the Unconscious.* Cambridge University Press, 1920, p. 176.

CHAPTER 7: THE CONSTRUCTIVE USE OF PAST CONDITIONINGS

1. MENZIES, R. "Further Studies in Conditioned Vasomotor Responses in Human Subjects." *Journal of Experimental Psychology.* 1941,29:457-482
2. HUDGINS, C. V. "Conditioning and the Voluntary Control of the Pupillary Light Reflex." *Journal of General Psychology,* 1933, 8: 3-51.

CHAPTER 8: RECONDITIONING AS ROOT THERAPY

1. WEISS, E, and ENGLISH, O. S. *Psychosomatic Medicine.* W. B. Saunders, Philadelphia, 1943, p.627.

2. FREUD, S. *The History of the Psychoanalytical Movement.* Nervous and Mental Disease Publishing Co., New York, 1917, p. 9.
3. PAVLOV, I. p. *Conditioned Reflexes and Psychiatry.* International Publishers, New York, 1941, p. 83.
4. In HEALY, W., BRONNER, A. E, and BOWERS, A. M. *Structure and Meaning of Psychoanalysis.* Alfred A. Knopf, New York, 1930, p. 299.
5. *Ibid.,* p. 309.
6. LANDIS, C. "Psychoanalytic Phenomena." *Journal of Abnormal and Social Psychology,* 1940,35: 17-28.
7. FREUD, S. *The Interpretation of Dreams.* Allen & Unwin, London, 1932, p.
8. *Insulin Shock Therapy.* Study by the Temporary Commission on [New York] State Hospital Problems, 1944.
9. DEUTSCH, A. Article in the newspaper *PM,* New York City, May 9, 1946.
10. *Ibid.,* May 6,1946.
11. *Ibid.,* June 9-10, 1946.
12. FREEMAN, W., and WATTS, J. W. *Psychosurgery.* Charles C, Thomas, Springfield, 1942, p. 312.
13. GELLHORN, E. *Autonomic Regulations.* Interscience Publishers, Inc., New York, 1943, p. 306.
14. GELLHORN, E., KESSLAR, M., and MINATOYA, H. "Influence of Metrazol, Insulin Hypoglycemia, and Electrically Induced Convulsions on Re-establishment of Inhibited Conditioned Reflexes." *Proceedings of the Society for Experimental Biology,* New York, 1942, 50: 260-262.
15. GELLHORN, E. "Further Investigations on the Recovery of Inhibited Conditioned Reactions." *Proceedings of the Society for Experimental Biology,* New York, 1942, 59: 155-161.

CHAPTER 10: SHYNESS AND THE WELL-BRED NEUROSIS

1. ROBERTSON, H. E. "Autohypnosis and Its Influence on Diagnosis." *Proceedings of the Staff Meetings of the Mayo Clinic.* Rochester, Minnesota, June 28, 1944, Vol. 19, No. 13: 336-340.
2. DUNLAP, K. *Habits, Their Making and Unmaking.* Liveright, Inc., New York, 1932, p. 78.

CHAPTER 11: THE MERRY-GO-ROUND OF LOW SELF-SUFFICIENCY

1. SUPER, D. E. "The Bernreuter Personality Inventory: A Review of Research." *Psychological Bulletin,* 1942, 39, 2: 94-125.
2. PAVLOV, I. P. *Lectures on Conditioned Reflexes.* Vol. 1. International Publishers, New York, 1928, pp. 285-286.
3. BECHTEREV, V M. *General Principles of Human Reflexology.* International Publishers, New York, translated from the Russian edition of 1928, p. 149.

CHAPTER 14 : STUTTERING

1. BENDER, J. F. *The Personality Structure of Stuttering.* Pitman Publishing Corporation, New York, 1939, p. 143. This book is based on the Bernreuter Personality Inventory.
2. Quoted in HOLLINGWORTH, H. L. *Abnormal Psychology.* Methuen & Co., London, 1931, p. 409. Elsewhere Ballard's data are often misinterpreted.
3. *Ibid.*
4. STARR, H. E. "The Hydrogen Ion Concentration of the Mixed Saliva Considered as an Index of Fatigue and of Emotional Excitation, and Applied to a Study of the Metabolic Etiology of Stammering." *American Journal of Psychology,* 1922,33:394-418.
5. STRATTON, L. D. "A Factor in the Etiology of a SubBreathing Stammerer." *Journal of Comparative Psychology,* 1924, 4: 325-345.
6. TRUMPER, M. *A Hemato-Respiratoiy Study of 101 Consecutive Cases of Stammering.* University of Pennsylvania Press, Philadelphia, 1928.
7. Kopp, G. A. "A Report on Bio-Chemical Studies of the Cause of Stuttering." *Speech Monographs,* 1934, 1: 117-132.
8. PALMER, M. E, and GILLETT, A. M. "Sex Differences in the Cardiac Rhythms of Stutterers." *Journal of Speech Disorders,* 1938, 3: 3-12.
9. ROBBINS, S. D. "Plethysmographie Study of Shock and Stammering." *American Journal of Psychology,* 1919, 48: 3—19.
10. DUNBAR, H. F. *Emotions and Bodily Changes.* Columbia University Press, New York, 2nd edition, 1938, pp. 125, 179, 192-197.
11. FLETCHER, J. M. "An Experimental Study of Stuttering." *Journal of Applied Psychology.* 1914,25:201-249.

12. TRAVIS, L. E. "Disintegration of the Breathing Movements during Stuttering." *Archives of Neurology and Psychiatry,* 1927, 18: 673-690.
13. PAVLOV, I. p. *Lectures on Conditioned Reflexes.* Vol. 1. International Publishers, New York, 1928, p. 333.
14. WATSON, J. B. "The Unconscious of the Behaviorist." In *The Unconscious A Symposium.* Introduction by E. S. Dummer. Alfred A. Knopf, New York, 1928, PP- 91-113.

CHAPTER 15: THE ADDICTIONS

1. M ASSERM AN, J. H, JACQUES, M. G., and NICHOLSON, M. R. "Alcohol As a Preventive of Experimental Neuroses." *Quart. J. Stud. Alcohol.,* 1945, 6:281-299 281-299.
2. MASSERMAN, J. H. and YUM, K. S. "An Analysis of the Influence Alcohol on Experimental Neuroses in Cats." ***Psychosomatic Medicine,*** 1946, 8:36-52.
3. STRECKER, E. A., and CHAMBERS, F. T., JR. *Alcohol, One Man's Meat.* The Macmillan Company, New York, 1939, pp. 42, 46-47.
4. LEMERE, F., VOEGTLIN, W. L., BROZ, W. R., O'HOLLAREN, R.TUPPER, W. E. "The Conditioned Reflex Treatment of Chrome Alcoholism. VIII. A Review of Six Years' Experience with This Treatment of 1526 Patients. *Journal of the American Medical Association,* 1942, 120. 2
5. *Ibid.*
6. KANT, F. "The Conditioned-Reflex Treatment in the Light of our Knowledge of Alcohol Addiction." *Quart. J. Stud. Alcohol., 1944, 5: 371-377*
7. *CARLSON, A. J. "The* Conditioned-Reflex Therapy of Alcohol Addiction."
   Quart. J. Stud. Alcohol., 1944, 5:212-215.
8. VOEGTLIN, W. L., and LEMERE, F. "The Treatment of Alcohol Addiction: A Review of the Literature." *Quart. J. Stud. Alcohol.,* 1942, 2: 717-803.
9. PAVLOV, I. P. *Lectures on Conditioned Reflexes.* Vol. I. International Publishers, New York, 1928, p. 331.
10. RUBENSTEIN, C. "The Treatment of Morphine Addiction In Tuberculosis by Pavlov's Conditioning Method." *Amer. Rev Tuberc.,* 1931, 24: 682-685.
11. FINNEGAN, J. K., LARSON, P. S., and HAAG, H. B. "The Role of Nicotine in the Cigarette Habit." *Science,* 1945, 102: 95-96.

12. PEARL, R. "Tobacco Smoking and Longevity." *Science,* Vol. 87, No. 2253, March 4, 1938,216-217.

13. HAMMOND, E. C, and HORN, D. "Smoking and Death Rates—Report on Forty-Four Months of Follow-up of 187,783 Men." *Journ. Amer. Med. Assoc.,* 1958, 166: 1159-1172; 1294-1308.

14. DORN, H. F. "Tobacco Consumption and Mortality from Cancer and Other Diseases." *Pub. Health Rep.,* 1959, 74: 581-593.

15. See CORNFIELD, J., HAENSZEL, W., HAMMOND E. C., LILIENFELD, A. M., SHIMKIN, M. B., and WYNDER, E. L. "Smoking and Lung Cancer: Recent **Evidence and a Discussion** of Some Questions. *Nat. Cancer Inst.,* 1959,22: 173-203 .

This paper thoroughly disposes of the "criticisms directed against the conclusion that tobacco smoking, especially cigarettes," has a significant role in the increase of cancer.

In the words of Cornfield *et al.* (page 198), "If would be desirable to have a set of findings on the subject of smoking and lung cancer so clear-cut and unequivocal that they were self-interpreting. The findings now available on tobacco, as in most other fields of science, particularly biologic science, do not meet this ideal. Nevertheless, if the findings had been made on a new agent, to which hundreds of millions of adults were not already addicted, and on one which did not support a large industry, skilled in the arts of mass persuasion, the evidence for the hazardous nature of the agent would be generally regarded as beyond dispute. In the light of all the evidence on tobacco, and after careful consideration of all the criticisms of this evidence that have been made, we find ourselves unable to agree with the proposition that cigarette smoking is a harmless habit with no important effects on health or longevity. The concern, shown by medical and public health authorities with the increasing diffusion to ever younger groups of an agent that is a health hazard seems to us to be well founded."

The following statement by the board of directors of the American Cancer Society was printed in the *Journal of the American Medical Association* on March 26, 1960.

"In 1959 the death rate from lung cancer among men in the United States was over 10 times as high as it was in 1930. The disease is now one of the most common and most lethal of all forms of human cancer. This tremendous increase in number of deaths and the reported association of cigarette smoking with lung cancer has led the American Cancer Society to pursue an aggressive program of research on lung cancer and to disseminate new evidence bearing on the subject to the medical profession and to the public.

"In October, 1954, the board of directors of the American Cancer Society declared that 'the presently available evidence indicates an association between smoking and lung cancer.' In November, 1957, the board reviewed the report of the study group on smoking and health and agreed with its conclusions that 'the evidence of a cause-effect relationship is adequate for considering the initiation of public health measures.'

"The board now believes that it has a further responsibility both to the medical profession and to the general public to state that in its judgement the clinical, epidemiologic, experimental, chemical, and pathological evidence presented by the many studies reported m recent years indicates beyond reasonable doubt that cigarette smoking is the major cause of the unprecedented increase in lung cancer. The board further believes that all organizations and agencies concerned with cancer have a responsibility to formulate programs of action based on this information in order to reduce the incidence of this largely preventable disease.

"The strong association between cigarette smoking and lung can has been established by an extraordinarily large amount of evidence. Twenty-eight studies have indicated that a history of smoking is more common among lung cancer patients than among those without the disease. Three follow-up studies of smokers and nonsmokers have demonstrated that the death rate from lung cancer among cigarette smokers is about 10 times as great as among nonsmokers. Epidemiologic indicate also that cigarette smoking is associated with about 75% of all cases of lung cancer. The incidence of the disease increase amount of cigarette smoking, and no threshold below which lung cancer will not occur has been identified.

"The fact that the association is one of cause and effect is well supported by several types of evidence. For example, in experiments condensates of tobacco smoke have produced cancers on the skin of mice and rabbits. After experimental exposure of mice to tobacco smoke or its condensates, abnormal cellular growths have been reported on mouse bronchial epithelium, in tissue cultures, and on the cervix. Cilia, one of the lung's major defenses against inhaled particulate matter, have been shown to be paralyzed by tobacco smoke. At least 10 chemical agents that have been identified in cigarette smoke have caused the development of cancer in laboratory animals. Studies of pathological changes in bronchial tubes of smokers have shown that abnormal cellular changes in the bronchi of the lung increase in degree and frequency as the amount of cigarette smoking increases and that in nonsmokers these changes are scarcely present at all....

"In presenting its conclusions the American Cancer Society recognizes that cigarette smoking is a personal habit and that the risk involved is at the option of the individual. The Society, nevertheless, believes that it has a responsibility to do everything possible within its established policies to reduce the alarming and rapidly increasing number of deaths from lung cancer."

16. OCHSNER, A. *Smoking and Cancer.* Julian Messner, Inc., New York, 1954, pp. 60-61.

CHAPTER 16: ANXIETY

1. MOWRER, O. H. "A Stimulus-Response Analysis of Anxiety and its Role as a Reinforcing Agent." *Psychological Review,* 1939, 46: 553-565.
2. GANTT, W. H. *Experimental Basis for Neurotic Behavior.* Paul B. Hoeber, Inc., New York, 1944, p. 187.
3. SHAFFER, L. F. "Fear and Courage in Aerial Combat." *Journal of Consulting Psychology,* 1947, 11: 137-143.
4. PAVLOV, I. P. *Conditioned Reflexes.* Oxford University Press, 1927, pp. 290-291.
5. MAIER, N. R. F. "Animal Neuroses." In *Encyclopedia of Psychology,* edited by P. L. Harriman. Philosophical Library, New York, 1946, pp. 33-38. Maier is referring to:
——, *Studies of Abnormal Behavior in the Rat. Harper & Brothers, New York,* 1939.
——, "Two Types of Behavior Abnormality in the Rat." *Bulletin of the Menninger Clinic,* 1943, 7: 141-147.
——, and KLEE, J. B. "Studies of Abnormal Behavior in the Rat: XVII. Guidance versus Trial and Error in the Alteration of Habits and Fixations." *Journal of Psychology,* 1945, 19: 133-163.
PAVLOV, I. P, *Lectures on Conditioned Reflexes.* International Publishers, New York, 1928.
MASSERMAN, J. H. *Behavior and Neurosis.* University of Chicago Press, Chicago, 1943.

LIDDELL, H. S. "Conditioned Reflex Method and Experimental Neurosis." In *Personality and the Behavior Disorders*. Vol. 1. Edited by J. McV. Hunt, The Ronald Press Company, New York, 1944, pp. 389-412.

6. BLEULER, A. *Textbook of Psychiatry*, Authorized English edition by A. A. Brill. The Macmillan Company, New York, 1939, p. 561.

7. PAVLOV, I. P. *Conditioned Reflexes and Psychiatry*. International Publishers, New York, 1941, p. 39.

CHAPTER 17: BODILY CORRELATES OF INHIBITION

1. CARR, H. A. *Psychology*. Longmans, Green & Co., New York, 1925, p. 6.

2. HEIDBREDER, E. *Seven Psychologies*. D. Appleton-Century, New York, 1933, p. 412.

3. DUNBAR, F. *Psychosomatic Diagnosis*. Paul B. Hoeber, Inc., New York, 1943, p. 119.

4. WEISS, E., and ENGLISH, O. S. *Psychosomatic Medicine*. W. B. Saunders, Philadelphia, 1943.

5. BURNHAM, R. W, "Logic in Psychosomatic Medicine." *Psychological Review*, 1944, Vol. 51, No. 4: 257-258.

6. PETROVA, M. K. (Russian) "Skin Diseases in Experimental Dogs; Their Origin and, Therapy." *Trud. fiziol. Lab, Pavlov.*. 1945, 12; 33-48. English summary pp. 47-48.

7. ——. (Russian) "Inhibition As a Factor of Restoration of Nervous Activity." *Trud. fiziol. Lab. Pavlov.*, 1945, 12: 106-127. English summary pp. 126-127.

8. GANTT, W. H. *Experimental Basis for Neurotic Behavior*. Paul B. Hoeber, Inc., New York, 1944, p. 158.

9. WATSON, J. B. *Behaviorism*. W. W. Norton & Company, New York, 1925, pp. 244-246. Rev. Ed., 1930, pp. 298-300.

10. HOLLINGSWORTH, H. L. *Abnormal Psychology*. Methuen & Co. Ltd., London, 1931, p. 299.

11. FISHBERG, A. M. "Sympathectomy for Essential Hypertension;' *Journal of the American Medical Association*. 1948, Vol. 137, No. 8:670-674

12. NEWBURGH, L. H. "Obesity. I. Energy Metabolism." *Physiological Review*. Jan. 1944, 24: 18-30.

13. FREED, S. C. "Psychic Factors in the Development and Treatment of Obesity." *Journal of the American Medical Association, 1947, vol.133, No. 6: 369-373.*

14. COHEN, M., R., and NAGEL, E. *An Introduction to Logic and Scientific Method. Harcourt, Brace and Company, New York, 1936, p. 397.*

CHAPTER 18: MASOCHISM AND SEX

1. LORENZ, A. *My Life and Work.* Scribners Sons, New York, 1936, p.84.
2. PAVLO, *I. P. Lectures on Conditioned Reflexes.* Vol. I, International Publishers, New York, 1928, p. 216.
3. EROFEEW [EROFEEVA], M. "Contribution à l'étude des reflexes conditionnels destructifs." *Comptes Rend. Soc. Biol. de Paris*, 1916, 79:239-240.
4. SLUTSKAYA M. M. [Russian] "Converting Defensive into Food Reflexes in Oligopnrenics and in. Normal Children." *Zhurnal Nevropatologii*, 1928, 21: 2 10. Original not seen. The quotation and procedure are from: *RAZRAN, G. H. S. "Conditioned Responses in Children." Archives of Psychology, 1933, 148: 86.*
5. GANTT, *W. H. Experimental Basis for Neurotic Behavior.* Paul B. Hoeber, Inc., New York, 1944, p. 180.
6. KINSEY, A. C., POMEROY. W. B., and MARTIN, C. E. *Sexual Behavior in the Human Male.* W. B. Saunders, Co., Philadelphia, 1948, pp. 164.165.
7. MAX, L. W. "Breaking Up a Homosexual Fixation by the Conditioned Reaction Technique.*" Psychological Bulletin*, 1935, 32: 734.
8. GUTHRIE, E. R. "Personality in Terms of Associative Learning." *In Personality and the Behavior Disorders, Vol. I, edited by J. McV. Hunt, The Ronald Press Co., New York, 1944, p. 64.*
9. PAVLOV, *I. P. Conditioned Reflexes.* Oxford University Press, *1927, pp. 33-44.*
10. *Ibid.*
11. HULL, C. L. *Principles of Behavior.* D. Appleton-Century Company, New York, 1943, p. 94.
12. MEIGNANT, P. "Réflexes conditionnels et psycho-pathologie: Quelques remarques concernant les perversions et les anomalies sexuelles." *Gazelle Médicale de France*, 1935: 327-332.
13. PAVLOV, 1. P. Op. *cit.*, p. 44.
14. MEIGNANT, P. Op. *cit.*
15. PAVLOV, I. P. Op. *cit.*, p. 48.
16. *Ibid.*, p. 68.
17. *Ibid.*, p. 68.
18. *Ibid.*, p. 106.
19. TERMAN, L. M., et al. *Psychological Factors in Marital Happiness.* McGraw-Hill Book Co., New York, 1938, p. 375.

20. LANDIS, C., et al. *Sex in Development.* Paul B. Hoeber, Inc., New York, 1940, p. 100.
21. DICKINSON, R. L. "Medical Analysis of a Thousand Marriages." *Journal of the American Medical Association,* 1931, 97, 8: 529-535.

CHAPTER 19: THE PSYCHOPATHIC PERSONALITY

1. KAHN, E. *Psychopathic Personalities.* Yale University Press, 1931.
2. HENDERSON. D. K. *Psychopathic States.* W. W. Norton & Co., New York, 1939.
3. CLECKLEY, H. *The Mask of Sanity.* C. V. Mosby Co., St. Louis, 1941.
4. KARPMAN, B. "A Yardstick for Measuring Psychopathy." *Federal Probation,* Oct...Dec. 1946, Vol. 10, No. 4: 26-31.
5. PREU, P. W. "The Concept of Psychopathic Personality." In *Personality and meBehavior Disorders,* edited by J. McV. Hunt. Vol. 2. The Ronald Press Co., New York, 1944, pp. 922–937.
6. KARPMAN, B. "On the Need of Separating Psychopathy into Two Distinct Clinical Types: The Symptomatic and the Idiopathic." Journal of Criminal *Psychopathology, 1941, 3: 112-137.*
7. ——— "Passive Parasitic Psychopathy: Toward the Personality Structure and Psychogenesis of Idiopathic Psychopathy (Anethopathy)." *The Psychoanalytic Review, 1947, 34: 102-118.*
8. ———. "Passive Parasitic Psychopathy: Toward the Personality Structure and Psychogenesis of Idiopathic Psychopathy (Anethopathy). Part II: Mechanisms, Processes, Psychogenesis." *The Psychoanalytic Review, 1947, 34: 198–222.*
9. KAVKA, J. "Between Psychosis and Psychopathy." *Journal of Nervous and Mental Disease, 1947, 106: 19-45.*
10. HEAVER, W. L. "A Study of Forty Male Psycho-pathic.Personalities Before, During and After Hospitalization." *American Journal of Psychiatry,* 1943, 100: 342-346.
11. GREENACRE, P. "Conscience in the Psychopath." *American Journal of Orthopsychiatry, 1945, 15: 495-509.*
12. LEVY, D. M. *"Primary Affect Hunger." American Journal of Psychiatry, 1937, 94: 643-652.*
——— "Psychopathic Personality and Crime." *Journal of Educational Sociology,* 1942, 16: 99...114.
13. BENDER, L. "Psychopathic Behavior Disorders in Children." *In Handbook of Correctional Psychology,* edited by R. M. Lindner and R. V. Seliger. *Philosophical Library, New York, 1947, pp. 360-377.*

14. *LOWREY. L. G "Personality Distortion and Early Institutional Care." American Journal of Orthopsychiatry, 1940, 10: 576-585.*

15. GOLDFARB, W. "Infant Rearing and Problem Behavior." *American Journal of Orthopsychiatry*, 1943. 13: 249.266. ——"The Effects of Early Institutional Care on Adolescent Personality." *Journal of Experimental Education*, 1943, 12i 106-129.

16. SCHMIDT, H. O., and BILLINGSLEA, F Y. "Test Profiles as a Diagnostic Aid: *The* Bernreuter Inventory." *"Journal of Abnormal and Social Psychology, 1945,* 40:70-76. Note: The 89.5 per cent B1-N score that I mention does not appear in this paper. I have calculated it from the average raw score of +47.50 given in the BI-N column in Table II of the original article, and interpolated in Bernreuter's norms for "adult men.

17. CALDWELL, J. M. "Neurotic Components in Psychopathic Behavior." *Journal of nervous and Mental Disease*, 1944, 99: 134...148.

18. *Ibid.*

19. *MEAD, M. Sex and Temper Temperament in Three Primitive Societies.* William Morrow & Co., Inc., New York, 1935, p. 189.

20. Quote from Shakespeare's Hamlet.

CHAPTER 20: ONLY SCIENCE, ABSOLUTE SCIENCE

1. MAIER, N. R. F "Animal Neuroses." *In Encyclopedia of Psychology,* edited by P. L. Harriman. Philosophical Library, New York, 1946, p. 38.

2. *PAVLOV, I. P. Lectures on Conditioned Reflexes. Vol. I. International Publishers, New York, 1928, p. 373.*

3. *Ibid.,* p. 126.

4. In *Personality and the Behavior menders. Vol* I. Edited by *l* MeV. Hunt The Ronald Press Company, New York 1944, p. *306.*

5. PAVLOV, I. P. Op. cit., p. 41.

ABOUT THE AUTHOR

Andrew Salter was born in Waterbury, Connecticut, in 1914, and died in Manhattan in 1996. He received his undergraduate degree in psychology from New York University in 1937. Professor Clark Hull of Yale University is credited with launching Salter's career in 1941 by agreeing to publish his article "Three Techniques of Autohypnosis" in the *Journal of General Psychology*, perhaps the leading academic psychology journal of the time, quite an endorsement for the work of a young man with no advanced degree. The article introduced the idea of and specific methods for self-hypnosis to an academic audience and received considerable coverage in the popular press as well. In 1944, Salter published *What is Hypnosis*, which demystified hypnosis by treating it as a product of suggestion, the now broadly accepted view. He had a lively clinical practice in New York from 1941 until a few months before his death.

In 1949 he published *Conditioned Reflex Therapy*, which moved well beyond hypnosis and articulated the ideas and many specific methods for what became known as behavior therapy, ideas developed in less than a decade of clinical work. It is generally considered a founding document of behavior therapy and its offshoots, including cognitive behavior therapy. It was widely reviewed, both positively and negatively. In 1952 *The Case Against Psychoanalysis* appeared, a vigorous attack on the then-dominant mode of psychotherapy. He was a founder of the American Association for Behavior Therapy (AABT, now the Association for Behavioral and Cognitive Therapies, ABCT) in 1966 and was awarded its lifetime achievement award in 1996.